The Economy–Security Nexus in Northeast Asia

T0313242

The dynamics of Northeast Asia have traditionally been considered primarily in military and hard security terms or alternatively along their economic dimensions. This book argues that relations among the states of Northeast Asia are far more comprehensible when the mutually shaping interactions between economics and security are considered simultaneously. It examines these interactions and some of the key empirical questions they pose, the answers to which have important lessons for international relations beyond Northeast Asia. Contributors to this volume analyze how the states of the region define their "security," and how bilateral relations in hard security issues and economic linkages play out among Japan, China, and the two Koreas. Further, the chapters interrogate how different patterns of techno-nationalist development affect regional security ties, and the extent to which closer economic connections enhance or detract from a nation's self-perceived security. The book concludes by discussing scenarios for the future and the conditions that will shape relations between economics and security in the region.

This book will be welcomed by students and scholars of Asian politics, Asian economics, security studies, and political economy.

T.J. Pempel is Professor and Forcey Chair of Political Science for the Study of East Asian Politics at the University of California, Berkeley, USA.

Politics in Asia series

ASEAN and the Security of South-East Asia
Michael Leifer

China's Policy towards Territorial Disputes
The case of the South China Sea islands
Chi-kin Lo

India and Southeast Asia
Indian perceptions and policies
Mohammed Ayoob

Gorbachev and Southeast Asia
Leszek Buszynski

Indonesian Politics under Suharto
Order, development and pressure for change
Michael R.J. Vatikiotis

The State and Ethnic Politics in Southeast Asia
David Brown

The Politics of Nation Building and Citizenship in Singapore
Michael Hill and Lian Kwen Fee

Politics in Indonesia
Democracy, Islam and the ideology of tolerance
Douglas E. Ramage

Communitarian Ideology and Democracy in Singapore
Beng-Huat Chua

The Challenge of Democracy in Nepal
Louise Brown

Japan's Asia Policy
Wolf Mendl

The International Politics of the Asia-Pacific, 1945–1995
Michael Yahuda

Political Change in Southeast Asia
Trimming the banyan tree
Michael R.J. Vatikiotis

Hong Kong
China's challenge
Michael Yahuda

Korea versus Korea
A case of contested legitimacy
B.K. Gills

Taiwan and Chinese Nationalism
National identity and status in international society
Christopher Hughes

State Making in Asia
Edited by Richard Boyd and
Tak-Wing Ngo

US–China Relations in the 21st
Century
Power transition and peace
Zhiqun Zhu

Empire and Neoliberalism in Asia
Edited by Vedi R. Hadiz

South Korean Engagement Policies
and North Korea
Identities, norms and the
sunshine policy
Son Key-young

Chinese Nationalism in
the Global Era
Christopher R. Hughes

Indonesia's War over Aceh
Last stand on Mecca's porch
Matthew N. Davies

Advancing East Asian Regionalism
Edited by Melissa G. Curley and
Nicholas Thomas

Political Cultures in Asia and
Europe
Citizens, states and societal
values
Jean Blondel and Takashi
Inoguchi

Rethinking Injustice and
Reconciliation in Northeast Asia
The Korean experience
Edited by Gi-Wook Shin, Soon-Won
Park and Daqing Yang

Foreign Policy Making in Taiwan
From principle to pragmatism
Dennis Van Vranken Hickey

The Balance of Power in
Asia-Pacific Security
US–China policies on regional order
Liselotte Odgaard

Taiwan in the 21st Century
Aspects and limitations
of a development model
Edited by Robert Ash and
J. Megan Green

Elections as Popular Culture
in Asia
Edited by Chua Beng Huat

Security and Migration in Asia
The dynamics of securitisation
Edited by Melissa G. Curley & Wong
Siu-lun

Political Transitions in Dominant
Party Systems
Learning to lose
Edited by Edward Friedman and
Joseph Wong

Torture, Truth and Justice
The case of Timor-Leste
Elizabeth Stanley

A Rising China and Security
in East Asia
Identity construction and security
discourse
Rex Li

Rise of China
Beijing's strategies and
implications for the Asia-Pacific
Edited by Hsin-Huang
Michael Hsiao and
Cheng-yi Lin

Governance and Regionalism
in Asia
Edited by Nicholas Thomas

The Economy–Security Nexus in Northeast Asia

Edited by T.J. Pempel

Routledge
Taylor & Francis Group

LONDON AND NEW YORK

First published 2013
by Routledge
2 Park Square, Milton Park, Abingdon, Oxfordshire OX14 4RN

Simultaneously published in the USA and Canada
by Routledge
711 Third Avenue, New York, NY 10017

First issued in paperback 2014

Routledge is an imprint of the Taylor & Francis Group, an informa business

British Library Cataloguing in Publication Data
A catalogue record for this book is available from the British Library

Library of Congress Cataloging in Publication Data
The economy-security nexus in Northeast Asia / edited by T.J. Pempel.
    p. cm. – (Politics in Asia series)
    Includes bibliographical references and index.
    1. East Asia–Economic policy. 2. National security–East Asia.
      I. Pempel, T. J., 1942-
HC460.5.E38 2012
330.95–dc23   2012024764

ISBN 978-0-415-62914-0 (hbk)
ISBN 978-1-138-85184-9 (pbk)
ISBN 978-0-203-10008-0 (ebk)

Typeset in Times New Roman
by Cenveo Publisher Services

Contents

Figures and tables

Figures

Tables

Contributors

Tai Ming Cheung is director at the University of California Institute on Global Conflict and Cooperation (IGCC), where he leads the institute's Study of Technology and Innovation (SITC) project. Cheung is a long-time analyst of Chinese and East Asian national security and technology policy issues. He received his Ph.D. from the War Studies Department at King's College, London University. His latest book, *Fortifying China: The Struggle to Build a Modern Defense Economy*, was published by Cornell University Press in 2009. He is also an associate professor in residence at the School of International Relations and Pacific Studies at UC San Diego, where he teaches courses on Asian security and Chinese security and technology.

Jong Kun Choi is assistant professor at the Department of Political Science and International Studies and associate dean of the Graduate School of Public Administration at Yonsei University. He also serves as chair for the Nordic Research Program at the Institute of East–West Studies. Choi specializes in international relations theory, Northeast Asian security, political psychology, and public opinions on national identity and foreign policy attitudes.

Keisuke Iida is professor in the Graduate School for Law and Politics at the University of Tokyo. He holds a Ph.D. from Harvard University and has taught at Princeton University and Aoyama Gakuin University. His major publications include *Legalization and Japan: The Politics of WTO Dispute Settlement* (2006) and *International Monetary Cooperation among the United States, Japan, and Germany* (1999). He has also published in major journals such as *Global Governance, International Organization, International Studies Quarterly*, and *Public Choice*. His current research interests include the politics of regional integration in East Asia, the comparative study of dispute-settlement institutions in the world, and the political economy of financial and currency crises.

Professor **Hiroko Imamura** is the director of the Center for Far Eastern Studies, University of Toyama. Previous publications include "North Korean Economic Reform: Comparison with China and Vietnam," *Far Eastern Studies* 4 (2005): 35–49, and *Kitachosen—Kyokou no Keizai* [*Fictional North Korean Economy*]

(Tokyo: Shuueisha, 2006). Her current research interests include the economic relationship between China and North Korea and the Chinese economy.

Scott L. Kastner is an associate professor in the Department of Government and Politics at the University of Maryland.

Min Gyo Koo is an associate professor in the Graduate School of Public Administration at Seoul National University. He is the author of a book, *Island Disputes and Maritime Regime Building in East Asia: Between a Rock and a Hard Place* (2009, Springer). He is also the co-editor (with Vinod K. Aggarwal) of the book, *Asia's New Institutional Architecture: Evolving Structures for Managing Trade, Financial, and Security Relations* (2007, Springer). Aside from many book chapters, he has published his research in a wide range of internationally recognized journals, including *The Pacific Review*, *International Relations of the Asia-Pacific*, *Pacific Affairs*, *Asian Perspective*, *European Journal of East Asia Studies*, and *Journal of East Asian Studies*.

Mie Oba is an associate professor at the Tokyo University of Science. She obtained her M.A. and Ph.D. in international relations at the University of Tokyo. She is a specialist on regionalism in Asia as well as on theories of regionalism. Her publications include "ASEAN's External Relations and the Changing Regional Structure in East Asia: Can ASEAN Stay in the 'Drivers' Seat'?" *ASEAN Study Group Report*, March 2010, and *Ajia Taiheiyo Chiiki Keisei heno Dotei: Kyokai-Kokka Nichi-Go no Aidentiti Mosaku to Chiiki-Shyugi* [*The Invention of the Asia-Pacific Region: A History of Regionalism and Search for Identity by Japan and Australia as Liminal Nations*] (Minerva Shobo, 2004).

T.J. Pempel is Jack M. Forcey Professor of Political Science at the University of California, Berkeley. His research has been on Japanese political economy, Asian regionalism, and security questions in Northeast Asia. His most recent book is *Security in Northeast Asia: Architecture and Beyond*, with Routledge.

Acknowledgments

This volume is the outcome of a more extensive project involving security in Northeast Asia conducted by the Institute for Global Conflict and Cooperation (IGCC) at the University of California and the Policy Alternatives Research Institute (PARI) at Tokyo University. Of the many debts of gratitude incurred, the greatest is to the John D. and Catherine T. MacArthur Foundation's Asia Security Initiative for the funding that made the entire project possible. Matthew Stumpf and Amy Gordon of the foundation were particularly instrumental in helping us move this project forward.

There was valuable staff support from both the IGCC and PARI. At the IGCC Susan Shirk, Tai Ming Cheung, and Heidi Serochi deserve special thanks. Lynne Bush provided critical editorial assistance on the final manuscript. At Tokyo University, Kiichi Fujiwara was instrumental in helping to organize the Japanese researchers in the project. Fujiwara contributed greatly to the organizational and intellectual shape of the final project. Ryo Sahashi and Lully Miura provided critical administrative support throughout.

T.J. Pempel would like to give special thinks to Chris Reinhardt and Seung-youn Oh, both of whom provided research help throughout the project. Stephanie Rogers and Hannah Mack at Routledge have been extremely helpful in shepherding this volume through its various iterations.

1 Introduction

The economic–security nexus in Northeast Asia

T.J. Pempel

Security analysts typically assess the dynamics of the Northeast Asian region primarily in military and hard security terms. This book begins from a different premise. It is a shared consensus among the contributors to this volume that relations among the states of Northeast Asia are far more comprehensible when the interactions between economics and security are considered simultaneously. Beyond the simple empirical light that these chapters shed on regional relationships however, they also utilize the experiences of Northeast Asia to shed light on a central puzzle that has ensnared political scientists and policymakers since at least the time of Immanuel Kant and Adam Smith: how do economic and security relations interact? Northeast Asia, we believe, provides a tantalizing laboratory within which to examine the relationships between economics and security primarily because of the complex but sustained interactions between the two within the region. More explicitly stated, this book begins with two related goals: first, to examine the linkages between economics and security in an effort to understand more fully the complex relations among the major states of Northeast Asia; and second, to utilize an empirical examination of those relationships to shed more light on the often studied linkages between economics and security at a general level.

At least three elements are central to our analysis and to the general puzzle of how economics and security are connected. First, Northeast Asia has long been plagued by a trove of security tensions that make it, in the oft-cited phrase of Aaron Friedberg (1993), a region "ripe for rivalry." Second, particularly in the period since the Asian Financial Crisis of 1997–98, economic interdependence has risen sharply in Northeast Asia as the result of cross-border investments, financial coordination, trade, and the development of transnational production networks. Third, and ironically, despite its deep security and geopolitical fissures, Northeast Asia has been free of any actual state-to-state wars since the Korean armistice was signed in 1953. Add to these still a fourth fact—that the region has for at least a decade been undergoing an extensive power transition based on the rapid development of China—and the relationships between security and economics within the region defy easy linear conclusions about causal connections, particularly in so far as the power transition may well mean that past experiences are but weak predictors of the future.

Among the empirical questions that the region poses: What is the role of economics in how the states of the region define their "security?" How do bilateral relations in hard security issues such as territorial disputes or more culturally-rooted issues such as historical memories, between China and Japan, Japan and Korea or China and Korea link to the bilateral economic relations among these countries? How do different patterns of techno-nationalist development play into regional security ties? Do closer economic connections enhance or detract from a nation's security, questions being asked, for example, in Taiwan, Korea, and Japan vis-à-vis deeper ties with China?

Answers to such questions can shed important light on a series of more abstract questions addressed usually at the global, rather than the regional level, by scholars of international relations: How much does economic interdependence account for the absence of shooting wars, a claim many adherents to commercial peace theory might suggest? Do the costs of geopolitical confrontation simply become too high as a consequence of the region's rapidly growing economic linkages? If so, how does one explain the persistence of security tensions short of overt warfare? Are outbreaks of periodic saber-rattling and bellicose rhetoric simply examples of geostrategic brinksmanship, signaling, and efforts at satiating domestic public opinion, but with the final escalatory step to shooting wars being jointly avoided? Does enhanced economic interdependence actually have a slow moving but generally positive spillover in the reduction of military tensions or conversely, do states respond to ongoing security challenges by attempting to leverage their enhanced economic ties into geostrategic bargaining chips? And to what extent do the answers to any of these questions lose predictive power in the face of a global or regional power transition?

This book attempts to shed light on these and other empirical and more abstract questions about the interactions between economics and security. To set the stage for the chapters that follow I begin by outlining the four points noted above—the security tensions that continue to bedevil the region; the region's growing economic interdependence; the absence of state-to-state warfare; and the shifting power relationships.

Security tensions in Northeast Asia

Northeast Asia has one of the world's heaviest concentrations of lethal military force. Three of the five permanent members of the United Nations Security Council, all of whom were original nuclear weapons states (the United States, China, USSR/Russia), have an ongoing security presence in the region. The DPRK has twice tested nuclear devices and has also demanded recognition as a nuclear power. Meanwhile, at least three other governments (the Republic of Korea (ROK), Taiwan, and Japan) have the technical capability to "go nuclear" on short notice. Conventional armaments are extensive with China (1.6 million), the United States (1.4 million), and the DPRK (1.1 million) having the most extensive active-duty military forces with additional numbers in active reserves.

Conventional weapons for air and sea combat are also sophisticated and extensive (e.g. International Institute for Strategic Studies 2010; Cordesman 2011). Furthermore, "both the U.S. and China have nuclear-armed aircraft and ICBMs, IRBMs, MRBMs, and SRBMs with boosted and thermonuclear weapons" (Cordesman 2011: 10). The DPRK, in addition to its nuclear weapons and conventional armaments, has extensive chemical weapons and is suspected of possessing biological weapons. Add in such items as extensive and integrated command and control system as well as communications, anti-ballistic missile defenses, satellites, cyber-warfare capabilities, and the like and it becomes very clear how extensive the dispersion of extremely sophisticated military capabilities across the region really is.

These militaries have been built up partly in response to, but also serve to exacerbate, tense relations in a variety of flashpoints. Since the reunifications of Vietnam and Germany, Northeast Asia now contains the largest concentration of divided polities in the world (Kim 2004). Incomplete national consolidation struggles are the pivot for relations between the two Koreas and between China and Taiwan. Cross-Straits tensions have ebbed and flowed as the two governments on either side have challenged the very legitimacy of the unsteady status quo. Since the inauguration of Ma Ying-jeou as Taiwan's president, cross-Straits relations have been far less frosty, but the People's Republic of China (PRC) as recently as 2005 passed a law threatening to use military force to reunite Taiwan with the mainland if it presses its case for independence too vigorously. Taiwan has hardly been militarily oblivious to the security posture of its gargantuan neighbor and purchases of sophisticated arms, particularly from the United States, are used to offset possible PRC threats.

Relations between the two Koreas have been equally mercurial and as of this writing are being heavily shaped by the sinking of the ROK's naval vessel, the *Cheonan* (March 2010), and by the DPRK's shelling of Yeonpyeong Island (September 2010). The ROK blames the DPRK for what it claims were unprovoked attacks while the North denies involvement with the *Cheonan* and blames ROK and U.S. military maneuvers in contested waters as the reason for the shelling of Yeonpyeong.

Beyond these two cases of divided nations, the region is rife with a number of unresolved territorial disputes, most of them legacies of World War II and the Cold War. These remain sources of ongoing rancor and military threats. So too do a number of historical memories of past wars, occupations, and military actions. These regularly poison contemporary relations while divergent political and economic systems, along with religion and culture, also fragment rather than bring together the region's diverse states. It is little wonder that scholars refer to Northeast Asia not only as a "region ripe for rivalry" (Friedberg 1993), but also as a "cockpit of great power rivalry" (Holbrooke 1991: 48), "the cockpit of battles" (Van Ness 2003), and a system of long-run, unstable multipolarity (Mearsheimer 2001: 381) moving "forward to an unhappy future" (Buzan and Segal 1994: 18).

Economic interdependence

Economic development has become a major agenda item for virtually all of the political and business elites in Northeast Asia. Governments have in their diverse ways played a substantial role in the economic development of most of the economies in the region. Indeed, as Tai Ming Cheung shows in his contribution to this volume, all Northeast Asian governments have pursued extensive public policies designed to shape their explicit strategies of techno-nationalism. At the same time, the region has also manifested an extensive rise in economic interdependence driven primarily by waves of commercial integration. The combination of trade and foreign direct investment fueled the region's collective growth and its enhanced interdependence starting as early as the 1980s. Simultaneously, as East Asia's economies moved toward greater interdependence, Asian-based multinationals also integrated themselves more efficiently into the global economy with the result that the region as a whole moved toward becoming an integrated "Asian factory" (Ravenhill 2008; inter alia).

Japanese corporations and the Japanese government, bolstered by the rapidly rising Japanese currency, were the initial drivers of these regional production networks (Katzenstein and Shiraishi 1997; Pempel 1997; inter alia). In Japan's case, the regionalization and internationalization of manufacturing became evident when in 1995 Japanese-owned companies were manufacturing more overseas (¥41.2 trillion) than they exported from the home islands (¥39.6 trillion) (Kubota 1994; *Far Eastern Economic Review* 4 July 1996: 45). Soon, however, investment from firms based in Taiwan, South Korea, Hong Kong, Singapore, and elsewhere was also flowing across national borders. Individual companies from countries with rapidly escalating currencies began heavy investments in other Asian countries that could offer cheaper land and labor, thereby diversifying their production processes across several different countries. Simultaneously, ethnic and family ties among diasporadic Chinese business people became the basis for linking together what Naughton (1997) has called the "China circles" across "Greater China" (Katzenstein and Shiraishi 1997; Pempel 2005). Equally, China's rise expanded economic opportunities for firms from Japan, South Korea, Hong Kong, and Taiwan (Perkins 2007: 47), while more recently, China itself has become increasingly the source of considerable outgoing FDI.

Intra-East Asian investment has taken a sharp turn upward, particularly since the mid-1990s, and the cumulative effect of these moves has been a substantial increase in cross-border production. This in turn has bolstered enhanced intra-Asian trade and a deeper East Asian interdependence while at the same time reducing the previous East Asian dependence on exports to the United States. By 2008, intra-Asian trade had risen to 56 percent of total Asian trade, a figure close to that of the EU while Asian reliance on the U.S. market was on a downward trend (see Figure 1.1). Interdependence in trade within Northeast Asia more specifically has risen in tandem, creating an extensive economic interdependence among Japan, China, and the ROK (see Figure 1.2).

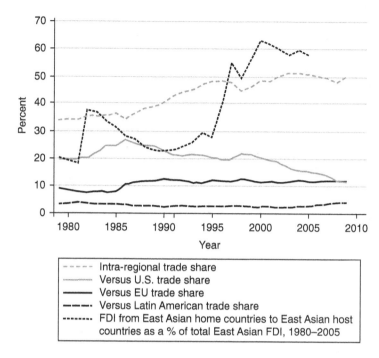

Figure 1.1 East Asia's linked trade and investment.
Source: Goldstein and Mansfield 2011.

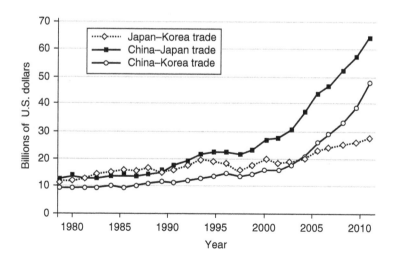

Figure 1.2 Intra-regional trade in Northeast Asia.

The states of Northeast Asia have also been moving in many common strategic directions and closer cooperation in the area of finance. China, Japan, and the ROK have all opted for strategies of expanded foreign reserve holdings in the aftermath of the Asian Financial Crisis that Gregory Chin (2010) has labeled "self-insurance" and "regional insulation" against the previously disruptive forces of global capital and "hot money" that were such a challenge to much of East Asia in 1997–98.

Financial cooperation has also been shown in the development of the Chiang-Mai Initiative and its subsequent multilateralization (CMIM). CMIM has put in place a currency swap mechanism for the region. Its establishment showed a particularly high level of financial cooperation among the ROK, China, and Japan in which the three reached collective agreement on the division of financial contributions that each would make. Similar financial cooperation was also shown in the development of the Asian Bond Markets Initiative aimed at reducing the region's dependence on global capital financing in U.S. dollars and/or on the London and New York exchanges, instead moving toward the use of Asian capital for Asian development projects.

Northeast Asian governments have also been active in the pursuit of preferential trade agreements (PTAs). Many of these have expanded existing corporate-based trade links; others seek to expand the economic linkages to include economic cooperation and technology-sharing arrangements as well (Dent 2003, 2005; Aggarwal and Urata 2006; Pempel and Urata 2006; Aggarwal and Koo 2008; Oba 2008; inter alia). And as Koo (2009) demonstrates persuasively, the pursuit of such PTAs has been a fundamental element in the regional and economic strategy of several countries, but most particularly, the ROK.

In striking contrast to these webs of economic interdependence, North Korea has stood out as a conspicuous exception. As Imamura's detailed analysis shows, there would be numerous economic reasons for the North to have tried emulating China's and Vietnam's economic reforms. But the combination of political fears, a focus on diverting limited resources to military forces, along with deep-seated agricultural and technical incompetence has left the North's economy in a shambles that contrasts starkly with the far more successful economies of its neighbors.

Two separate trends should be underscored. First, there is growing economic interdependence, much of it driven by the actions of individual corporations based in different Northeast Asian countries. Certain elements of corporate activity have been further spurred by government actions such as Taiwan's loosening of restrictions against investment in the PRC, export-import bank financing and bureaucratic structuring and information assistance in both Korea and Japan, PRC policies creating export-free zones and encouraging incoming FDI, and the like. The result has been enhanced regional production and trade.

A second trend should be highlighted as well, and that is actual government cooperation efforts such as those witnessed in the formation of CMIM or in the forging of preferential trade agreements. It is clear that despite the issues that often divide them, and despite the many testy exchanges across national borders, the governments of China, Japan, Taiwan, and the ROK have not let those issues derail their growing economic interdependence and indeed, in many instances, they have actively fostered closer economic linkages even with neighboring countries with whom they have unresolved geopolitical tensions.

The 'puzzle' of regional peace

The economic–security nexus in Northeast Asia is marked by the apparent contradiction between, on the one hand, the region's numerous structural security tensions; the overall military robustness; the episodic military skirmishes with their occasional loss of lives; as well as the frequent and cacophonous nationalist vitriol hurled across its many borders; and on the other, the fact that beneath all these potential sources of warfare, the region has seen no state-to-state military conflicts since the armistice that ended the Korean conflict in 1953. (In a related vein, since Chinese troops pulled out of Vietnam in 1979 neighboring Southeast Asia has also been free of any open warfare between states.) Thus, as Muthiah Alagappa (2003: 1–33) and others (e.g. Kang 2003; Cha 2007: 110; Goh 2007–08: 113) have shown, even though all governments in Northeast Asia and East Asia more broadly confront a smorgasbord of ongoing internal and international security tensions, the absolute number of these problems has decreased, and most of the region's disputes and conflicts have at least been stabilized. Many have actually been resolved; for example, China and Russia have solved their multiple border disputes and demilitarized their 2,640-mile shared border; and commercial interactions between the two (including increased military sales) have increased steadily (Weitz 2007: 53). The currently conflictual dyads in Northeast Asia trace to the end of World War II and the Cold War; many have been softened. No new dyads of conflict have emerged. Equally, a series of confidence-building measures have been taking place across the region, suggesting an official willingness to explore the possibilities for defusing, rather than escalating, military tensions.

Etel Solingen underscores the ongoing improvements in East Asia's improved security climate:

> Existing disputes have been restrained as never before in recent history, and major powers have normalized diplomatic relations despite continued tensions … Military modernization has not undermined macroeconomic and regional stability. Military expenditures relative to GNP have declined from 2.6 percent (1985) to 1.8 percent (2001), lower than world averages of 5.4 percent (1985 and 2.5 percent (2001)), with parallel declines—in most states—in military expenditures relative to central government expenditures (2007: 757).

Steven Chan (2010) provides more detailed country-by-country data to show the same pattern (see Table 1.1). Kivimaki (2010) also provides compelling support for the emerging relative peace in the region.

How is one to interpret these seemingly contradictory realities—high geopolitical tension with lots of military mobilizations and periodic skirmishes yet no

Table 1.1 Defense burden (military expenditures as percent of gross domestic product)

	1990	1995	2000	2005
Australia	2.00	1.91	1.74	1.78
Brunei	6.75	5.75	6.52	4.50[1]
Cambodia	3.12	5.78[2]	3.23	1.78
China	2.71	1.73	1.83	1.98
Indonesia	1.81	1.57	1.00	0.94
Japan	0.94	0.96	0.98	0.97
Korea, South	3.56	2.78	2.50	2.58
Laos			2.03	0.50[1]
Malaysia	2.56	2.75	1.70	1.90
Myamar	3.40	3.56[2]	2.31	2.10[1]
Mongolia	5.66	1.74	2.56	1.74[3]
New Zealand	1.82	1.41	1.23	1.01
Papua New Guinea	2.13	1.02	0.87	0.53
Philippines	1.35	1.44	1.08	0.82
Singapore	4.89	4.36	4.67	4.68
Taiwan	4.90[4]	3.85[4]	3.70[4]	2.20[1]
Thailand	2.63	2.26	1.45	1.14
Vietnam		7.91	2.65[2]	2.50[1]

Source: Chan 2010.

Notes: 1. http://www.cia.gov/cia/publications/factbook; for Brunei the figure is for 2006; 2. These figures are for 1994; 3. This figure is for 2004; 4. Council for Economic Planning and Development 2002.

actual state-to-state wars for over fifty years? Has Northeast Asia somehow managed to forge an East Asian Peace? Certainly, in the deft wording of Miles Kahler (2011: 19), Northeast Asia's enjoys at best, a *"peace of the prudent*, not a peace grounded in deeper levels of trust or predictability [emphasis added]." Or in Algappa's (2003) terms, the security order in Northeast Asia is "instrumental" rather than "normative" or "solidarist." With its many geopolitical fissures and its deep levels of cross-border mistrust, the region remains far short of being a security community based on mutual trust and a common multinational project. Northeast Asia is still far from a region in which war among the members is as "unthinkable" as most would suggest is the case for the countries of the European Union or North America. Yet the absence of outright war and the emergence of a peaceful security order, however limited it may be, must be acknowledged as a significant break with the region's numerous wars in the last part of the nineteenth and the first half of the twentieth centuries. A definite break with the sustained combat and military occupations of the past is undeniable.

There is little consensus as to why the shooting has subsided in Northeast Asia. Certainly powerful neo-realist arguments have been advanced arguing for the importance of the U.S. alliance system as a key factor in the regional peace (e.g. Christensen 2003; Lake 2009; inter alia). In a related vein, others point to the regional "balance of power" and/or to the United States as "offshore balancer" (Mearsheimer 2001). And it would be foolish to ignore the reality that the destructive power of nuclear weapons makes wars between the holders of such weapons exceedingly costly—regardless of their economic interactions. Such contributions are difficult to refute since these conditions have largely been consistently present since the end of the Korean War. As a result we have not witnessed a Northeast Asia *without* these conditions thus preventing a more conclusive verdict on what if anything would change in their absence.

Nevertheless, important as a military balance may be, this volume and the research behind it point to the numerous cases in which the multiple tension spots about which East Asian governments become viscerally animated, typically prove to be flashes in the pan or ritualistic exchanges of longstanding charges and countercharges with no military options being enlisted. Rarely do they capture enough sustained political attention to divert from their political elites' ongoing focus on issues of domestic economic development and enhanced interaction with the global economy. Geopolitical considerations and security worries have by no means vanished from the agenda of Northeast Asian political elites but the temptation to seek their resolution through military force remains low on the list of policy options most government leaders are actually considering (Pempel 1999; Woo-Cumings 1999; Frost 2008; Mahbubani 2008; Overholt 2008; inter alia).

The compelling reality is that throughout the region political elites have increasingly seen that economic security is as critical to their nation's overall security as well as to their own political legitimacy. Military protection from foreign invasions or substantial exchanges of fire remain of concern but, over time, these have faded in priority as they appear ever less likely.

The DPRK remains an undeniable exception, but political and business elites across the remainder of the region have been operating from the shared conviction that national economic development has become a positive-sum game for the region as a whole, as a consequence of which it has risen to being a principal focus of their domestic and foreign policies, if not the preeminent focus. In essence rather than worrying about *relative* power gains among neighboring states, multiple Asian political leaders realize that it is possible for both their country and others in the region to achieve simultaneous economic gains that make all more powerful in *absolute* terms. In the apt phrasing of Etel Solingen (2007: 760), East Asia's rulers "pivoted their political survival on economic performance, export-led growth, and integration in the global political economy." In the process, Northeast Asian states have advanced simultaneously in absolute wealth and power. In the process the region has taken the shape noted above, namely as a natural economic zone with ever-expanding and integrated production linkages transcending national borders and bringing regional economic benefits to mass and elite alike.

Across Northeast Asia there has been a pervasive embrace of national economic growth as a powerful tool capable of enhancing a nation's power and prestige as well as in mitigating potential domestic divisions. As a consequence, states have collectively reduced their focus on military might as the principal driver of enhanced national influence and as a consequence have forged a less militarily brittle region. This shift is well captured by William Overholt's crisp phrasing:

> For centuries, the principal route to wealth and power had been conquest of neighboring territory. Wealth came from seizing neighbors' golden temples and taxing their peasants. The dawn of the Asian miracle transformed this ancient reality. Now wealth and power accrued to whoever grew the faster by reforming the domestic economy. Conversely, the arrival of modern military technology put the quest for power through war at risk of achieving Pyrrhic victories (2008: 18–19).

As a consequence, as Armstrong (2006: 257–8) has noted,

> although historical animosities and distrust among China, South Korea, and Japan, not to mention Russia, persist, in recent years, the conversations among the respective governments have tended to focus more on free trade areas and increasing cooperation at all levels.

The result is that, despite periodic bursts of nationalist bombast and occasional military skirmishes, a shared Northeast Asian prioritization of economic development continues, for the moment at least, to hold official precedence and to serve as a powerful check on irredentist territorial conflicts and military freelancing.

Causal connections between economics and security in Northeast Asia remain far from unidirectional, however. During the early phases of the Cold War, East Asian security tensions were particularly high while cross-border economic interactions were limited by the sharp bipolar divisions across the region and by the military and economic dependence of Korea, Taiwan, and Japan on both the U.S. military and U.S. export markets. The region's last five decades or so, however, suggest that an easing of the worst security tensions permitted the region's political and economic elites to gain confidence about previous external security threats and to shift their focus to domestic economic development.

As former Singaporean President Lee Kwan Yew (2007) has effectively argued, the easing of these security tensions began with the U.S. defeat in Viet-Nam. This gave countries across the region the opportunity to explore paradigms of economic growth based neither on Chinese or Soviet communism nor on U.S. laissez-faire market stratagems. Governments forged their national economic policies using mix-and-match policy approaches with relative ideological impunity. In most cases heavy doses of state leadership and an export orientation drew substantially on the blueprint that had undergirded Japan's success (for example, Woo-Cumings 1999).

Even more dramatic was the situation in U.S.–China–Japan relations. The improved regional security climate was further fostered by the Nixon visit to China in 1972 and normalization of relations between China and Japan that same year. These laid the groundwork for China's subsequent escape from the straightjacket of Maoist economics, in turn allowing for Deng's shift to domestic economic development based on a mix of market principles and CCP political control. The prior economic successes of Japan, the ROK, Singapore, Hong Kong, and Taiwan held out for China's leaders a tantalizing alternative growth model along with the promise that China might plug into and benefit from what was increasingly becoming a region-wide economic miracle (World Bank 1993; Zweig 2002). And as China's new economic fortunes improved and the search for enhanced foreign investments continued, the PRC was more readily able to normalize its diplomatic relations with the ROK (despite DPRK opposition and the lack of similar normalization of either U.S.–DPRK or Japanese–DPRK relations) (Yahuda 2004: chap. 3; Overholt 2008; inter alia).

Over time, the region's mounting economic successes have contributed to the region-wide reduction in security tensions by allowing most governments in Northeast Asia to prioritize the improvement of the economic well-being and wealth of their countries rather than to enhancement of their military budgets in the interest of territorially-based confrontations with their neighbors. In effect, for most of the countries in the region over the last two decades or more, economic growth and a reduction in security tensions were linked in a mutually constitutive positive spiral. Security frictions have hardly disappeared, but they have been greatly relaxed and the probabilities of imminent military conflicts have been greatly reduced. Equally importantly, as economics has become an ever more important indicator of national power, it is possible to envision a future in which geopolitical and security balances become increasingly concentrated on enhancing national economic muscle.

Greater economic security also contributed to a softening of other bipolar rigidities, among the most prominent being the recognition of the ROK by the PRC in 1992. Equally, while relations across the Taiwan Straits were periodically tense, the last PRC missiles were fired over Taiwan in 1996, and rhetorical saber-rattling aside, the two sides have moved toward a strategic standoff sans shooting and even rapid improvement in economic, tourism, and communications links since the 2009 election of Taiwanese president Ma Ying-jeou, topics explored in greater depth in Scott Kastner's chapter.

Moreover, contrary to some predictions (e.g. Mearsheimer 2001), there has been no East Asian "balancing" against the now single superpower, the United States. The most persistent security threats in the region continue to center around the regime in North Korea and what its leaders would describe as their unending and uphill struggle to ensure national safety from rapacious outsiders but what most objective observers would portray as little more than a cyclical pattern of regional provocation and a rejection of economic improvements that might threaten the privileges of an authoritarian political and military elite (Cha and Kang 2003; Funabashi 2007; Chinoy 2008).

Thus, while East Asia's collective economic growth may have been initially contingent on the improved security climate across the region, economic development has subsequently fostered further reductions in the most overt arms races and security flare-ups. Governments have become freer to forgo massive military build-ups and territorial confrontations and to devote both policy-making and budgetary resources to domestic economic development. Improved security and enhanced economic performances have become mutually interdependent.

Nevertheless, particularly within Northeast Asia, national rivalries remain even as pursuit of national economic growth has become a commonly chanted mantra. National governments remain the ultimate repositories of power and the primary building blocks within the region and territoriality and national governmental priorities continue to trump any potentially integrative forces of cross-border economics. Nor has economic interdependence obliterated the appeals of economic nationalism. Governments continue to joust with one another on a host of diplomatic and security issues—as well as economic issues—despite their growing economic interdependence.

Historical memories continue to cast a long shadow over relations between Japan on the one hand and China and the ROK on the other. Just as historical legacies lay beneath the surface of many problems, so too is the fact that China seems to be "rising" while Japan is at best "stagnant." This latter dynamic has played out particularly as a Japan–China rivalry in the economic sphere.

Under Roh Moo-hyun, Seoul began cooperating with the PRC on military matters. Moreover, both China and Korea issued declarations indicating their opposition to Japan's bid for a permanent seat on the UN Security Council, making it clear that economic ties among the three countries did not eliminate national concerns about power balances and prestige (Korea's President Roh actually came out explicitly in favor of a seat for Germany, ignoring Japan's claims). Then in April 2005, President Roh announced that his country would seek to be a "balancer" in the Asian region, a role that implied a new proximity to China at the expense of Korea's prior ties to the United States and Japan.

Thus Northeast Asia presents a far from simple picture of the relationship between economics and security. Initially, a reduction in many of the worst security tensions fostered a collective national focus on economic growth and regional interdependence. And as the economies of most Asian countries improved, the most threatening security tensions subsided, although they hardly disappeared. Economic interdependence proceeded in tandem with a general improvement in the security climate, pockmarked by parenthetic outbursts of nationalism, cross-border insults, and bombast. Even though the region's nation-states are interconnected by growing commercial and investment linkages, security relations, particularly in Northeast Asia, remain palpably tense and far more subject to national differences in goals, despite the relatively low probability of overt military confrontations. Clearly economics and security have been closely linked and mutually interdependent over the last several decades in Northeast Asia. But at the same time, one presents a picture of the "glass half full" while the other remains a "glass half empty." Or as I have argued elsewhere (Pempel 2005): East Asian security conditions suggest a region whose future, though uncertain, remains in the words of Aaron Friedberg (1993) "ripe for rivalry" while economic linkages suggest a region "ripe for cooperation."

Power transition

The three factors noted above can appear overly linear or static. Clearly Northeast Asia is a highly dynamic region, and concerns about the future direction of the economic–security nexus in Northeast Asia must confront the question of whether recent trends involving a mixture of economic interdependence and reduced security tensions will continue. Will security tensions continue to soften or, instead, will one or more of the smoldering areas of friction ignite, sparking major military conflagration? Answers to such questions will be heavily shaped by the currently huge shifts in power relations within the region and how one evaluates the broad literature on "power transitions." A vast body of literature contends that such power transitions will almost automatically spawn conflicts between the demands of the rising power for changes in the status quo to better reflect its interests and efforts by existing powers to retain the system which ensures their primacy (Organski 1965, 1968; Organski and Kugler 1980; Gilpin 1981; Mearsheimer 2001; inter alia).

Northeast Asia is currently in the midst of a power transition driven primarily by the rising economic strength of China. No single fact has been more important in the economic–security nexus within Northeast Asia since the turn of the century than the so-called rise of China. Since throwing off the ideological shackles of Maoist economics in 1978, China's growth rate has consistently been at or above 10 percent per year and total GDP has risen four-fold. The country has marched steadily from its rural and agricultural roots to one that is vastly more urban and industrialized. By the end of 2010, the country's GDP had catapulted into second place globally, ahead of Japan and Germany; it is currently closing in quickly on the world's leader, the United States.

China's share of world economic output in 2010 had risen to more than 13 percent in U.S. dollars, up from less than 4 percent two decades earlier. As late as 1975 China's per capita income was one of the lowest in the world and even as late as 1990 it was 30 percent below the average of sub-Saharan Africa. In 2010 that figure was $4,500 per capita, establishing the country as an undeniably middle-income country (Lin 2011). China's growth was fueled by expanding exports and the country's share of world exports of goods and services which had been barely above 1 percent as late as 1990 was more than 8 percent in 2011. And as China's exports have grown, and as domestic consumption has been held down, foreign reserves have ballooned. In 1990 these were only $11.1 billion, roughly enough to cover three months of imports. Today those reserves stand at a gargantuan $3 trillion plus, the largest in the world by far, and a powerful indicator of China's enhanced global financial might.

Related statistics could be rattled off for pages; they all tell portions of the same story. China has undergone a massive economic transition, in the process of which it has gained a vastly larger influence within the region. Furthermore, China's growth is rapidly becoming more sophisticated, moving the country from its labor-intensive assembly orientation toward one that is increasingly reliant on enhanced productivity and in which the country has become the final consumer and the engine of regional economic growth, as well as the final exporter of finished products to North America and Europe. Without question, the ability of Chinese leaders to continue this economic blitzkrieg is far from guaranteed, if not highly problematic, but even if it is not sustained, past growth has given Chinese leaders a far more robust and influential economy than the country enjoyed as little as twenty years earlier (Shirk 2007).

The presumptive regional leadership that Japan had demonstrated during the 1980s with its economic prowess, foreign aid, and massive outgoing investments has become a distant memory in the region, overshadowed by China's robust economy paralleled by twenty years of declining productivity and slow-to-no growth in Japan. Nor is the economic muscle of the United States any longer as potent as it once was. A decade marked by two expensive and draining wars; the erosion of fiscal balance through massive tax cuts by the Bush administration; and most recently, the self-inflicted wounds from a collapsing housing bubble, the Lehman crisis, and the bizarre political gridlock induced by the so-called debt crisis, have collectively catalyzed a strong sense of *schadenfreude* among Chinese leaders. China is by far the largest single holder of the ever-mounting U.S. debt with roughly $1.2 trillion in U.S. Treasuries or about 8 percent of the total, and is also its largest supplier of imported goods ($364 billion), leading to a facile but nonetheless compelling claim that America's economy is based on borrowing from China to buy goods made in China. Although neighboring countries may have a more nuanced view of the U.S. economy, the overriding message is clear—American economic muscle is atrophying while that of China is bulking up.

The massive surge in China's absolute and relative economic strength has substantially enhanced the country's regional influence. For example, by 2001 China had become the ROK's number one target for outgoing investments and in 2002 China–Hong Kong became South Korea's largest export market (*China Daily* 2 February 2002), replacing the United States, which had long occupied first place. China has also replaced the United States as Japan's number one trading partner and has become a major destination for outgoing Japanese FDI; Japanese firms based in China have become a key engine in Japan's still limp economic growth. In addition, China is the major destination for Taiwanese FDI and is far and away Taiwan's leading economic and trade partner, as Scott Kastner's chapter in this volume details at great length.

In a break from the focus on bilateral foreign relations, concentrated mostly on larger powers until the turn of the century, China has also become more active recently in the development of multilateral regional linkages. As Oba shows in Chapter 6 and Pempel demonstrates in Chapter 9, China has played key roles in the ASEAN Plus Three process, including the development of the financial swap arrangements under the Chiang Mai Initiative (CMI) and CMI's subsequent multilateralization (CMIM). Japan plus China–Hong Kong are the co-largest contributors to CMIM, with each contributing 32 percent of the fund's total capital. China was a founding member and a key energizer behind the Shanghai Cooperation Organization (SCO) and Beijing serves as the headquarters for SCO's secretariat as well as being the major coordinator and host of the Six

Party Talks. China has also been active in a host of Track II processes and has developed a number of preferential trade pacts, the most notable being with ASEAN. At present, as Iida's detailed description of the trilateral process has shown, China is in study groups with both Japan and Korea to evaluate the possibilities for a trilateral FTA which would include both. Such multilateral activity not only has demonstrated China's willingness and ability to work cooperatively with its neighbors but it has also provided China with regional forums through which to influence the region's future course of development.

China's economic strength has allowed the country to make substantial increases in military modernization and defense expenditures. Official figures from the PRC for its 2011 military budget indicate expenditures of s $91.5 billion, which would be the second largest absolute expenditure in the world. Chinese estimates are well below U.S. Department of Defense (DoD) calculations, which are roughly $150 billion. SIPRI puts the figure for 2010 at $114 billion, higher than the official number but below the estimates of DoD (SIPRI 2011). Beyond the dispute over specific numbers, it is quite clear that China is expending substantial portions of its new wealth on modernizing and enhancing its military capabilities. At the same time, it is helpful to keep the numbers and percentages in regional perspective.

The SIPRI estimates have China's total military expenditures second only to those of the United States, which they calculate at $698 billion; however, the United States still spends roughly six times what China spends. Official Chinese figures put defense spending at about 1.4 percent of the nation's GDP; other studies put the figure at between 1.9 and 2.4 percent. Such proportions indicate that Chinese budgeters clearly give greater priority to military expenditures than does the budget of neighboring Japan (1 percent of GDP). The U.S. figure is strikingly larger at 4.7 percent of GDP while that of Taiwan is 2.2–2.4 percent and that of the ROK is about 2.9 percent, although obviously with much smaller economies and budgets the absolute expenditures of the ROK and Taiwan are but a portion of these of the PRC.

Much of the rise in China's military expenditure is linked to its broader economic growth. Thus, the country slowed its rate of increase in military spending considerably in 2010 (3.8 percent in real terms compared to an average of 9.3 percent from 2001 to 2009), with the lower increase specifically linked by the Chinese government to weaker economic growth in 2009 (SIPRI 2011).

Regardless of how much one attempts to downplay the significance of China's military budget or to justify it in the context of other countries' "larger" expenditures, it is clear that China's escalating military expenditures and increased sophistication challenge the current military balance of power in the region, and as a consequence they have catalyzed considerable speculation about the long-run implications of such increases (Jacques 2009; Friedberg 2011; inter alia). Surely for military planners, the enhanced sophistication of the Chinese military remains something to be "planned for." Of particular concern to such planners in the United States is the fact that the PRC is advancing its capabilities for area access deniability, thus making it militarily more difficult for the U.S. military to enjoy the complete freedom of movement in and around the Chinese coasts that it once had.

Yet, while potential business competitors and many national leaders worry about the ways in which China's economic growth might challenge them, for the most part, they have welcomed an economically stronger China for its ongoing contribution as an engine of continued regional growth. And even when they express misgivings about a regional economy dominated by China, most accept its inevitability.

In arguing that power transition is underway in Northeast Asia, it is vital to recognize that this transition has been moving forward on two rather separate tracks and timetables. China's enhanced economic strength has unquestionably catapulted it to vastly new powers in the region. These, however, are still far from being matched by its much slower improvements in military capabilities. The United States remains by far the most powerful state militarily in the region, a position it is unlikely to yield for at least another decade or two even as its military planners focus on the many ways in which even a somewhat more militarily powerful China might pose security problems for the United States and its goals across the region. At present however, China has been quite reluctant to utilize its emerging military capabilities to shape events in the region; virtually all of its geo-diplomatic activities have traded on its enhanced economic strength.

International relations, Northeast Asia, and the economic–security nexus

How does the economic–security nexus in Northeast Asia inform the broader debates in international relations? A central premise among realist and neo-realist scholars has been the extent to which international relations remains driven by the anarchic nature of the world and the preeminence of individual states acting in pursuit of their self-defined national interests as well as their relative power vis-à-vis potential adversaries. The national state and military security are presumed to be the ultimate drivers of intra-state relations. National governments are taken as ultimately interested in advancing their material and security gains vis-à-vis one another. In the anarchic world of competing states, political relations are consequently seen as largely zero sum. From such perspectives, a nation's economic might is surely a part of its overall resource armory but it is typically seen as a far less useful weapon when the security chips are down than are guns, bullets, missiles, and military might.

In strong contrast are arguments that put greater emphasis on economic strength and more importance on the economic interactions and economic interdependence of states. The broad conclusion typically arrived at is that enhanced economic interdependence works to reduce the inclination for any single state to act militarily because economic interdependence makes the costs of combat actions too high due to the damage that would be done to trade and investment ties. Such arguments are central to neoliberal analysis, and undergirding such approaches is the belief that interdependent states can simultaneously advance their absolute gains through economic cooperation rather than focusing on relative gains vis-à-vis one another.

Beyond this classic epistemological battle, there has been extensive examination of the more particularistic ways in which economics and security interact, the major question being whether economic interdependence does indeed make warfare more unlikely. To date, the bulk of the efforts to resolve debates have been global in nature and have relied on huge worldwide data sets measuring such things as trade and investment, dyadic conflicts, the escalation and resolution of conflicts, and the like.

This vast body of literature, despite some progress, has agreed on no definitive resolution of the central issue of whether economic interdependence fosters military peace. This book does not begin from, nor does it seek to resolve, these macro-debates per se. Clearly Northeast Asia is affected by the global balance of power and the region is undoubtedly a part of any world system one can envision. Nevertheless, we begin from the premise that Northeast Asia functions largely as a regional security complex, a rather self-contained security ecosystem if you like, in which state-to-state relations are shaped far more heavily by intra-regional relations and links to one's immediate neighbors (including as a permanent East Asian presence, the United States) than to the broader globe as a whole (Buzan 2003).

In this regard, this project resonates with the provocative question posed by Acharya and Buzan (2007): "Why is There no non-Western International Relations Theory?" They observe that the vast bulk of contemporary international relations theorizing was done in a Western context, devoid for the most part from the diverse experiences of East Asia. Some efforts (e.g. Ikenberry and Mastanduno 2003) have been made to examine East Asia and international relations theories in an interactive process, but these have been relatively few. We hope that by addressing the particular relationships among economics and security in the detailed confines of Northeast Asia we will be able to expose the far more nuanced interactions.

Undergirding all the research that follows is the presumption that within Northeast Asia, a nation's self-defined "security" is rarely if ever restricted simply to shooting wars, defense budgets, military prowess, and state-to-state conflicts. If Northeast Asia has anything to teach international relations more broadly, it is that the states in the region have typically defined their national security in far broader terms that include security in economics, energy, the environment, epidemics, and a host of other non-traditional security areas that could threaten the nation's well-being. And as will be clear in the chapters themselves, economic well-being and security are typically at the top of each nation's list of "security" concerns.

Rather than positioning ourselves on one side or the other of debates about whether or not economic interdependence dramatically reduces the chances of war, this volume addresses the more nuanced questions of how well or how poorly states interact with one another in geopolitics and how this is (or is not) affected by their economic relations. Thus, Taiwan's leaders have put considerable attention on protecting Taiwan's sovereignty, not just in avoiding military confrontations. China in turn has been concerned with preventing any increased manifestations of Taiwanese independence. And as Scott Kastner shows in Chapter 2, leaders on both sides of the Straits have tried to shape their economic interactions with one another in ways that will allow each to advance their competing views. Political relations between Taiwan and China are heavily shaped by their economic interactions and their economic interactions are also shaped by the political relations between the two sides. But there is nothing like a linear relationship, in large part because both sides are engaged in political competition and diplomatic arm-wrestling that is far more nuanced than simply engaging in military conflict or avoiding it.

In like manner, Hiroku Imamura shows in Chapter 3 how the ROK has sought to shape the military and nuclear behavior of the DPRK though economic carrots under the Kim Dea-Jung and Roh Moo-hyun regimes but has shifted to using economic sanctions as sticks under the Lee Myung-bok administration. The North in turn has frequently shifted its short-term behavior in response to economic blandishments but its military and security behavior has been only episodically affected by such external economic sanctions or inducements, quite probably because of the willingness to the PRC to continue providing bilateral economic investments and trade and to resist the imposition of sanctions by the ROK, the United States, Japan, and others. She also shows how domestic political and economic choices in the North have kept it from the successful pursuit of economic reforms such as were carried out by China and Vietnam.

Staying on the Korean peninsula, Min Gyo Koo provides an extensive treatment in Chapter 7 of how the ROK has adopted a highly positive attitude toward FTAs as a strategy for economic change at home and global integration abroad. In doing so, the ROK has shown much more domestic openness than its Japanese neighbor, most recently entering into FTAs with the European Union and the United States, two of its major trade partners.

Equally complicating for any linear projections about economic ties reducing conflicts, Jong Kun Choi (Chapter 5) shows how political tensions in Northeast Asia among Japan, the ROK, and China have been substantially shaped by issues of historical memory linked to Japan's aggressive behaviors during the earlier part of the twentieth century. But he shows as well that these tensions have rarely achieved more than a subsidiary role in shaping ties and that economic interdependence has jumped phenomenally even in the face of frequent nationalist vituperations about issues of historical memory.

Still a different nuance on the economic–security nexus is presented by Tai Ming Cheung (Chapter 4), who demonstrates that the states of Northeast Asia have adopted very different grand strategies concerning the acquisition and use of technology. At different times the several countries of Northeast Asia have pursued military technologies and civilian technologies with quite different views about techno-nationalism, techno-globalism, and possible fusions between the two. Here technology serves both a military and a civilian-developmental set of goals simultaneously and the two are rarely in conflict.

In addition to economic interdependence, both Keisuke Iida and T.J. Pempel's chapters show that the countries of Northeast Asia have become more institutionally linked. Pempel, in Chapter 8, examines the broad pallet of East Asian and Northeast Asia institutions that have been created largely in the wake of the financial crisis of 1997–98. These exist predominantly in the economic and financial spheres. At the same time, he argues that there is functional spillover from such bodies into the improved security climate. In Chapter 9 Iida looks in more detail at one such body—the relatively new trilateral leaders meeting among China, Japan, and Korea—and shows how it has become more deeply institutionalized and how it is laying the groundwork for a trilateral trade agreement as well as a trilateral investment treaty. These measures have moved forward despite the frequent geopolitical disputes that emerge among them. He argues, and I personally would agree, that these three have come to a collective realization that they have more to gain from cooperation, particularly in the economic sphere, than they do by contestation.

At the same time, Mie Oba (Chapter 6) reminds us that whatever tentative conclusions we may draw about the economic–security nexus in Northeast Asia, this remains a region in flux. The financial crises of 1997–98 and the more recent crisis of 2008–09 have played a large part in structuring economic relations both within Northeast Asia and between the states of Northeast Asia and the broader global financial community. In the midst of both crises, China in particular has emerged as the most successful economic player. Additionally, China's overall regional influence has risen considerably as the consequence of its successful maneuvering through both crises while the prestige and economic influence of the United States have been sharply reduced.

These chapters converge on one central point: Northeast Asian economic and security relations are marked by numerous and nuanced facets. The behavior of major states is far from whimsical or the result of ever-shifting winds. Deep structural patterns are identifiable. Yet, the behavior of the major players is often more complicated and nuanced than efforts at global generalizations typically acknowledge. Northeast Asia clearly has important lessons for international relations more broadly. Most significantly, the region demonstrates the need to recognize the driving power of economic linkages among the key states in Northeast Asia. Thus, any examination of the economic–security nexus generally, we believe, must start in particular regions and remain sensitive to that region's specifics as well as to the changes that occur as power shifts among its key players.

References

Acharya, Amitav and Barry Buzan. 2007. Why Is There No non-Western International Relations Theory? An Introduction. *International Relations of the Asia-Pacific* 7 (3): 287–312.

Aggarwal, Vinod K. and Min Gyo Koo, eds. 2008. *Asia's New Institutional Architecture: Evolving Structures for Managing Trade, Financial, and Security Relations*. Berlin: Springer-Verlag.

Aggarwal, Vinod K. and Shujiro Urata, eds. 2006. *Bilateral Trade Agreements in the Asia-Pacific: Origins, Evolution, and Implications*. London: Routledge.

Alagappa, Muthiah, ed. 2003. *Asian Security Order: Instrumental and Normative Features*. Stanford, CA: Stanford University Press.

Armstrong, Charles K., Gilbert Rozman, Samuel S. Kim, and Stephen Kotkin, eds. 2006. *Korea at the Center: Dynamics of Regionalism in Northeast Asia*. Armonk, NY: M.E. Sharpe.

Buzan, Barry. 2003. Security Architecture in Asia: The Interplay of Regional and Global Levels. *The Pacific Review* 16 (2): 143–73.

Buzan, Barry and Gerald Segal. 1994. Rethinking East Asian Security. *Survival* 36 (2): 3–21.

Cha, Victor D. 2007. Winning Asia: Washington's Untold Success Story. *Foreign Affairs* 86 (6): 98–113.

Cha, Victor D. and David C. Kang. 2003. *Nuclear North Korea: A Debate on Engagement Strategies*. New York: Columbia University Press.

Chan, Steve. 2010. An Odd Thing Happened on the Way to Balancing: East Asian States' Reactions to China's Rise. *International Security Review* 12: 387–412.

Chin, Gregory T. 2010. Remaking the Architecture: The Emerging Powers, Self-insuring, and Regional Insulation. *International Affairs* 86 (3): 693–715.

Chinoy, Mike. 2008. *Meltdown: The Inside Story of the North Korean Nuclear Crisis*. New York: St. Martin's Press.

Christensen, Thomas J. 2003. China, the U.S.–Japan Alliance, and the Security Dilemma in East Asia. In *International Relations Theory and the Asia Pacific*, G. John Ikenberry and Michael Mastanduno, eds. New York: Columbia University Press.

Cordesman, Anthony H. 2011. *The Korean Military Balance: Comparative Korean Forces and the Forces of Key Neighboring States*. Washington, DC: Center for Strategic and International Studies.

Council for Economic Planning and Development. 2002. *Taiwan Statistical Data Book 2002*. Taipei: Council for Economic Planning and Development.

Dent, C.M. 2003. Networking the Region? The Emergence and Impact of Asia-Pacific Bilateral Trade Agreement Projects. *Pacific Review* 16 (1): 1–28.

———. 2005. Bilateral Free Trade Agreements: Boon or Bane for Regionalism in East Asia and the Asia-Pacific? *European Journal of East Asian Studies* 4 (2): 287–314.

Friedberg, Aaron. 1993. Ripe for Rivalry: Prospects for Peace in a Multipolar Asia. *International Security* 18 (3): 5–33.

———. 2011. *A Contest for Supremacy: China, America, and the Struggle for Mastery in Asia*. New York: Norton.

Frost, Ellen L. 2008. *Asia's New Regionalism*. London: Lynne Rienner.

Funabashi, Yoichi. 2007. *The Peninsula Question: A Chronicle of the Second Korean Nuclear Crisis*. Washington, DC: Brookings Institution.

Gilpin, Robert. 1981. *War and Change in International Politics*. Cambridge: Cambridge University Press.

Goh, Evelyn. 2007–08. Great Powers and Hierarchical Order in Southeast Asia. *International Security* 32 (3): 113–57.

Goldstein, Avery and Edward D. Mansfield. 2011. Peace and Prosperity in East Asia: When Fighting Ends. *Global Asia* 6 (2): 9–15.

Holbrooke, Richard. 1991. Japan and the United States: Ending the Unequal Partnership. *Foreign Affairs* 70 (5): 41–57.

Hughes, Christopher. 2009. "Super-Sizing" the DPRK Threat: Japan's Evolving Military Posture and North Korea. *Asian Survey* 49 (2): 291–311.

Ikenberry, G. John and Michael Mastanduno, eds. 2003. *International Relations Theory and the Asia Pacific*. New York: Columbia University Press.

International Institute for Strategic Studies. 2010. *The Military Balance, 2010*. London: Routledge.

Jacques, Martin. 2009. *When China Rules the World: The End of the Western World and the Birth of a New Global Order*. New York: Penguin Books.

Kahler, Miles. 2006. Territoriality and Conflict in an Era of Globalization. In *Territoriality and Conflict in an Era of Globalization*, Miles Kahler and Barbara Walter, eds. Cambridge: Cambridge University Press.

———. 2011. Weak Ties Don't Bind: Asia Needs Stronger Structures to Build Lasting Peace. *Global Asia* 6 (2): 18–23.

Kang, David. 2003. Hierarchy and Stability in Asian International Relations. In *International Relations Theory and the Asia Pacific*, G. John Ikenberry and Michael Mastanduno, eds. New York: Columbia University Press.

Kaplan, Fred. 2004. Rolling Blunder: How the Bush Administration let North Korea Get Nukes. *Washington Monthly*, May. Available at <http://www.washingtonmonthly. com/features/2004/0405.kaplan.html>.

Kato, Kozo. 1999. Open Regionalism and Japan's Systematic Vulnerability. In *Asian Regionalism*, Peter J. Katzenstein, ed. Ithaca, NY: Cornell East Asia Series.

Katzenstein, Peter J. and Takashi Shiraishi. 1997. *Network Power*. Ithaca, NY: Cornell University Press.

Kim, Samuel S. ed. 2004. *The International Relations of Northeast Asia*. Lanham, MD: Rowman & Littlefield.

Kivimaki, Timo. 2010. East Asian Relative Peace—Does it Exist? What is it? *The Pacific Review* 23 (4): 503–26.

Koo, Min Gyo. 2009. *Island Disputes and Maritime Regime Building in East Asia: Between a Rock and a Hard Place*. Heidelberg: Springer.

Kubota, Isao. 1994. Economic Integration is Increasing in Asia. *Japan Times* 20 June.

Lake, David A. 2009. *Hierarchy in International Relations*. Ithaca, NY: Cornell University Press.

Lin, Justin Yifu. 2011. China and the World Economy. Remarks at the 20th Anniversary of the University of Science and Technology, Hong Kong, 23 March. Available at <http://www.bm.ust.hk/chinaforum/pdf/prof_lin_speech.pdf>.

Mahbubani, Kishore. 2008. *The New Asian Hemisphere: The Irresistible Shift of Global Power to the East*. New York: Public Affairs.

Mearsheimer, John J. 2001. *The Tragedy of Great Power Politics*. New York: Norton.

Naughton, Barry. 1997. *The China Circle: Economics and Technology in the PRC, Taiwan, and Hong Kong*. Washington, DC: Brookings Institution.

Oba, Mie. 2008. Regional Arrangements for Trade in Northeast Asia: Cooperation and Competition between China and Japan. In *Asia's New Institutional Architecture: Evolving Structures for Managing Trade, Financial, and Security Relations*, Vinod K. Aggarwal and Gyo Koo Min, eds. Berlin: Springer-Verlag.

Organski, A.F.K. 1958. *World Politics*. New York: Alfred A. Knopf.

Organski, A.F.K. 1965. *The Stages of Political Development*. New York: Knopf.

Organski, A.F.K. and Jacek Kugler. 1980. *The War Ledger*. Chicago: University of Chicago Press.

Overholt, William H. 2008. *Asia, America, and the Transformation of Geopolitics.* Cambridge: Cambridge University Press.

Pempel, T.J. 1997. Transpacific Torii: Japan and the Emerging Asian Regionalism. In *Network Power*, Peter J. Katzenstein and Shiraishi Takashi, eds. Ithaca, NY: Cornell University Press.

———. 1999. Regional Ups; Regional Downs. In *The Politics of the Asian Economic Crisis*, T.J. Pempel, ed. Ithaca, NY: Cornell University Press.

———. 2005. *Remapping East Asia: The Construction of a Region.* Ithaca, NY: Cornell University Press.

Pempel, T.J. and Shujiro Urata. 2006. Japan: A New Move Toward Bilateral Trade Agreements. In *Bilateral Trade Agreements in the Asia-Pacific: Origins, Evolution, and Implications*, Vinod K. Aggarwal and Urata Shujiro, eds. London: Routledge.

Perkins, Dwight H. 2007. East Asian Economic Growth and its Implications for Regional Security. *Asia-Pacific Review* 14 (1): 44–53.

Ravenhill, John. 2008. Asia's New Economic Institutions. In *Asia's New Institutional Architecture: Evolving Structures for Managing Trade, Financial, and Security Relations*, Vinod K. Aggarwal and Min Gyo Koo, eds. Berlin: Springer-Verlag.

Shirk, Susan. 2007. *China: Fragile Superpower.* Oxford: Oxford University Press.

SIPRI (Stockholm International Peace Research Institute). 2011. Recent Trends in Military Expenditure. Available at <http://www.sipri.org/research/armaments/milex/resultoutput/trends>.

Solingen, Etel. 2007. Pax Asiatica Versus Bella Levantina: The Foundations of War and Peace in East Asia and the Middle East. *American Political Science Review* 101 (4): 757–80.

Van Ness, Peter. 2003. *The North Korean Nuclear Crisis: Four-Plus-Two—An Idea Whose Time Has Come. Keynote* No. 4. Department of International Relations, Australian National University, Canberra, Australia. Available at <http://rspas.anu.edu.au/ir/pubs/keynotes/keynotes-04.htm>.

Weitz, Richard. 2007. China and Russia Hand in Hand: Will it Work? *Global Asia* 2 (3): 52–63.

Woo-Cumings, Meredith, ed. 1999. *The Developmental State.* Ithaca, NY: Cornell University Press.

World Bank. 1993. *The East Asian Miracle: Economic Growth and Public Policy.* Oxford: Oxford University Press.

Yahuda, Michael B. 2004. *The International Politics of the Asia-Pacific, 1945–1995.* 2d ed. London, New York: Routledge Curzon.

Yew, Lee Kuan. 2007. The United States, Iraq and the War on Terror. *Foreign Affairs* 86 (1): 2–7.

Zweig, David. 2002. *Internationalizing China: Domestic Interests and Global Linkages.* Ithaca, NY: Cornell University Press.

Part 1

Economics and security in Northeast Asia

Geographical interfaces

2 Drinking poison to quench a thirst?

The security consequences of China–Taiwan economic integration

Scott L. Kastner

Introduction

Despite what at times has been an extremely tense political relationship, economic ties between the People's Republic of China (PRC) and Taiwan have grown rapidly since the 1980s. Bilateral trade flows ballooned from less than US$1 billion per year in the mid-1980s to over US$120 billion by 2010.[1] Many estimate that accumulated Taiwan investment in the PRC far exceeds US$100 billion. The PRC is Taiwan's largest trading partner and, by far, the primary destination of the island's outbound foreign direct investment. Economic integration across the Taiwan Strait proceeded even though former Taiwan presidents Lee Teng-hui (1988–2000) and Chen Shui-bian (2000–2008) were deeply skeptical that expanding economic ties with the PRC benefit Taiwan economically or politically. The current Ma Ying-jeou (2008–present) administration, on the other hand, unambiguously welcomes cross-Strait economic integration. Since becoming president, Ma's government has signed numerous economic agreements with Beijing. These agreements have—among other things—opened direct shipping and air transport links with the PRC, opened Taiwan to PRC tourists, and increased financial cooperation between the two sides. In the summer of 2010, the two sides signed a more sweeping Economic Cooperation Framework Agreement (ECFA), which provides a roadmap for future negotiations over cross-Strait economic liberalization and includes an "early harvest" list of products subject to accelerated tariff reduction schedules.[2]

Ma's liberalization of Taiwan's economic policies toward China has sparked sharp criticism from his political opponents, some of whom have issued dire warnings about the security implications of deepening cross-Strait economic exchange. Some fear that Taiwan's growing economic dependence on China has the potential to undermine Taiwan's sovereignty. For example, former president Lee Teng-hui warned that Beijing's interest in an ECFA is politically motivated, and is part of a larger plan to use deepening economic ties as a means to facilitate eventual unification. As such, Lee asserts that Ma's pursuit of an ECFA with China represents his "most serious mistake." Tsai Ing-Wen, former chairperson of the opposition Democratic Progressive Party (DPP) and the DPP's nominee for president in 2012, has argued along similar lines: "China has maintained a consistent economic strategy against Taiwan that involves making it part of the greater China economic sphere and enslaving Taiwan to China's economy."[3]

The Ma administration counters that economic cooperation with mainland China not only can help Taiwan's economy (particularly during a global economic downturn), but it also helps to lay the groundwork for a more stable cross-Strait political relationship. Ma believes that cooperation in economic arenas has the potential to spill over into political arenas by building trust and understanding. As he put it in a 2008 interview: "Only by more contact, more understanding, more exchange [can] we reduce the historical hostilities across the Taiwan Strait."[4] Officials in the Ma administration also believe that normalization of cross-Strait economic relations—including the reaching of the ECFA agreement—will make it easier for Taiwan to reach free-trade agreements with other countries, and hence will help to protect Taiwan from marginalization as other countries in East Asia move toward regionalism.[5] In this way, improved economic relations with the PRC can actually make Taiwan more secure.

There are clearly substantial differences in how key political players in Taiwan view the security consequences of cross-Strait economic integration. What drives these differences? A cynic might contend that the arguments advanced by both sides of the political spectrum in this regard are post hoc and self-serving. Cross-Strait trade, as is the case with international trade more generally, has distributional consequences in Taiwan. And those most threatened by cross-Strait trade—relatively unskilled labor, small enterprises, farmers—often support the opposition DPP, while those who benefit most from cross-Strait exchange (such as businesses with operations in the PRC) appear to lean toward the governing Nationalist Party (the Kuomindang, or KMT).[6] As such, it is perhaps not surprising that the DPP would be skeptical of Ma's efforts to further liberalize Taiwan's cross-Strait economic policy; nor is it surprising that pan-green leaders would reference national security concerns in making their case in this regard. That Ma would stress the potential security-related upside is not especially surprising either.[7]

Nevertheless, while it is true that both sides of this debate certainly have good reasons unrelated to national security to take the positions that they do on cross-Strait economic exchange, it does not follow that China–Taiwan economic integration therefore has no security implications for Taiwan. To the contrary, I believe that economic integration across the Taiwan Strait does have important security consequences, though these effects do not always operate in straightforward ways. In this chapter I develop several hypotheses in this regard. First, China–Taiwan economic integration can have an important influence on cross-Strait tensions, but whether growing economic ties are on balance stabilizing or not hinges in part on the political party governing Taiwan. When Taiwan's governing party is essentially happy with the status quo in the cross-Strait political relationship (today's KMT), growing cross-Strait economic ties are stabilizing; but when Taiwan is governed by a party seeking to revise the status quo in a way contrary to Beijing's preferences (today's DPP), economic integration may actually be destabilizing. Second, over the long term, economic integration probably makes Taiwan independence harder to achieve, which helps to explain both the DPP's unease with deepening cross-Strait economic ties, and the PRC's support of deeper ties. Finally, the long-term implications of cross-Strait economic exchange for political unification between Taiwan and the PRC are ambiguous; as such, from the KMT's vantage, the downside security risks of cross-Strait economic ties are limited since the party does not support formal Taiwan independence.

Are cross-Strait economic ties a source of stability?

Whether international economic ties have a pacific effect or not is a controversial issue in the broader international relations literature. Proponents of the commercial liberal argument contend that economic integration raises the costs of war, and hence encourages restraint (Polachek 1980; Russett and Oneal 2001). Commercial exchange increases understanding, and can help to create powerful domestic lobbies that favor stability in relations with key trading partners. And economic ties give governments coercive tools other than military violence: they can, for example, impose economic sanctions instead of resorting to the gun (Morrow 1999; Gartzke *et al.* 2001). Skeptics counter that economic ties at the bilateral level are rarely important enough to act as a significant constraint on state behavior—particularly when great powers are contending over vital interests (Mearsheimer 2001). Economic ties are unlikely to flourish in the most hostile political environments in the first place (Pollins 1989; Gowa 1994), and when economic ties do arise among competing states, they can just as easily generate new frictions as they can alleviate existing ones (Waltz 1979). Witness, for instance, the economic frictions that have arisen in the U.S.–China relationship.[8]

Some scholarship has further advanced the debate by seeking to understand the specific conditions under which economic integration is likely to be stabilizing, and when it is not.[9] My approach here falls into this mold because it is my contention that cross-Strait economic integration has differential effects on the level of cross-Strait tensions depending on the political preferences of Taiwan's leadership. More specifically, I hypothesize that cross-Strait economic integration has a stabilizing effect when Taiwan's leadership is generally happy with the cross-Strait status quo, but that this effect disappears when the Taiwan leadership hopes to revise the status quo in the direction of a formally independent Taiwan. Indeed, in the latter case, economic integration can actually have a destabilizing effect. Below I use a very simple model of the cross-Strait relationship to explain the reasoning behind this hypothesis. I then explore some further implications of the model for cross-Strait relations.

A simple model of cross-Strait relations

Figure 2.1 presents a very stylized model of the relationship across the Taiwan Strait.[10] In relations between China and Taiwan, the core area of contention concerns Taiwan's sovereign status: the extent to which Taiwan is, or should be, an independent, sovereign nation-state. While Beijing denies Taiwan's sovereign

a. An independence/unification continuum, with status quo and expected outcome from fighting a war

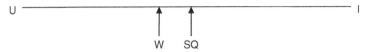

b. Factoring in that war is costly

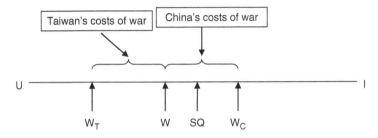

c. Factoring in the increased costs of war generated by cross-strait economic integration

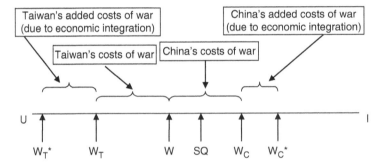

Figure 2.1 A stylized model of cross-Strait economic integration and the prospects for war.

status, and insists that formal unification with mainland China must ultimately occur, both of Taiwan's major political parties insist that Taiwan (for the DPP) or the Republic of China (for the KMT) is a sovereign state, and that the issue of formal unification is one that must ultimately be decided on by the Taiwanese people. It is therefore useful to think of a continuum that defines the range of possible constructions of Taiwan's sovereign status, ranging from formal unification with mainland China (U) on one end to formal independence for Taiwan at the other end (I); see Figure 2.1a. Moreover, it makes sense to think of the current status quo (SQ) as lying near the middle of the continuum: Taiwan enjoys de facto independence, but is not recognized internationally as independent.

The current Ma administration subscribes to a weak version of a one-China principle,[11] but insists on no steps toward independence or unification while Ma is president. Now assume that if the two sides were to fight a war, the outcome would result in some shift toward unification, to point W on the chart (the logic of the discussion to follow is not sensitive to the precise location of W).

War, however, is costly, in terms of lives lost and assets destroyed. It can also wreck political careers and bring down regimes. The costliness of war, then, must detract from the attractiveness of the war outcome for both China and Taiwan. Accounting for these costs on a sovereignty continuum is obviously tricky; however, for simplicity, assume that these costs can be expressed in sovereignty "units." Once these costs are factored in, China's utility for war shifts from W to W_C, and Taiwan's from W to W_T (see Figure 2.1b).[12] China prefers all outcomes to the left of W_C over fighting a war, and Taiwan favors all outcomes to the right of W_T over fighting a war.[13] The space between W_C and W_T thus represents the range of outcomes that both Taiwan and China prefer over fighting a war.

In practice, Taiwan can essentially claim a certain level of sovereignty, to which the PRC must respond. Thus, so long as Taiwan claims a level of sovereign status to the left of W_C, China prefers to accept it rather than fighting a war to try to attain something better. In the case presented in 2.1b, China prefers the status quo to war: even though, in this example, it can use military force to coerce an outcome closer to unification, the costs of doing so make it a less attractive option than the status quo. In this scenario, then, if a Taiwan government is happy with the current status quo, then the cross-Strait relationship should be characterized by relative stability.

But what if a Taiwan government is unhappy with the current status quo, and hopes instead to move the status quo to a position closer to independence? If we assume that Taiwan's leadership knows roughly where W_C lies, then it has a strong incentive to move Taiwan's status closer to that point. Former president Chen Shui-bian, for example, appeared to be pursuing this sort of strategy. He argued that cross-Strait relations should be thought of as "one country on each side of the Strait;" dissolved Taiwan's National Unification Council; and championed a referendum seeking endorsement for entering the United Nations under the name "Taiwan." These policies aimed, at least in part, to bolster Taiwan's sovereign status, but not so much that it provoked a war with China: Chen, for example, steered clear of a formal declaration of independence. In practice, moving the status quo just to the left of W_C is risky for Taiwan, simply because it is hard to know for certain how Chinese leaders assess the likely outcome and costs of war. Even if a Taiwanese leader plays it safe, efforts to push the status quo at all toward independence would be expected to generate harsh rhetoric and perhaps even saber-rattling from Beijing, as Chinese leaders sought to communicate the resolve to fight a war if Taiwanese leaders cross W_C, and, indeed, to try to convince Taiwanese leaders that W_C lies farther left than might really be the case. This sort of expectation is quite compatible with Chinese behavior during the Chen administration. Chinese leaders warned, for instance, that they were willing to pay "any costs" to prevent Taiwan independence.

Now consider the effects of increased economic integration. Assume that growing economic linkages across the Taiwan Strait raise the costs of war for both sides (though, perhaps, not in a symmetrical fashion). After factoring in these increased costs, Taiwan now prefers all outcomes to the right of W_T^* over fighting a war, and China favors all outcomes to the left of outcome W_C^* over fighting a war. What does this mean for the level of tension likely to be seen in cross-Strait relations?

If we imagine first a Taiwan government that is basically satisfied with the current status quo, this change should help to further reduce cross-Strait tensions. The pro-status quo Taiwan government can now feel more confident that it is operating within the confines of acceptable behavior from Beijing's perspective. It can pay somewhat less attention to small exogenous changes, such as a shift of W to the left as Beijing's military capabilities improve. Meanwhile, knowing that it is dealing with a pro-status quo Taiwan government, Beijing need not worry about its war utility shifting to the right (toward independence): such a Taiwan government has no incentive to try to take advantage of this shift by claiming a greater level of sovereign status. In short, when a pro-status quo government is in power in Taiwan, growing economic links across the Taiwan Strait should be stabilizing and tension reducing: the increased costs of war lead to greater confidence in Taiwan that Beijing will not attack, without generating anxiety in Beijing that Taipei will try to capitalize on China's growing reluctance to use force. This prediction is consistent with the views that Ma Ying-jeou—who has explicitly endorsed the status quo on sovereignty issues—has put forth on the effects of cross-Strait economic integration.

Consider now how the model's predictions change if a government more dissatisfied with the current status quo were to come to power in Taiwan. More specifically, imagine that a government favoring formal Taiwan independence were to come to power; since such a government would hope to revise the current status quo, I will out of simplicity refer to such a government as revisionist. In this case, the model suggests that growing economic ties are not necessarily a source of stability, and can paradoxically lead to increased tensions. The reasoning here is straightforward: a revisionist Taiwan government might conclude that growing economic ties, because they raise the cost of war for China, give Taiwan more leeway to claim a greater degree of sovereign status. In Figure 2.1c, a pro-independence Taiwan government might conclude that it can now push the status quo all the way to W_C^*. Beijing, of course, would likely respond with bellicose rhetoric, saber-rattling, and other threatening steps (changed military deployments, increased military spending, and so forth), aiming to deter Taiwan from moving farther toward independence. For Beijing, the hope would be to convince Taiwan leaders that it remains highly resolved, and that the increased costs of war generated by deeper economic integration do not affect its war utility as much as Taiwan leaders might believe. Moreover, steps such as increased military expenditures, by increasing the probability that China would prevail in a military conflict, can have the effect of moving W to the left (and hence shifting W_C^* to the left as well). As such, if Beijing concludes that Taiwan's leaders are likely to try to capitalize on economic interdependence-induced increased costs of war to push farther toward independence, Chinese leaders might try to counteract these effects by bolstering military capabilities or increasing force deployments near Taiwan. Thus, in cases where a revisionist government is in power in Taiwan, growing economic ties across the Taiwan Strait can actually be destabilizing and tension-creating on the margins.[14]

Whether past revisionist Taiwan presidents Lee Teng-hui and Chen Shui-bian actually viewed growing economic ties as providing an opportunity to push farther on sovereignty issues is unclear, though some statements from the Lee administration are suggestive. For example, shortly after declaring in 1999 that the China–Taiwan relationship should be considered "special state-to-state relations," Lee pointed to China's own economic difficulties in downplaying the risk that his policies might provoke a war. His defense minister, Tang Fei, likewise saw war as unlikely because China was "concerned about international pressure and economic growth." In this case at least, Taiwanese officials seemed to be closely gauging China's expected costs of war in assessing how risky their policies were. That China's costs of war were seen as high meant that Taiwan could adopt policies at odds with PRC interests without fearing a military response. Moreover, Taiwanese officials clearly factored economic costs borne by the PRC into their considerations in this regard. Not surprisingly, cross-Strait tensions increased dramatically after Lee's 1999 declaration, as the PRC sought to signal its resolve in preventing Taiwan independence.[15]

Further implications and qualifications

A key assumption in the simple model presented above is that, ceteris paribus, economic integration raises China's costs of war, and hence makes China willing to accept a wider range of bargains than would otherwise be the case. But it may be worthwhile to consider the possibility that different Chinese leaders might view the costs associated with war in the Taiwan Strait, including the added costs associated with economic integration, in different ways. It is conceivable, for instance, that a future Chinese leadership could view Taiwan as a much more pressing issue than does the current leadership; such a leadership, in turn, might view the costs of war in the Taiwan Strait as lower relative to the benefits of a cross-Strait relationship more to Beijing's liking. In terms of the model, W_C^* would shift left.[16]

The possibility that W_C^* might shift during times of leadership change in the PRC further underscores the potential risks of revisionist policies in Taiwan. To the extent that growing economic interdependence encourages revisionist Taiwan leaders to push Taiwan's status closer to W_C^*, then it leaves Taiwan more vulnerable to what might be termed a "leadership shock," or a sharp shift left in W_C^* arising from a new leadership with different priorities coming to power in China. If W_C^* were to shift to the left of Taiwan's actual status, then China would prefer to fight a war over accepting the status quo. Such a scenario would likely lead to a showdown in the Taiwan Strait. Again, this type of scenario is less likely to unfold if status quo leaders are in power in Taiwan, since such leaders are not interested in capitalizing on growing economic ties to claim a greater level of sovereignty for Taiwan: that is, they would not have pushed Taiwan's status closer to W_C^* in the first place.

It also worth emphasizing that W is probably moving to the left as China continues to become more powerful militarily: that is, the likely outcome of a war in the Taiwan Strait is probably moving closer to China's ideal point. This, in turn, raises an interesting possibility: W_C^* can actually move left even as the distance between W_C^* and W_C continues to grow due to the increased costs of war associated with deepening economic integration. If W_C^* is moving left (or begins to move left in the future) despite growing economic ties, then the effects of economic integration on cross-Strait political bargaining are subtly different. In this scenario, economic integration continues to allow Taiwan to achieve a level of sovereign status that is greater than would be possible absent economic ties. But, growing economic ties wouldn't allow revisionist Taiwan governments to push Taiwan's status farther to the right in absolute terms. Instead, growing economic ties merely enable Taiwan to retreat more slowly on sovereignty issues than would otherwise be necessary. The implications are straightforward: revisionist governments, when in power, would be forced by power realities to adopt policies progressively less revisionist over time. As W_C^* inched closer to SQ, moreover, we might expect a convergence in the cross-Strait polices (if not preferences) adopted by status quo and revisionist parties when actually in power in Taiwan. Absent transformation in the underlying preferences of the parties in Taiwan, once (if ever) W_C^* moves left of SQ, then both revisionist and status quo parties would seek, when in power, to keep Taiwan's level of sovereignty as close to W_C^* as possible.

Summary

The simple model sketched out in this section suggests that the relationship between China–Taiwan economic integration and cross-Strait political tensions is contingent on the political preferences of the Taiwan government. When a Taiwan government—such as the current Ma administration—favors the status quo in cross-Strait relations, increased economic ties act as a stabilizing force. They build confidence in Taiwan that the PRC will not attack; meanwhile, the status quo preferences of the Taiwan government mean that the PRC need not saber-rattle to deter steps toward independence. On the other hand, if a revisionist government—such as the previous Chen Shui-bian administration—is in power in Taiwan, growing economic ties can lead to increased tensions. Taiwanese officials may be tempted to push closer to independence than would have been possible absent economic integration, which in turn is likely to generate bellicose rhetoric and hostile actions from Beijing. Over the longer term, however, these differences between the two parties may dissipate if the increased costs of war associated with cross-Strait economic integration come to be overwhelmed by changes in the military balance of power across the Taiwan Strait.

Economic integration and the future of the cross-Strait political relationship

While economic integration may make it more feasible for a revisionist Taiwan government to move Taiwan's status closer to independence, such "envelope pushing" behavior is unlikely to be popular with those actors in Taiwan who benefit economically from the burgeoning economic ties across the Taiwan Strait. Tensions will spike (for reasons detailed in the previous section) which in turn might undermine the confidence of those engaged in cross-Strait economic activities. For example, businesspeople might feel more uneasy about traveling to or investing in the PRC during a time of high tensions. Those with a stake in the cross-Strait economic relationship, then, are likely to oppose revisionist policies that could increase tensions.[17]

Furthermore, as cross-Strait economic ties expand, a growing constituency in Taiwan has a stake in the bilateral economic relationship. By 2005, for example, over 81 percent of Taiwan's manufacturers had investments or business operations in China, up from less than 73 percent three years earlier.[18] Likewise, as the two sides reach agreements on tourism and financial services, more actors in these sectors will also come to have a direct stake in the bilateral relationship. In turn, as more actors in Taiwan have a vested interest in a stable cross-Strait political relationship—and, indeed, as Taiwan's broader economy becomes more vulnerable to spikes in cross-Strait tensions—politicians advocating revisionist policies may find it harder to win elections in Taiwan. Robert Ross (2006) has even pointed to growing cross-Strait economic ties as an important factor undercutting the appeal of the DPP's cross-Strait policies under Chen Shui-bian. Over the long term, then, deepening economic integration across the Taiwan Strait potentially makes it less likely that elected Taiwan governments will push for independence, because it may make it less likely that strongly pro-independence politicians will be elected in the first place. This sort of a dynamic may have been at play in the 2012 presidential election: DPP candidate Tsai Ing-wen appeared to have difficulty convincing centrist Taiwan voters that she would be able to maintain stable cross-Strait relations given her rejection of the "1992 consensus" and the vagueness of her proposed alternative "Taiwan consensus." While Ma's re-election was undoubtedly a consequence of many other factors, Tsai's defeat did lead some to argue that the DPP needed to rethink its cross-Strait policies.[19]

But Taiwan's opponents of increased cross-Strait economic ties often make a stronger claim: that deepening economic dependence on the PRC will lead to political *unification*. During the 2008 Taiwan presidential campaign, for example, DPP candidate Frank Hsieh Chang-ting harshly criticized KMT vice-presidential candidate Vincent Siew Wan-chang's idea of a cross-Strait common market as a "one-China market." Likewise, one criticism of the ECFA is that it could lead to a loss of sovereignty for Taiwan.

It is indeed possible to imagine, in theory, at least two ways through which cross-Strait economic integration might ultimately lead to political integration.

First, economic integration potentially gives Beijing more coercive tools through which to maneuver Taiwan into unification: the PRC, that is, can potentially threaten or implement economic sanctions to force Taiwan to the bargaining table. Second, economic integration may come to have a transformative impact on Taiwanese attitudes toward unification: actors with a stake in the cross-Strait economic relationship in particular may come to favor a closer cross-Strait political relationship.

In practice, however, there is good reason to be skeptical that either of these mechanisms linking increased economic integration to political unification will come to materialize. While Taiwan's economic dependence on the PRC does potentially make Taiwan more vulnerable to PRC economic coercion, such coercion—to quote a recent RAND study—is a "tricky weapon to use" (Tanner 2007). Economic sanctions, for instance, would be very costly for the PRC, both economically and politically (Cheng 2005). Perhaps even more fundamentally, sanctions directed against Taiwan firms would punish most directly the very actors in Taiwan who tend to favor stability in cross-Strait relations. In this regard, sanctions could be deeply counterproductive for Beijing's unification dreams, as they could potentially alienate the actors—those who already have a stake in the cross-Strait relationship—whose support (or acquiescence) would be most critical if Beijing ever hoped to rule Taiwan.[20] Meanwhile, while those with a stake in the bilateral economic relationship may favor a stable cross-Strait political relationship, whether these actors will come over time to support *unification* is far from clear cut. Indeed, even Taiwan businesspeople living in mainland China often maintain a strong sense of Taiwan identity (Cheng 2005). When they have become involved in political issues, these businesspeople have typically emphasized practical concerns such as restrictions on cross-Strait interactions; the notion that they might become a "fifth column" advocating unification seems, in other words, unlikely (Bush 2005: 237–8; Cheng 2005).

Furthermore, it is worth mentioning that at the aggregate level, there is very little support for unification within Taiwan despite burgeoning economic ties. Indeed, trends suggest that support for unification has been in decline. One regular survey sponsored by Taiwan's Mainland Affairs Council, for instance, finds that—when given a range of possible scenarios for cross-Strait relations—the percentage of respondents favoring immediate or eventual unification has declined over the past decade.[21] While in the early 2000s it was common to find support for unification approaching (or even exceeding) 20 percent, more recent surveys have found support hovering closer to 10 percent.[22] Other surveys have found consistently minimal support in Taiwan for Beijing's "one country, two system" proposal.[23] Moreover, there has been a steady decline in the percentage of Taiwan's population that self-identifies as exclusively "Chinese," while the percentage self-identifying as exclusively "Taiwanese" (as opposed to both Taiwanese and Chinese) has grown sharply since the early 1990s.[24]

In sum, deepening cross-Strait economic integration has uncertain implications for the prospects of eventual unification, even though there are good reasons to think it makes Taiwan independence less likely over the long term.

Conclusion: liberalization and its discontents

The analysis presented in this chapter helps to make greater sense of the positions that Taiwan's major political parties, along with the PRC, have taken on cross-Strait economic ties in recent years. As should be clear, a party's view of the security consequences of economic integration depends on that particular party's preferences relating to Taiwan's sovereign status.

First, this chapter's analysis is consistent with the well-known PRC view that cross-Strait economic integration accords with China's strategic interests: even if economic integration may give a revisionist Taiwan government marginally more leeway in the short term, it probably makes formal Taiwan independence harder to achieve in the long term.[25] Since the late 1970s, Beijing has consistently supported increased cross-Strait economic exchange. For instance, many of the PRC's major policy initiatives relating to Taiwan—including the 1979 "Message to Taiwan Compatriots," Jiang Zemin's 1995 "Eight Points," and even the 2005 Anti-secession Law—have emphasized the desirability of increased cross-Strait economic ties.[26] Meanwhile, statements by Chinese officials have at times been quite frank in emphasizing that economic integration with Taiwan furthers Beijing's political goals vis-à-vis the island. For example, in an overview of PRC policy toward Taiwan, Deputy Director of the Taiwan Affairs Office Sun Yafu noted that expanding cross-Strait economic, personnel, and cultural exchanges are consistent with Beijing's efforts to check Taiwan independence: they constitute a "driving force for the development of cross-strait relations and an important factor for curbing 'Taiwan independence.'"[27] Not surprisingly, the PRC has embraced liberalization of cross-Strait economic exchange since the Ma Ying-jeou administration came to power in Taiwan.

This chapter's analysis likewise helps to make sense of the KMT's generally positive view of the security consequences of cross-Strait economic exchange: since the party does not support Taiwan independence, the long-term effects are not especially troubling. In the short term, economic integration should be conducive to stability and confidence-building in the Taiwan Strait. There are, of course, other non-security-related factors that make liberalization attractive to the KMT. As noted in the introduction, those actors in Taiwan who benefit most directly from cross-Strait economic integration tend to support the KMT. Moreover, the liberalization process under Ma has received fairly strong support within the broader population.[28] As such, from the standpoint of the KMT, there is relatively little political or security downside to pursuing cross-Strait economic liberalization, and the KMT has strongly supported liberalization since Taiwan's political parties realigned after 2000. This stance, in turn, has translated into enthusiastic support for cross-Strait dialogue since the party returned to power in 2008, and has led to significant liberalization in a variety of areas. The Ma Ying-jeou administration, it should be emphasized, continues to take a cautious approach on political issues in its dealings with Beijing: Ma, for instance, has signaled that he is in no hurry to sign a peace agreement with China, and he is certainly in no hurry to negotiate over issues relating to Taiwan's final status.[29]

This caution relating to political issues is likely to continue during Ma's second term in office. In sum, the Ma administration continues to adopt a largely pro-status quo approach to the cross-Strait sovereignty dispute; but since economic integration does appear to undermine the status quo, and because integration offers additional political benefits to the Ma administration, Ma has sought to cooperate with the PRC on cross-Strait economic issues.

Finally, the DPP—which takes a more assertive role on sovereignty issues than the KMT (and officially backs formal Taiwan independence)—tends to be more concerned about the security consequences of deepening cross-Strait economic ties, which again is quite consistent with the analysis presented in this chapter. From the DPP's standpoint, even if economic integration affords Taiwan with more leeway in the short term to claim a greater level of sovereign status than would otherwise be possible, over the longer term it makes formal Taiwan independence harder to achieve. Indeed, independence may become harder to achieve in part because a growing number of Taiwanese will be more reluctant to vote for a party that will pursue policies that put Taiwan's deepening economic ties with China at risk: the DPP, that is, may come to see its own stand on cross-Strait sovereignty issues as untenable if it hopes to compete in elections. Furthermore, as with the KMT, the party's view on the security consequences of cross-Strait economic ties dovetails with the economic interests of much of the party's base: farmers and relatively unskilled labor in southern Taiwan are most threatened by deepening economic integration with the PRC (see Chen 2004 on this point). Thus, the DPP has strong ideological and political reasons to register opposition to continued liberalization of cross-Strait economic ties, and indeed the party has tended to take a more skeptical approach to cross-Strait economic liberalization than the KMT. Since Ma came to power, the DPP has been critical of the dialogue between the Straits Exchange Foundation (SEF) and the Association for Relations across the Taiwan Straits (ARATS), and the party spearheaded opposition to the ECFA. In the fall of 2008, for instance, the party organized large-scale protests that disrupted the second round of talks—held in Taipei—between the SEF's P.K. Chiang and the ARATS's Chen Yunlin.[30] The DPP likewise organized protests during the fourth round of talks, held in Taichung in December, 2009. Party leaders, including Tsai Ing-wen, criticized Ma's plans to move forward with an ECFA during the protests.[31]

Ultimately, of course, the DPP was unable to block the ECFA. Furthermore, it is worth emphasizing that even though the DPP is more skeptical than the Ma administration concerning the security and economic consequences of continued cross-Strait economic integration, the simple reality that the economies of China and Taiwan have already become deeply intertwined means that there has been little appetite in the DPP for broad new restrictions on cross-Strait economic exchange.[32] The economic and political costs would simply be too high. As such, the parameters of debate in Taiwan over cross-Strait economic relations have, since the late 1990s, centered primarily on the scope and speed of liberalization: as Rigger (2005421) writes, "there is broad agreement [among Taiwan's parties] that cross-strait economic ties are indispensible if Taiwan's economy is to thrive." For the foreseeable future, cross-Strait economic integration is here to stay.

Notes

1. Trade statistics come from *Cross-Strait Economic Statistics Monthly*, various issues, available online from Taiwan's Mainland Affairs Council: http://www.mac.gov.tw/ct.a sp?xItem=88227&ctNode=5934&mp=3.
2. The text of the agreement, and the early harvest list and schedule, are available on the webpage of Taiwan's Ministry of Economic Affairs: http://www.moea.gov.tw/Mns/populace/news/News.aspx?kind=1&menu_id=40&news_id=19723.
3. For Lee's comments: "Lee Teng-hui Criticizes Ma's ECFA Plans" (*China Post*, 17 May 2009); For Tsai's comments: "CECA Comes with Big Hidden Costs," (*Taipei Times*, 1 March 2009: 8). These arguments, of course, are not new. As cross-Strait economic integration accelerated in the early 1990s, warnings about Taiwan's economic dependence on the PRC—and its political implications—became more common and helped to motivate policies meant to slow the pace of cross-Strait economic integration during the Lee Teng-hui administration.
4. Ma also argued: "when you have more trade, more investment, more contact—cultural, educational—particularly among the young people, when they make friends with their contemporaries on the other side of the Taiwan Strait, I'm sure friendship…, cooperation instead of hostility, will grow." See "An Interview with President Ma Ying-jeou" (*New York Times*, 19 June 2008). Official U.S. policy is to encourage cross-Strait economic integration for reasons similar to those articulated by Ma. For example, in January 2006, a State Department spokesman summarized U.S. policy as follows: "We support expansion of transportation and communication links across the Strait aimed at increasing political, economic, social and cultural exchanges with a view to increasing mutual understanding and diminishing the chances of miscommunication or misunderstanding" (see *Taipei Times*, 1 February 2006: 1).
5. Owing largely to pressure from Beijing, Taiwan has found it difficult to negotiate free-trade agreements with other countries (outside a handful of Latin American states that recognize the Republic of China (ROC) diplomatically), even as other countries in East Asia have moved aggressively to negotiate new FTAs. The Ma administration argued, prior to signing the ECFA, that Beijing would be more amenable to Taiwan signing FTAs with other countries if Taipei first were to reach a similar arrangement with the PRC. See, for instance, "Interview: ECFA Will Help Taiwan Catch Up with Asia: Ma." And, in fact, shortly after the ECFA was signed Taiwan and Singapore agreed to "explore the feasibility of an economic cooperation agreement." Taiwan is also exploring the possibility of trade agreements with other ASEAN countries. See "Taiwan, Singapore Mull Trade Accord" (*Taipei Times*, 6 August 2010) available at: http://www.taipeitimes.com/News/front/archives/2010/08/06/2003479720.
6. For a good discussion, see Tanner (2007: 125). Tanner suggests that Taiwan businesspeople working in China most likely supported the KMT over Chen Shui-bian in the 2004 election, though by margins less dramatic than sometimes assumed by both the PRC and the KMT.
7. Both sides, naturally, do emphasize as well the *economic* consequences of deepening cross-Strait economic cooperation, with pan-green officials highlighting the negative consequences for Taiwan's workers and farmers, and KMT officials emphasizing studies that point to increased growth and net job increases in Taiwan if an ECFA were to go into effect. For an example of the former, see Tsai Ing-wen, "CECA Comes with Big Hidden Costs." For an example of the latter, see "Interview: ECFA Will Help Taiwan Catch Up with Asia: Ma."

8. For empirical analyses that raises some doubts on the commercial liberal argument, see also Ripsman and Blanchard (1996/1997), Barbieri (2002), and Keshk *et al.* (2004). But see Hegre *et al.* (2009) for a powerful rebuttal in this regard. Mansfield and Pollins (2003) provide a good collection of works on the subject.

9. See, for instance, Papayoanou (1996), Mansfield and Pevehouse (2000), and McDonald (2004).

10. A similar model is presented in Kastner (2009). The model's logic is drawn from Fearon (1995), Morrow (1999), Gartzke *et al.* (2001), and Powell (2002).

11. Based on the "'92 Consensus," with both Beijing and Taipei accepting a "one-China" principle but each adopting its own interpretation of the term.

12. That is, once the costs of war are accounted for, China's utility for war moves away from its ideal point (unification). For Taiwan, the costs of war mean that Taiwan's utility for the war outcome is equivalent to something even closer to unification.

13. Assuming, of course, that Taiwan's ideal point is formal independence. Below I'll discuss the possibility that a Taiwan government might have an ideal point at SQ.

14. While this sort of a scenario gives rise to increased tensions, it is not clear that the probability of *war* is affected: war, in the model, would occur if a revisionist Taiwan government moved the status quo to the right of W_C (prior to economic ties) or W_C^* (with increased economic ties). Even revisionist Taiwan leaders have, in this model, obvious incentives to avoid war (because of its high cost), and so they prefer to avoid triggering that outcome. Indeed, it is possible that because increased economic integration raises the costs of fighting for Taiwan as well, increased economic ties will induce some increased caution on the part of Taiwan's leaders, so that they avoid trying to approach W_C^* too closely (out of fear of crossing the line). In this scenario, increased economic ties would generate increased tensions but a reduced likelihood of actual war.

15. For a more extended discussion of the 1999 episode, and sources for quotes, see Kastner (2009: 114–15).

16. There are certainly indications that different leaders have weighted Taiwan's importance, relative to the importance of other issues, differently. Shirk (2007: 191), for instance, writes that Jiang Zemin was "impatient" on the Taiwan issue, as he viewed significant progress on unification as something that would help cement his legacy as a great Chinese leader. On the other hand, Hu Jintao was more cautious in tying his legacy to the Taiwan issue, and as such was willing to accept delay (ibid.: 207).

17. For example, a 2006 survey of Taiwan's 1000 largest enterprises found that 70 percent of respondents saw cross-Strait tensions as their biggest concern over the next three years. See "Taiwan's CEOs Say China Presents Biggest Challenge, Urge Direct Links" (*Taipei Times*, 3 May 2006). During the 2012 election campaign, a number of businesspeople with a stake in China were quite vocal in their concerns that a victory by Tsai Ing-wen (who refused to endorse the 1992 consensus) could lead to a more tense cross-Strait relationship—with potentially disastrous economic consequences. See, for instance, "Business Leaders Come Out in Support of Ma" (*China Post*, 12 January 2012), available at: http://www.chinapost.com.tw/taiwan/national/presidential-election/2012/01/12/328786/Business-leaders.htm. Foxconn CEO Terry Gou reportedly offered extra leave and free flights home to Taiwanese employees working in China so that they could vote in the election; Gou was outspoken in his support for Ma. See "Big Business Tries to Sway Increasingly Tense Taiwan Election" (*Sydney Morning Herald*, 6 January 2012), available at: http://www.smh.com.au/world/big-business-tries-to-sway-increasingly-tense-taiwan-election-20120105-1pmvp.html.

18. "More Taiwan Makers Head to China Despite Lackluster Profits: MOEA" (*Taiwan Central News Agency*, 5 January 2006).

19. Others, of course, disputed the view that the DPP needed to move even closer to the KMT in order to be electorally viable. Indeed, Tsai's approach to cross-Strait issues

could already be characterized as quite centrist. For a good discussion of some of the election's implications, see deLisle (2012).

20. I elaborate on this point in Kastner (2009). See also Kastner (2006) and Tanner (2007).

21. Results are available at www.mac.gov.tw. The survey presents respondents with the following scenarios, and asks which they lean toward: unification as soon as possible; maintain the status quo and unification later; maintain the status quo and decide on unification or independence later; maintain the status quo indefinitely; maintain the status quo and independence later; independence as soon as possible. The vast majority of respondents choose some version of the status quo, and in recent surveys over 60 percent either favor maintaining the status quo indefinitely or maintaining the status quo and deciding later. The surveys, of course, do not address the issue of conditional preferences; for instance, would respondents be more supportive of independence if it could be achieved without war? Would they be more supportive of unification if the PRC were to become democratic? For studies that address these sorts of issues, see Chu (2004) and Niou (2004).

22. Of those indicating support for unification, the vast majority say they favor "maintaining the status quo and unification later." Those supporting "unification as soon as possible" have generally represented less than 3 percent of respondents throughout the past decade.

23. In surveys conducted for the Mainland Affairs Council since 2000, the percentage of respondents agreeing that one country, two systems is applicable to solving problems across the Taiwan Strait has rarely exceeded 15 percent (with those disagreeing usually making up more than 70 percent). In an August 2008 survey, over 80 percent disapproved of one country two systems, while only 8.1 percent approved of the formula; it should be noted, however, that the question was framed by a statement emphasizing that the ROC would cease to exist if one country, two systems were to be implemented. Findings posted at: www.mac.gov.tw.

24. In the most recent survey asking about identity conducted by National Chengchi University's Election Study Center, over 52 percent of respondents self-identified as "Taiwanese." Only 4 percent identified solely as "Chinese," while 39 percent self-identified as "both Chinese and Taiwanese." See Election Study Center, N.C.C.U., Important Political Attitude Trend Distribution, available at: http://esc.nccu.edu.tw/eng/data/data03-2.htm.

25. Of course, cross-Strait economic integration dovetails with the PRC's broader development strategy centered on integration into global markets, and as such should also be welcomed for the economic benefits it brings to China.

26. For a summary of major points in the Message to Taiwan Compatriots and Jiang's Eight Points, see Taiwan Wenti Duben (2001: 50–1, 66–7). For the text of the Anti-secession Law, see "Full Text of Anti-secession Law" (*People's Daily Online*, 14 March 2005), available at: http://english.people.com.cn/200503/14/eng20050314_176746.html.

27. Sun Yafu, "Sincerely Work for the Well-being of the Compatriots on Both Sides of the Strait and for Peace in the Taiwan Strait Region (Studying and Implementing the Spirit of the 17th Party Congress)" (*Renmin Ribao*, 27 November 2007).

28. For instance, after the third round of talks between the PRC's Chen Yunlin (of the Association for Relations across the Taiwan Straits) and Taiwan's P.K. Chiang (of the Straits Exchange Foundation) which were held in the spring of 2009, over 73 percent of respondents to a Mainland Affairs Council sponsored poll indicated that they supported "the handling of cross-strait exchange issues through institutionalized negotiations between the two sides." Substantial majorities also indicated satisfaction with the agreements relating to crime, air transport, and financial cooperation that were reached at the talks. In a September 2009 poll, 57 percent of respondents indicated that they thought that the "current pace of opening cross-strait exchanges" was either "just

right" or "too slow." Only 33 percent thought things were moving "too fast." Over 54 percent of respondents in the same poll indicated that they approved the "promoting" of an ECFA, while only 26 percent disapproved. However, it is important to be at least somewhat cautious about reading too much into these numbers. For instance, in an August 2008 poll conducted by the Election Study Center at National Chengchi University, even though 52 percent of respondents indicated that they supported the government's promotion of relaxed cross-Strait economic interaction, over 65 percent thought that the management of cross-Strait economic and trade exchanges should be tightened—which Wang (2009) has interpreted as indicating unease among Taiwan's citizens about the security consequences of cross-Strait economic ties. All polling data are available on the Mainland Affairs Council webpage: www.mac.gov.tw.

29. See, for instance: "No Rush to Engage in Political Talks with China: President" (*Taiwan Central News Agency*, 19 November 2009).
30. "Thousands in Taiwan Protest Talks with China" (*New York Times*, 26 October 2008).
31. "Tens of Thousands March to Protest Trade Pact with China" (*Taiwan Central News Agency*, 20 December 2009).
32. And indeed, during the campaign for the 2012 election, Tsai and the DPP essentially accepted (if not embraced) the ECFA. See, for instance, "Tsai Details DPP's Cross-Strait Policies" (*Taipei Times*, 24 August 2011), available at: http://www.taipeitimes.com/News/front/archives/2011/08/24/2003511508.

References

Barbieri, Katherine. 2002. *The Liberal Illusion: Does Trade Promote Peace?* Ann Arbor, MI: University of Michigan Press.

Bush, Richard C. 2005. *Untying the Knot: Making Peace in the Taiwan Strait*. Washington, DC: Brookings Institution.

Chen, Ming-chi. 2004. Sinicization and its Discontents: Cross-Strait Economic Integration and Taiwan's 2004 Presidential Election. *Issues and Studies* 40 (3/4): 334–41.

Cheng, T.J. 2005. China–Taiwan Economic Linkage: Between Insulation and Superconductivity. In *Dangerous Strait: The U.S.–Taiwan–China Crisis*. NancyBernkopf Tucker, ed. New York: Columbia University Press.

Chu, Yun-han. 2004. Taiwan's National Identity Politics and the Prospect of Cross-Strait Relations. *Asian Survey* 44 (4): 484–512.

deLisle, Jacques. 2012. Taiwan's 2012 Presidential and Legislative Elections: Winners, Losers, and Implications. *Foreign Policy Research Institute E-Notes* January. Available at <http://www.fpri.org/enotes/2012/201201.delisle.taiwan.html>.

Fearon, James D. 1995. Rationalist Explanations for War. *International Organization* 49 (3): 379–414.

Gartzke, Erik, Quan Li, and Charles Boehmer. 2001. Investing in the Peace: Economic Interdependence and International Conflict. *International Organization* 55 (2): 391–438.

Gowa, Joanne. 1994. *Allies, Adversaries, and International Trade*. Princeton, NJ: Princeton University Press.

Hegre, Havard, John R. Oneal, and Bruce Russett. 2009. Trade Does Promote Peace: New Simultaneous Estimates of the Reciprocal Effects of Trade and Conflict. *Leitner Working Paper* 2009–07. Available at http://www.yale.edu/leitner/resources/docs/HORJune09.pdf.

Kastner, Scott L. 2006. Does Economic Integration across the Taiwan Strait Make Military Conflict Less Likely? *Journal of East Asian Studies* 6: 319–46.

———. 2009. *Political Conflict and Economic Interdependence across the Taiwan Strait and Beyond*. Stanford, CA: Stanford University Press.

Keshk, Omar M.G., Brian M. Pollins, and Rafael Reuveny. 2004. Trade Still Follows the Flag: The Primacy of Politics in a Simultaneous Model of Interdependence and Armed Conflict. *Journal of Politics* 66 (4): 1155–79.

McDonald, Patrick J. 2004. Peace through Trade or Free Trade? *Journal of Conflict Resolution* 48 (4): 547–72.

Mansfield, Edward D. and Jon C. Pevehouse. 2000. Trade Blocs, Trade Flows, and International Conflict. *International Organization* 54 (4): 775–808.

Mansfield, Edward D. and Brian M. Pollins, eds. 2003. *Economic Interdependence and International Conflict: New Perspectives on an Enduring Debate*. Ann Arbor, MI: Michigan University Press.

Mearsheimer, John J. 2001. *The Tragedy of Great Power Politics*. New York: W.W. Norton.

Morrow, James D. 1999. How Could Trade Affect Conflict? *Journal of Peace Research* 36 (4): 481–9.

Niou, Emerson M.S. 2004. Understanding Taiwan Independence and its Policy Implications. *Asian Survey* 44 (4): 555–67.

Papayoanou, Paul A. 1996. Interdependence, Institutions, and the Balance of Power: Britain, Germany, and World War I. *International Security* 20: 42–76.

Polachek, Solomon William. 1980. Conflict and Trade. *Journal of Conflict Resolution* 24: 55–78.

Pollins, Brian M. 1989. Does Trade Still Follow the Flag? *American Political Science Review* 83 (2): 465–80.

Powell, Robert. 2002. Bargaining Theory and International Conflict. *Annual Review of Political Science* 5 (June): 1–30.

Rigger, Shelley. 2005. Party Politics and Taiwan's External Relations. *Orbis* 49 (3): 413–28.

Ripsman, Norrin M. and Jean-Marc F. Blanchard. 1996/7. Commercial Liberalism under Fire: Evidence from 1914 and 1936. *Security Studies* 6: 4–50.

Ross, Robert S. 2006. Taiwan's Fading Independence Movement. *Foreign Affairs* 85 (2): 141–8.

Russett, Bruce and John R. Oneal. 2001. *Triangulating Peace: Democracy, Interdependence, and International Organizations*. New York: W.W. Norton.

Shirk, Susan L. 2007. *China, Fragile Superpower: How China's Internal Politics Could Derail its Peaceful Rise*. New York: Oxford University Press.

Taiwan Wenti Duben (Reader on the Taiwan Question). 2001. Beijing: Central Party School.

Tanner, Murray Scot. 2007. *Chinese Economic Coercion against Taiwan: A Tricky Weapon to Use*. Santa Monica, CA: RAND Corporation.

Waltz, Kenneth N. 1979. *Theory of International Politics*. Reading, MA: Addison-Wesley.

Wang, T.Y. 2009. Economic Rationality and National Security: Taiwan's New Government and the Global Economic Recession. In *Taiwan and the Global Economic Storm. Asia Program Special Report* No. 143, Bryce Wakefield, ed. Washington, DC: Woodrow Wilson International Center for Scholars.

3 The North Korean economy and international society

Hiroko Imamura

Introduction

For decades the North Korean regime has been a puzzle and a problem for most of its neighbors. Its military activities and most recently its missile tests and nuclear programs have precipitated varying degrees of condemnation by all countries in the region. But there has been widespread disagreement on how best to wean North Korea from its longstanding policy directions. For many, the solutions lie in transforming the North Korean economy through a mixture of internal reforms based perhaps on the successful changes in China and Vietnam as well as greater integration with the other, more successful, economies of the region. Yet the North has moved only episodically in such directions, far more often demonstrating greater concerns about regime preservation than about improving the performance of the domestic economy.

This chapter examines the economy of the Democratic People's Republic of Korea (DPRK) in an effort to unravel the country's links between its perceived security and its economics. In the process it explores the mix of economic measures taken by the North and sanctions undertaken by others as a way of demonstrating how the countries of the region have dealt with the perceived threat from North Korea's military actions.

The chapter is divided into four parts. The first part examines the main characteristics of the DPRK's economy including its own internally-driven efforts at marketization. It then compares the "market reforms" attempted by the North with those undertaken by two other former communist states, China and Vietnam. It analyzes why the North Korean measures were so much less successful than those of the other two countries. The third section examines the economic sanctions brought against the North and shows why these proved largely unsuccessful in changing the North's economic and security behaviors. The chapter finishes with a brief conclusion about the logical ways forward.

The nature of the North Korean economy?

What is the nature of the economy in North Korea, the country that launched missiles in April, July, and October 2009, and carried out a nuclear test in the same year? How should the international community approach a country such as

North Korea? It has been a while since the North Korean economic hardships were first reported to the world, so it is not hard to imagine that the country's high military expenses greatly affect the DPRK's economy. According to one report, as much as $700 million was invested solely on missile launches and the first nuclear test.

It was in the mid-1990s that the deterioration of the North Korean economy started to gain global attention. Catastrophic floods in 1995 and 1996 brought a remarkable food shortage that forced North Korea to request food support from the international community. Graphic images of children wasting away or people falling in the street from malnutrition were broadcast, clearly showing the miserable state of affairs in North Korea.

However, the North Korean economy had not gotten suddenly worse in the mid-1990s. The North's troubles trace back at least to the time of the oil shock (1973), which depressed the global prices of lead and zinc, two key export items from North Korea, and consequently prevented North Korea from receiving the amounts of foreign currency it expected. In the 1970s, North Korea imported industrial plants from Japan and Western Europe, which it has not yet paid for. Although a debt rescheduling was negotiated, only a small part of the debt was ever repaid. If borrowings from the former Soviet Union and Eastern European countries are included, North Korea's debt amounted to an estimated $11.9 billion ($4.55 billion to former Western bloc countries and $7.35 billion to former Eastern bloc countries (*Nihon Keizai Shimbun*, 10 May 1999)). These conditions, which indicate a nearly broken national economy, have essentially continued to this day. Moreover, North Korea confronted this trade balance problem in its internal economy as far back as the 1950s and 1960s, and thus the economy of North Korea has become steadily impoverished by its unchanging economic system.

There is no doubt that the North Korean economy is in trouble. However, this does not mean that its development level is also low. Consider the following: 1) industrial facilities for heavy manufacturing were built at the founding of the nation thanks to aid from socialist countries including the Soviet Union; and 2) heavy industrial production accounts for a large part of the North Korean industrial system. Clearly, North Korea is far more industrialized than others in the general category of "developing countries."

In many developing countries with little capital, economic development cannot advance due to the inability to industrialize. This in turn prevents deeper economic transformation. Even when the economy improves in the aggregate, it is often difficult to increase per capita GDP because, despite economic development leading to improved public hygiene and a lower infant mortality rate, many developing countries simply switch from "high rates of birth and infant mortality" to "high rates of birth and low infant morality." The result is an explosive increase in population leaving per capita GDP relatively stagnant. In the economics of development, this situation, where minor economic development is cancelled out by increased population, is called either a "malignant cycle of poverty" or a "low-level equilibrium trap;" it is conventionally believed that escaping such a situation requires a huge one-time investment, called a "big push."

However, the DPRK's poverty cannot be attributed to this type of economic phenomenon. The constant food shortage since before the 1990s and the continual natural disasters such as heavy flooding in the middle of the 1990s make it clear that North Korea's economic problems are not due to any such explosive population increase nor the resultant "low-level equilibrium trap."

Then what is the cause of North Korea's widespread starvation? One of the causes of starvation brought on in the Ukraine in the early 1930s and in China in the late 1950s was fast and furious consolidation of agricultural lands. In North Korea, such consolidation was fully in progress after the Korean War, and it was rapidly pushed forward to exceed a rate of 80 percent in 1956. The speed of North Korea's consolidation is obvious when one realizes that even China took 7 years, the Soviet Union took 13 years, and Eastern Europe, aside from East Germany and Albania, more than 20 years to exceed this 80 percent level (Koh Sungyo 1989). The inefficiencies in such consolidation and the lack of economic incentives were evident from the beginning. Even Kim Il-Sung, the country's founder, pondered the question, "Why do people skimp when they work in a cooperative livestock barn but bring up cows carefully when they are allocated to each family?" (Kim Il Sung 1980). Moreover, due to unscientific and insufficient methods of raising agricultural crops, such as failure to plant closer together or failure to introduce widespread rice-terracing yields continued to go down.[1] The already small yields became smaller because of the failure to follow basic procedures like "husk rice after it's harvested" or "hull wheat when it's well dried" (Lee Uhong 1989). Accordingly, starvation in North Korea can be traced heavily to human failures.

In the early 1990s, the DPRK was hit by many adverse events at the same time: 1) the Soviet Union and China each established diplomatic relations with South Korea; 2) the Soviet Union and East European countries collapsed; 3) Kim Il-Sung passed away in 1994; and 4) the country was struck by many natural disasters. North Korea suffered from food shortages throughout the 1990s.

The first challenge demonstrated the one-sided fulfillment of the planned mutual recognition theory during the detente of the 1970s. Expectations then were that Japan and the United States would recognize North Korea while China and the Soviet Union would recognize South Korea. But Russia and China's recognition of the Republic of Korea (ROK) was not matched by similar legitimation of the North by the United States and Japan. In the second event, North Korea not only lost the support of two longstanding allies, but also lost key export markets and aid donors. After the death of Kim Il-Sung, his son seized the reins of power in a succession system that had already been fixed in the 1970s, with notice given to China and the Soviet Union in the 1980s. Yet, even so, Kim Jong-il officially seized power only after a two-year period of mourning (3 years, according to Confucian numeration). Finally, the series of natural disasters that plagued the DPRK involved not only flood damage in 1995 and 1996 but also hailstorms in 1994 and drought in 1997.

The main source of revenues in North Korea, which claim to have abolished taxes, are proceeds from state-owned enterprises (Figure 3.1). Therefore, the size of the budget helps to reflect, at some level, the conditions of industrial manufacturing.

However, conditions had become so bad that the country did not even announce the national budget in 1995 and 1996, while the national budget in 1997 had fallen to about half its 1994 level. Only in 1999 did the North Korean economy start to achieve positive growth once again, and improvements in economic administration were initiated in 2002.

Marketizing a communist economy

In July 2002, North Korea carried out a policy shift labeled "Remedies for Economic Administration." When this was publicly broadcast, government officials proclaimed that the move "resembles the beginning of economic reform in China." However, the "remedies for economic administration" in North Korea were in fact widely divergent from the reform and open-door policies of China in three ways.

First, the reform policies in China originated as a full refutation of China's Great Cultural Revolution. In China, even the general public knew that the country had changed its entire economic approach. However, in North Korea, the

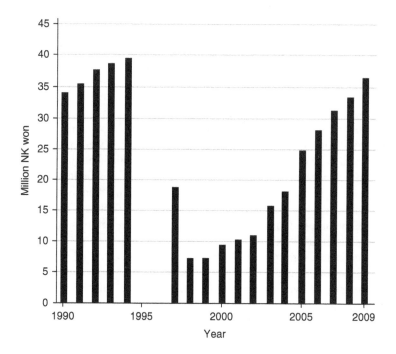

Figure 3.1 North Korean revenue.

Source: Officially announced figures of North Korea or calculated by announced rate of increase.

Note: North Korea does not announce absolute budget amounts; since 2002 only the rate of increase has been announced. Thus, these figures were calculated according to the announced rate of increase. North Korea has been hit by hyperinflation due to its 2002 "Remedies for Economic Administration," so the absolute amount is surely much greater than shown in this figure.

political system continued from Kim Il-Sung to Kim Jong-Il in an unbroken line. Even after the dawning of the Kim Jong-Il era, Kim Il-Sung was still a subject of worship. Although the political leadership might declare that there was some particular "instruction" from Kim Il-Sung, specific economic changes barely took hold unless the general public felt assured that they could engage in "money-making" without reservation. And the leadership gave few signs of any meaningful break with the North's past policies, where money-making was scorned.

Second, in the economic reform of China, domestic reforms and open-door policies were conducted at the same time. Because foreign direct investment was invited in simultaneously with domestic economic reforms, the country could escape falling into capital deficit, which often happens to developing countries. Open-door actions with no internal reforms would have left foreign enterprises at risk of carrying out unprofitable operations, and China would have been unable to offer the attractive investment market that it did.

Third, although overall prices were raised through North Korea's "Remedies for Economic Administration," no steps were taken to enhance domestic incentives aimed at increasing total production. By way of contrast, in Chinese agricultural production, for example, procurement prices were increased with the adoption of a contract system. Moreover, surplus production received another 50 percent premium at procurement, while the price increase for contracted amounts was only 20 percent. Accordingly, farmers worked hard to increase production so that they would ensure, and benefit personally from, surplus production. North Korea's "Remedies for Economic Administration" merely asked farmers to acquire "actual profit concomitant with costs," an uninspiring message that did nothing to promote increased production. Meanwhile, increased wages were paid in factories in July and August 2002, but since these factories, having no materials or energy, did nothing to increase production, no wages were paid after September. Indeed, workers were later asked to give back their earlier wages. Because the government raised prices without increasing production, North Korea was hit by hyperinflation. Thus the "Remedies for Economic Administration" was a reform that neglected the logical sequence of events. Table 3.1 compares "Remedies for Economic Administration" in North Korea, the reforms in China, and the Doi Moi reform in Vietnam.

Regarding sequencing, reforms began with the agricultural sector in both China and Vietnam. China was a classic developing country when reform and open-door policies were first started, with less than US $220 per capita GDP and with 76.3 percent of the population belonging to the agricultural community. In China, therefore, reforms originated in the agricultural community. These reforms centered on the adoption of a contract system, which was natural for a developing country whose major industry was in the primary sector. But this was not the only reason that reforms started in agriculture. Having sufficient food can make people feel richer. In addition, with modern industries or assembly-line operations, it is difficult to know who is responsible for increases in production, and a related problem is how to evaluate those working in management. In fact, in China, it did not work out well when the contract system was introduced in the industrial sector.

Table 3.1 Comparison of economic reform measures taken in North Korea, China, and Vietnam

	North Korea	*China*	*Vietnam*
Prior conditions	Decline of Sino–Soviet assistance Economic deterioration Establishment of Kim Jong Il system	End of Cultural Revolution Re-emergence of Deng Xiaoping	Slowdown of rapid socialization of the south; change to a market economy Resistance of conservatives
Procedure	Not known	Gradual	Gradual; shock treatment in 1989
Sequence	Price reform first	Agriculture→ Industry→ Finance→Labor	Agriculture and industry→Change to market economy (price reform, etc.)
Agriculture	Team system	Contract system Raising purchase price	New contract system in 1981, but collectivization in South; Output stagnation Contract system in 1988 (including private farms)
Industry	Central control	Partial decentralization in 1985	Expansion of output plan and finance autonomy in 1987
FDI	Joint venture law in 1984	Joint venture law in 1979	Foreign investment law in 1977
Foreign trade	Devaluation against the dollar in 2002	Permitting the use of foreign exchange by some local and other authorities	Unifying foreign exchange rate in 1989
Money and finance	Unknown	Tax-replacing profit and bank loans in 1985 Divided tax system in 1994	Tax reform in 1991

Source: Compiled by author. For Vietnam, see Ohizumi 1999.

Chinese reforms were developed smoothly and adoption of the contract system succeeded thanks to the fact that Chinese reforms started in a field that would show immediate effects and where those effects were widely felt among the general public.

North Korea, on the other hand, was hit by hyperinflation due to the lack of incentives to increase production and shortages of materials, despite actions to raise prices. Taking rice as an example, after the changes in economic administration in

July 2002, the price was raised from 0.08 won per kilogram to 44 won, a 550-fold increase. However, since production was not boosted, in January 2005 prices continued to escalate; for example, reaching 1150–1280 won in Hanagyeogna-do (Moon-Soo Yang 2007).

Indeed, both China and Vietnam had been hit by inflation following their economic reforms, but the inflationary effects in these two countries were far different from that in North Korea. In socialist countries, because of official price controls, apparent inflation is rare. However, under a supply shortage, it is natural to have "hidden inflation." The shortage of goods often stimulates the emergence of an underground economy and is the main reason for many long queues in front of stores. Shortages under price control have also brought about fiscal deficits in these countries because government fiscal subsidies are needed to maintain the price controls. When China and Vietnam introduced partial market economies and increased open relations with the world economy they were forced to change their existing pricing systems.

In Vietnam, at the beginning of the 1980s, materials and commodities in the state sector were sold at a price much lower than the free market price, and, therefore, state subsidies were forced to increase and budget deficits kept increasing (Nguyen Thanh Bang 1992). This system of double pricing fostered a thriving underground economy and new black-market merchants.

On the other hand, as Vietnam's trading partners shifted in 1981 from primarily members of COMECON to Western countries, domestic prices became more closely linked to world market prices and thus price subsidies began to be discontinued. A number of adjustments in prices and wages since 1981 and a 5- to 7-fold increase in prices in 1984 caused market prices to increase sharply as real value decreased. Consequently, a policy of price and wage freezes was introduced in June 1985. Inflation continued, however, because no freeze on the issuance of currency was implemented, and the money supply kept increasing. Because banks provided loans to enterprises at an interest rate far below the inflation rate, enterprises earned large profits simply by taking out loans from banks and using these funds to accumulate materials and commodities.

Under these circumstances, inflation continued in Vietnam, and the rate of price increase was 91.6 percent at the end of 1985, the amazingly high level of 487.6 percent at the end of 1986, and 310.9 percent at the end of 1987. Reacting to these phenomena, in 1989, on the advice of the IMF and World Bank, Vietnam completely eliminated price controls, implemented a single exchange rate, reduced subsidies, and introduced a high rate of interest. This collective "shock treatment" (Ohizumi 1999) had dramatic effects: the rate of inflation decreased to 35 percent in 1989 and to a mere 2.9 percent in January 1990.

There is a similarity between the recent North Korean "reform" and the Vietnamese policy of bringing black market prices, which had caused hyperinflation, into the open and making them official prices, as well as raising wages to accompany the price increases. Yet Vietnam was able to control its inflation under strict management, mixed with diplomatic pressure from the IMF and the World Bank. Even more significantly Vietnam, although poor and in short supply of key goods, had a grain output that allowed self-sufficiency and even allowed it to become a rice-exporting country in 1989. As a result, the country was never in North Korea's desperate situation where the lack of food put subsistence itself at risk. In North Korea, where the state can continue to print money if it wishes (under no outside control) and where the level of poverty reached the point of starvation, there is neither a guarantee that hyperinflation can be avoided nor that any available measure to contain inflation will in fact take place.

North Korea also tried to initiate reforms in agriculture. "Remedies for operation of consolidated farms based on divided group management system" was announced officially in 1996 and implemented in 1997. The new policy inaugurated three major changes: 1) it decreased the size of a work group, as a unit of production, to 7–8 people per group from the previous 20–25 people; 2) it lowered the annual production quota to 90 percent of the calculated weighted mean average of an average crop yield from 1993 to 1995 and that of the 10 years from 1983 to 1993; and 3) it allowed surplus production to be sold by group members in farmers' markets (Lin Jinshu 2000). The number of people in a group was decreased to prevent the problem of "free riders." Moreover, in 2005, the component of a work group was changed from an individual head count to 2–3 family units. The belief was that if the group consisted of relatives, farms would in practice be run by families (Nam 2007).

In addition the North sought improvements in the agricultural infrastructure that aimed, among other things, at placing the right production at the right spot and making the right production in the right season. Particularly significant was the goal of substantial improvements in potato production. The government stressed that potatoes are the same as white rice and carrying out a successful shift to potato production could solve the domestic food problem and provide economic insulation against powerful countries. But the production of potatoes per hectare in North Korea remained only 8,233.9 kg/ha, roughly one-third of that in South Korea, 25,765.6 kg/ha.[2] Potato cultivation, as well as other agricultural efforts, has been marked by problems such as the lack of fertilizer or replant failure.

Along with the Potato Revolution, additional policies were pursued: "Making a critical turning point in solving food problems by conducting double-crop farming with wet-rice farming, drastically increasing the areas for wheat and barley cultivation, and increasing the raising of plant-eating animals such as pigs and goats." Also proposed were solving the arable land shortage by multiple cropping and using the manure of pigs as fertilizer. However, since North Korea has a long frost period, multiple cropping could not work effectively, since multiple cropping simply made the land poorer. It is preferable to farm crops that would have the effect of improving the soil condition, such as peas, beans, and lentils.

Although the procurement prices of cereal crops were raised for the first time after the July 2002 announcement of "Remedies for Economic Administration," a usage charge for land, at 11–14 won per pyoung (about 3.3 square meters), was newly imposed at the same time. From 2003 onward, work groups were allowed to divide out a part of the collective farms into areas of about 300 pyoung (roughly 990 square meters) to individuals, separately from the farmland run by the work group. These individuals could then spend the needed hours on the individual farm. But South Korean researchers calculate that by taking the actual dimensions of agricultural land into account, this policy could not actually have been carried out.[3]

However, in the agricultural sector of North Korea, there is a much more serious problem than poorly designed reforms: It has become easy for floods to begin with only a little excessive rainfall. Over-exploitation of timber in the mountainous regions since the 1960s has transformed much of the land into rice terraces but these now lack soil binders, leading to landslides and rising riverbed levels. Once a flood occurs it is difficult to reclaim arable land since there is so little heavy machinery (and so little fuel oil). Furthermore, there is also replanting failure due to secret close-crop planting by farmers anxious to generate extra income. The shortage of chemical fertilizer has also been a production bottleneck. For example, North Korean production of chemical fertilizer was only 0.956 million tons, which permits an allocation of only 0.5 tons per hectare, with production output down by 55 percent compared to farmland having sufficient compost. The lack of feed keeps down the number of farming cattle, which in turn precludes deep tillage. Therefore, the production efficiency of farming in North Korea has sunk back to the level of the 1960s (Lin Jinshu 2000).

The North had also depended on imports of chemical fertilizer from South Korea or China to compensate for the small amount they were able to produce themselves. Chemical fertilizer support from South Korea was stopped in 2008, and imports from China were drastically decreased due to the imposition of export duties by China.

In summary, it is clear that North Korea's efforts to follow an economic reform path similar to that of China or Vietnam were deeply flawed. Reforms that were mutually interdependent were avoided, and incentives to enhance production and agricultural basics were ignored.

Opening the North Korean door

In 1984, legislation was promulgated to encourage foreign investment in North Korea. It was the year before the Plaza Accord, which seemed like the ideal time for such a move, but the introduction of foreign currency has never been fully achieved in North Korea. One of the underlying reasons for the lack of foreign currency and the low levels of foreign direct investment is the government's deep worry that such foreign investments would bring with them the introduction of new channels of information. For foreign investors North Korea is not an attractive market, because the population is small and the infrastructure is poor.

Although an Economic and Free Trade Zone was set up in Rajin Sonbong in 1991, the word "Free" was eliminated in 1998, making the label simply "Economic and Trade Zone," a poignant symbol of the decline in the hinted-at openness to greater economic freedom.

The legislation on the introduction of foreign investment in North Korea is, in large part, related to China. Although it greatly differs from legislation on the introduction of foreign investment in other developing countries, there were similarities to the corresponding legislation in China at the initial stages, such as: 1) permitting 100 percent foreign capital enterprises and only restricting the minimum ratio of foreign capital involved; 2) the mandatory export of production; 3) encouraging investment from fellow citizens residing abroad, as China had encouraged investment from Hong Kong residents or Chinese living abroad; and 4) the clear notification of the duration of joint venture corporations.

On the other hand, the North Korean approach offered some apparent advantages over those undertaken by China. China has had a nominally open-door policy for more than thirty years. Some of its initial regulations have changed, but in comparing North Korea's and China's early policies several traits were clearly favorable to North Korea: 1) the income tax rate was set at 25 percent in normal areas (versus 30 percent in China) and 14 percent in Economic and Free Trade Zones (versus 15 percent in China); 2) there was a three-year tax holiday, one year longer than that in China. Moreover, in China the tax holiday was limited to "two years after starting to make a profit," aggravating the problem of tax avoidance by encouraging businesses to declare a deficit every year. In North Korea the rule was simply "three years from first joining" in 1985 legislation, but in 1993 it was amended to "three years after starting to make a profit;" and 3) the North further lowered the income tax rate to 10 percent for activities such as the development of infrastructure, scientific research, or engineering achievements. There is no such provision in the Chinese legislation.

Although North Korea seemed to offer some advantages, the country was still not an attractive investment destination. Despite their nominal tax rate advantage the infrastructure was often inferior, thus escalating factory construction costs for foreign enterprises. In China, on the other hand, even at the beginning of foreign currency introduction, utilities such as waterworks, electricity, gas, and communication equipment were enhanced in the special economic zones. There was also a shortage of building materials in North Korea, as epitomized by the cynical comment of a Chinese entrepreneur who was going to build a factory there: "Not only cement and machines but also every single nail had to brought in from China."[4] Furthermore, North Koreans, who were not used to the business practices of Western countries, would, for example, after contracting to export products to joint ventures, sometimes export to another enterprise if and when the conditions seemed better. Moreover, it is doubtful whether pay levels in North Korea were truly low once overall productivity was considered.

In addition, a crucial difference from China is the country's attractiveness as a "market." Although China's "market of 1.3 billion people" remains a pipedream in practical terms, the country's growing affluent class makes it an undeniably attractive investment destination. Even if this class amounts to just 5 percent of the population, that still constitutes 65 million people, roughly the equivalent of the population of France. On the other hand, the entire population of North Korea is only 24 million. Considering not only this modest size but also the fact that most of the people have to spend the majority of their earnings on food, the country's meager disposable income virtually eliminates it as an appealing investment destination. Even more troubling, the stability of the country's politics remains precarious and its policies seem, from the viewpoint of outsiders, entirely inconsistent.

Economic sanctions and the North Korean economy

On 10 June 2009, in response to North Korea's second nuclear test, the United Nations adopted resolution 1874 which involved sanctions that included cargo inspections, the freezing of assets, travel restrictions, economic restrictions, and other measures, all to be taken immediately. How effective have these proven to be? What was the actual response of North Korea's various neighbors to the sanctions?

Turning first to China, the DPRK's closest military and economic supporter, Prime Minister Wen Jiabao visited North Korea in October 2009 to mark the 60th anniversary of the establishment of diplomatic ties between China and North Korea. An opening ceremony for the friendship year was held in March, and agreements on 60 joint programs were formalized before the closing ceremony in October.[5] Normally, it would have been considered disruptive of China's celebratory mood for North Korea to launch missiles and then to carry out a nuclear test right after the opening ceremony. However, China was reluctant to sever its relationship to North Korea or to diminish its role as North Korea's bridge to the international community. Therefore, the closing ceremony provided the best opportunity for the prime minister to visit North Korea, and North Korea also seized upon that opportunity. They expressed unusual hospitality by having Kim Jong-Il himself go to the airport to greet Prime Minister Wen Jinbao, and they showed a cooperative attitude toward either a bilateral or a multilateral conference on nuclear issues on the Korean Peninsula. Moreover, they signed an agreement of collaboration on industrial technology and even reached an agreement on the replacement of an iron bridge over the Yalu River. China provided no report on the total amount of support it gave, but according to a report from South Korea, Chinese support amounted to no less than $200 million, including the reconstruction of the bridge and supplies of food and crude oil.[6]

At the same time, China faces a major dilemma in its policy toward North Korea. There is a serious possibility of creating a huge inflow of refugees to the northeastern part of China if they constrict North Korea so tightly that citizens' lives become threatened. Too great a flow of refugees would raise the possibility of conflict between Koreans living in China and China's Han ethnic majority. China, which has recently experienced its own problems with ethnic minorities, would like to minimize the chances of an ethnic conflict near its North Korean border. However, failure to impose any restrictions would seem to indicate that China recognizes North Korea as a "nuclear nation." Therefore, it is difficult for China to find the right mix of sanctions.

China's ambivalence toward North Korea generally is reflected in the complexity of trade relations following the imposition of the sanctions. Trade between China and North Korea continued to expand after 2006, reaching its highest level in 2008, although some other aspects of the relationship must also be taken into

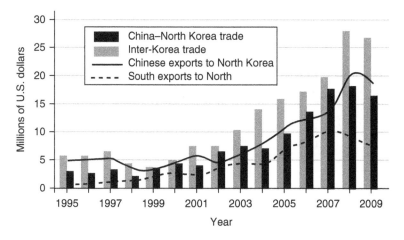

Figure 3.2 Chinese and South Korean trade with North Korea.

Source: Ministry of Unification, China monthly export and import data from December each year.

consideration (Figure 3.2). First, until the 1980s China–DPRK trade had been transacted under a clearance-account system.[7] This was later changed to a hard-currency clearance system, which increased the trade "amount" after 1992. Under the clearance-account system, the export amount on the Chinese side was potentially estimated to be lower so as to balance the export amounts of both countries. Exports from China might have been recorded with actual prices when the process was changed to the hard-currency clearance system.

An increase in the prices of natural resources, such as crude oil, was another reason for the increase in China's export "amount." Until the 1980s, crude oil and food were exported at "friendship prices" that were extremely low, usually only one-third to one-seventh of international prices. However, in the 1990s, instead of the friendship price, products were exported at prices closer to commercial rates, and sometimes even higher than the prices for other countries. In particular, the price of crude oil rose drastically after 2007 (Table 3.2).[8] Currently, China is a net importer of crude oil, and the limited export amounts are used strategically. China's crude oil exports to North Korea are reportedly part of what China itself had imported. The quantity exported also decreased to 0.3–0.5 million tons per year from 1–1.5 million tons during the 1970s and 80s. Crude oil exports in 2008 showed a fractional increase of 1 percent, at 0.529 million tons. On the other hand, within the framework of the Six-Nation Talks, heavy fuel oil, provided from countries other than Japan, has decreased by 39.4 percent, at a level of 74,600 tons. Although China certainly did carry out its responsibility to provide 50,000 tons, the actual amount of export has decreased, since there had been no net increase after 2007.

The export prices of grains to North Korea are also sometimes higher than China's average export price. China had begun a policy in 2008 aimed at

Table 3.2 Chinese crude oil export prices
(US$/barrel)

	World	DPRK
2004	30.4	35.4
2005	61.8	51.1
2006 1st half	54.6	62.9
2006 2nd half	69.9	77.4
2007 1st half	46.7	65.1
2007 2nd half	85.1	83.1
2008	108.5	106.0
2009 1st half	50.9	51.1

Source: Calculated by the author from *World Trade Atlas*.

suppressing the country's grain exports by imposing an export tax or export quotas; exports to North Korea naturally decreased as a result.[9] Rice was exported only from January to March, corn was exported only from January to March and in the months of June and July (June and July were support crops, not exports). Processed grain products such as instant noodles were exported instead to decrease the grains exported as border trade, but this did not make up for the overall decrease.

There was also a mysterious phenomenon in Chinese exports to North Korea, most notably a drastic export increase in items such as toys or fabric materials, which are hardly urgent or necessary goods.[10] The net increase of such peculiar items amounted to $130 million and it is possible that the items were exported via North Korea as a roundabout way for China to avoid being identified as the real exporter, considering that most of these items were the sources of conflicts between China and its other trade partners.

On the other hand, China's import prices paid for mineral ores remained low (Figure 3.3). For example, the import price of lead from North Korea dropped to 20 percent of the average international price in 2005, although this ratio had hovered around 70 percent until 2001, even when there were problems of quality or content or the materials involved compensation trade. The North Korean price increased by only 5 percent while the world price grew as much as 3.3 times higher during that period. Even as customers could gain a discount if they were willing to conclude long-term contracts, it seems that China was deliberately beating down the price. In addition, although mining mineral ore alone would not cause an economic ripple effect within North Korea, it could not be moved on to refining due to the lack of electricity.

As stated above, "special consideration" in Chinese exports to North Korea has become much smaller than it used to be. At the same time, China has provided some large-scale support, such as the glass factory in Tae An, given during the rule of President Hu Jintao, but the amount of official Chinese support for crude oil or grain support continues to remain far below the level actually needed by North Korea.

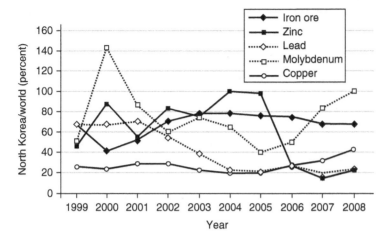

Figure 3.3 Chinese import comparison price of mineral resource prices.
Source: World Trade Atlas.

China has long sought to prod the North into making domestic economic reforms similar to those in China, usually with minimal success. As part of its inducement for changes in DPRK economic policies, the Chinese government is trying to reduce as much as possible the nation's involvement with items other than crude oil or grains. Foreign Minister Yang Jiechi, who visited North Korea in July 2007, stated that the relationship between China and North Korea would go forward on the following basis: "government makes guidelines, citizens participate, and the market moves." Furthermore, North Korea agreed to that statement implying that they also agreed to a market-based approach. The assistant secretary of China's Ministry of Commerce, who visited North Korea in August 2008, stated that the two countries would move ahead on economic cooperation under the policy of "government makes guidelines, enterprises become the principal players, and the market makes it work."[11] It seems that the Chinese side is trying its best to reduce the involvement of government and politics and ensure a more commercial relationship between China and North Korea.

The exporting enterprises in North Korea do not use banks; instead they have truck drivers transact deals in cash so as to prevent conspicuous financial flows or profits from being diverted by the government.[12] Restrictions on such activity have also become stricter. Nevertheless, a press report in July 2009 said, "[the amount of traffic has] drastically fallen, but is recovering gradually these days."[13] China may well be trying to reactivate its trade relationship with North Korea without opening up the same kind of debate that appeared at the time of sanctions in 2006.

Meanwhile, in the first half of 2009, trade between Yanji, a major hub of trade between China and North Korea reportedly decreased by as much as 43 percent.[14] However, this decline was not in reaction to the nuclear test since these data were for the first half of the year. As stated above, transactions between private sector entities in China and North Korea are typically done in cash, and the cash needed to make payments to China was typically acquired through South Korean tourism or the Government Corporation in Kaesong. However, North Korea experienced a shortage of foreign currency as relations between it and South Korea worsened, leading in turn to a decrease in North Korean trade with China.

By contrast, the "Dandong Branch Office of the Shenyang Consulate General" was set up in late August.[15] The establishment of this office was said to have been approved by the Chinese government at the beginning of 2009, but it seems to have been delayed due to the nuclear test in May. This office is scheduled to assume consular services such as issuing visas, which used to be handled by the Shenyang Consulate General of Liaoning Province. The movement of both people and trade between North Korea and China is accordingly being expanded with this office's opening. In addition, the development of Wi Wha Do, a North Korean free-trade zone accessible only to Chinese, was initiated.[16]

In July 2009, 70 kilograms of vanadium, a material needed for missile production, was about to be smuggled across the border into North Korea from Dangdong, China, but was detected.[17] This suggests that China is indeed carrying out United Nations' sanctions against the export of materials related to nuclear technology or weapons of mass destruction. But it is also clear that China's overall economic relations with the North reflected much greater complexity than the simple imposition of across-the-board sanctions.[18] China would clearly welcome a DPRK that was less regionally provocative militarily. To this end it has endorsed economic sanctions while also pressing the DPRK to make multiple shifts in its economic strategy so as to alleviate domestic economic deprivation. But China is also reluctant to act in ways that could seriously exacerbate the DPRK's economic plight—even when that plight is recognized as the consequence of economically rectifiable but politically unwelcome policy shifts by the DPRK.

Turning to trade between the Koreas, particularly exports from South Korea, it is clear that these too had increased somewhat in 2006.[19] But the relationship between the two Koreas worsened after Lee-Myung-bak became South Korea's president in 2008 and declared his policy of "Denuclearization, Openness, 3000" (a phrase promising that South Korea would help to raise the per capita national income of North Korea to $3000 in 10 years by cooperating with the international community if North Korea would make commitments to abolish its nuclear weapons and open up its economy). Lee broke sharply with the policies of his two presidential predecessors who provided generous economic assistance toward the North on the implicit assumption that the North would respond by reducing its insecurity, its military provocations, and its nuclear program. For Lee, any economic assistance from the South would be linked to changes in DPRK security and military behavior. Thus, sightseeing tours to the North's Mount Kumgang were called off because a South Korean tourist was shot and killed in July 2008. Government cooperation in Kaesong, another important North–South project, ceased after the North kicked out a resident South Korean official in March 2008. North Korea also detained workers of Hyundai Asan and demanded increases in North Korean workers' wages and land leases, implying that they "do not mind retreating from a project" if South Korea does not accept North Korean demands. Clearly the South under the Lee Myung-bak regime became far more vigorous than China in enforcing United Nations' sanctions and this has accorded with its overall tough line toward the North, a marked shift from its two predecessor regimes.

But since August 2009, North Korea has also tried to change its relationship with South Korea. Hyoen Jeongeun, a chairman of the Hyundai group, visited North Korea that month and, after having a long talk with Kim Jong-Il, secured the release of the detained Kaesong workers, reached a private agreement that included restarting the sightseeing business on Mount Kumgang and activation of the Kaesong industrial complex, and worked out a deal for reuniting separated families during the mid-autumn harvest festival. Moreover, North Korea sent a funeral delegation to South Korea after the death of former President Kim Dae-jung. They also announced that as of 21 August 2009 they would lift restrictions on time of stay and land road passage in the Kaesong industrial complex.[20]

It has been argued that foreign currency revenue from the Kaesong industrial complex or sightseeing tours to Mount Kumgung is roughly equal to the North's unfavorable trade balance. With such foreign currency revenue, North Korea could purchase the technologies they need (including military goods), but the North closed that route. Perhaps they judged that it would be an appropriate time to restart these activities, but they might also have been forced to restart them due to the continual economic crises they face.

Relations between the DPRK and the other members of the Six-Party Talks have been tense in part because of the tough-minded security focus of the Lee presidency. Only under the condition that North Korea perfectly reports all of its nuclear projects and seriously considers the dismantling of all existing nuclear facilities will the other countries provide economic, energy, or humanitarian support. Moreover the maximum amount will be equal to 0.95 million tons of heavy oil (this was finally agreed in July after the delay caused by the Banco Delta Asia problem).

Both China and Russia include aid supplies in their customs statistics. Exports of heavy oil from China are decreasing in the customs statistics, as described above. Furthermore, the export of heavy oil from Russia has also decreased by 68.7 percent from 133,046 tons in 2007 to 41,665 tons in 2008.

The relationship between North Korea and the United States has been particularly vital and the United States remains a country that North Korea is keen to talk to. For the United States as with China and South Korea, economic ties to the North are intimately connected to its security concerns. At the end of the Bush administration, the United States showed a conciliatory attitude by removing North Korea from its list of terrorism-supporting nations, but once North Korea launched missiles and refused to engage in the Six-Party Talks in 2009, the U.S. House of Representatives' Appropriations Committee zeroed out the entire budget devoted to normalization of relations with North Korea. This included $95 million to support energy in North Korea and $34.5 million needed for dismantling nuclear facilities.[21] But then former president Clinton visited North Korea in August 2009 to secure the release of two captured American news correspondents.

At that time, he also spoke with Kim Jong-Il. If its early set of hardline stances such as missile launches and the nuclear bomb test were designed to lay the groundwork for Kim's successor, the North appears to have switched over to a softer line following its initial posturing.[22]

Japan was once an important trade partner for North Korea, ranking second after China. However, following the nuclear test in 2006, Japan began to see the North as more of a security threat than an economic opportunity. Japan cut off all imports and exported only $7.61 million worth of goods in 2008, partly because of concerns over the abduction of Japanese citizens by the North and partly because Japan imposed and is enforcing its own additional sanctions beyond those imposed by the United Nations.

Grain support from the international community more broadly has also been decreasing. The World Food Program (WFP) was planning to supply grain to 6.2 million North Koreans by spending $504 million, but support drastically declined from 2009 onward and no new funds were added after the DPRK forced through its two nuclear bomb tests. That reduced funds to only 15 percent of the original plan, and the number of recipients of support decreased to 2.27 million.[23]

North Korea since the sanctions

Although it does nothing to improve the country's economy and just helps to sustain the ruling system, the quickest way for North Korea to acquire foreign currency has long been the export of weapons. If ocean shipping becomes difficult due to stricter ship inspections, the country might shift to a land route; however, weapons exports are likely to remain a major target for blockage no matter which route they take.

Economic development would seem to demand the introduction of foreign currency to compensate for North Korea's existing capital deficit. However, this will not be possible unless the DPRK itself becomes an attractive market for foreign currency.

Meanwhile, North Korea seems to have no consistent economic development policy, or it seems to have internal political conflicts, since policy keeps changing, as evidenced by a cycle of economic openness followed by closings. Actions may seem more consistent if one focuses on economics as a means of ensuring the survival of the Kim Il-Sung/Kim Jong-Il system. In all likelihood this same focus on regime survival will continue under Kim Jong-un. The leadership has shown that it will stop any reform that appears to be working against the continuation of the current regime, even if such reforms might be highly effective economically. For example, the integrated market in Pyongannam-to was closed again in the latter half of 2009, although it was invigorating the economy and providing daily benefits to the people.

On 30 November 2009, North Korea declared a major currency devaluation at a rate of 100:1. The upper limit of exchange from old currencies to new currencies is 150 thousand won per person (only $40 in real exchange rate terms). The redenomination came in response to rising inflation, widening income gaps, and the proliferation of de facto market mechanisms, following the reforms of July 2002. In response, market mechanisms were ignored. Since there is no trust yet for the new won, inflation is likely to increase drastically.

In conclusion: sanctions or engagement?

As mentioned above, maintaining the current system is the most important objective of the current government, in contrast to the desire of the rest of the international community to stabilize the Korean Peninsula and Northeast Asia in general. Most often those outside efforts have sought to reduce regional security tensions by encouraging DPRK economic reforms that would enhance citizen well-being and integrate the North more closely with the economies of the rest of the region. But to date the North has resisted such economic reforms and/or been incapable of bringing them to fruition. What should be done to achieve that stabilization? Which would be more effective, pressure or support? South Korea, which had followed a volatile policy of anti-communism and anti-North activities until the early 1980s, shifted under the Roh Tae-woo administration (1988–93) to push forward democratization, establish diplomatic relations with the Soviet Union and China, and take an ironic "northward policy" toward North Korea in the manner of the former Brandt administration in West Germany. This policy of reconciliation became even clearer under the Kim Dae-jung administration (1998–2003). A summit between North and South was held in 2000, and support for North Korea and economic exchanges were pushed forward. These policies were passed on to the Roh Moo-hyun administration, but their effects have been called into question ever since North Korea held its nuclear test in 2006. The enthusiastic engagement boom that began in 2000 has passed, and it has become harder for South Korea to take care of North Korean defectors as their numbers have become larger, while the portion of these defectors who cannot adjust to the "capitalist society" in the South has been growing. In addition, it has become obvious that North Korea has no intention of paying back ROK assistance, although most of the support from South Korea to North Korea requires reimbursement. For this reason, Lee Myung-bak, who became president in 2008, revised prior policies and hammered out his new policy of "Denuclearization, Openness, 3000," rejected out of hand by North Korea.

South Korean initiatives suggest that neither conciliatory economic nor punitive security policies have in isolation succeeded in achieving the denuclearization of North Korea. Clearly it is not a matter of choosing between these approaches if the North's nuclear capability enables it to maintain its system (although recall that Iraq was invaded even though it did not actually have nuclear weapons). The most important goal for North Korea remains keeping its system going.

How long can the present system continue? The protest movements in the Middle East and other parts of the Arab world in 2011 were caused largely by the dissatisfaction of poor people. In North Korea with its withered economy and lack of basic goods such as food, there is a strong possibility for similar unrest. Furthermore, economic disparity is increasing. Party officials, military authorities, and business people want for nothing, while the majority of people lead miserable lives.

There have been sporadic protest movements up to now, but North Korean citizens find it hard to communicate between different areas because mobile telephone and internet coverage is not widespread in North Korea; thus, compared with the Arabic countries small separate movements are unlikely to swell into larger ones. However dissatisfaction could reach a breaking point, resulting in mass protests which in turn could give rise to a severe military crackdown. Under such conditions, nuclear engineers may flee North Korea threatening the stability of Northeast Asia. In addition, when North Koreans migrate to China, they link up with ethnic Korean groups there, potentially creating a minority problem that is of ongoing concern to the Chinese government. In short, if economic disparity continues to increase in North Korea or the food situation does not improve, it may threaten the security of North Korea and Northeast Asia.

As a consequence, it is of paramount importance for outsiders to assure North Korean elites that their system will remain intact after denuclearization and to help them build a system that re-examines a variety of existing economic policies in a comprehensive fashion. Although it is also important to push forward democratization in North Korea, the stabilization of Northeast Asia and greater prosperity would first of all follow successful denuclearization, even if this may seem to be a circuitous strategy toward an eventual regime transformation.

Notes

1. Mountains in North Korea seen from China have no trees. Fields continue up to the tops of mountains just like patchwork, but bare, untended hillsides can be observed in some spots.
2. <http://faostat.fao.org/site/336/DesktopDefault.aspx?PageID=336>.
3. Hearing in Seoul, September 2007.
4. Hearing in Yanji, October 2008.
5. <http//bbsl.people.can.cn/post detaido?boarrdId=18view=1&id=92430375>.
6. <http://www.chousunonline.com/news/20091007000023>. One of the Chinese scholars said "Premier Wen Jiabao promised China would give 300 thousand tons of grain, 500 thousand tons of crude oil, and 800 thousand tons of coal."
7. It is sometimes mistaken as barter (give-and-take) trade, but the clearance-account system is designed to keep the export prices of both countries in account ledgers, with the country that has a balance in terms of imports paying cash at the end of each year.
8. In the first half of 2009, the price of crude oil (barrels) decreased by 51.8 percent compared to the same half of the previous year, partly due to the worldwide decrease in the price of crude oil. Exports from China to North Korea in the first half of 2009 amounted to $750 million, a decline of 8.4 percent from the previous year, but overall exports would have increased if the price of crude had remained at the same level as in the first half of 2008.
9. Refunds of 84 grains items, including whale meat and rice, were cancelled at the price of the additional export tax (*China Information News*, 20 December 2007), and an export-restrictive policy was adopted by imposing an export tax of 5–10 percent on grains or an export allocation of milled cereal flour (*International Business Daily*, 2 January 2008).

10. According to customs statistics, clothing (weaved) increased by 1010.3 percent (from $4.19 million to $46.83 billion), toys increased by 2178.8 percent (from $1.09 million to $24.78 million), leather products increased by 1227.7 percent (from $1.44million to $19.15 million), and umbrellas/walking sticks increased by 1164.4 percent (from $0.63 million to $8.63 million).
11. <http://www.gov.cn/jrzg/2008-10/14/content_1120529.htm>.
12. Since Chinese traders also do not believe in North Korean banks, they use cash transactions (according to a hearing in March, 2007).
13. <http://bbs1.people.com.cn/postDetail.do?boardId=1&view=1&id=93528517>.
14. Hearing in Yanji, September 2009. On the other hand, according to *Tumen Jiang Daily*, trade between Hunchun and North Korea during January to July was $114 million, an increase of 26.6 percent. However, the amount of trade conducted by government-owned companies decreased by 53.4 percent, although private enterprises, which have taken over about 70 percent of all business, increased by 32.4 percent.
15. *Nihon Keizai Shimbun*, 27 August 2009.
16. According to the interview in the Liaoning Academy of Social Sciences, September 2009, North Korea requested to call this off, although they suggested it in 2006.
17. <http:www.chousunonline.com/news/20090729000010>.
18. <http//bbsl.people.can.cn/post detaido?boarrdId=18view=1&id=92430375>.
19. Both South Korea and North Korea call this domestic marketing but actually consider it "foreign trade" for now.
20. <http://j.peopledaily.com.cn/94474/6735510.html>.
21. <http://www.chousunonline.com/news/20090509000017>.
22. There is some doubt about what, for the North, is actually orthodox here, as reported in Japan and South Korea.
23. *Nihon Keizai Shimbun*, 3 July 2009.

References

Ishihara, Kyouichi. 1988. Kakaku kaikaku (Reform of Price). In *Chugoku no Keizai Kaikaku* [*Economic Reform in China*], Reiitsu Kojima, ed. Tokyo: Keisoshobo.

Kim Il-Sung. 1980. *Kakumeiteki Taishu Rosen* [*The Policy of Revolutionary Mass*]. Tokyo: Hakuhou Bunko.

Koh Sunghyo. 1989. *Gendai Chosen Keizai Nyumon* [*The Introduction of Modern Korean Economy*]. Tokyo: Shinsensha.

Lee Uhong. 1989. *Donzoko no Kyowakoku* [*DPRK in Abyss*]. Tokyo: Aki Shobo.

Lin Jinshu. 2000. *Chaoxian Jingji* [*Economy of North Korea*]. Changchun, PRC: Jilin University Press.

Moon-Soo Yang. 2007. Haikyusei—kyoukyuu fusoku de seijyouka ha konnan [Rationing System—to Normalize due to the Lack of Supply]. In *Contemporary North Korea*, North Korea Research Association, ed. Tokyo: Iwanami-shoten.

Nam Sung Uook. 2007. Kitachousen no Nougyouseisan no Jitsujyou to Nougyou Kaikaku no Mitooshi [North Korean Agricultural Situation and the Outlook of Agricultural Reform]. *The Possibility of North Korean Reform* (*Bulletin of Seigakuin University*).

Nguyen Thanh Bang. 1992. Vietnam no keizai kaikaku—process, naiyou to hyouka [Economic Reform in Viet Nam—Process, Content, and Evaluation]. In *Gendai Vietnam Keizai* [*Modern Vietnamese Economy*], Sueo Sekiguchi and Tran Van Tho, eds. Tokyo: Keisoshobo.

Ohizumi, Keiichiro. 1999. Vietnam. In *Ajiakeizairon* [*Asian Economics*], Yousuke Hara, ed. Tokyo: NTT Shuppansha.

Part 2

Economics and security in Northeast Asia

Functional interfaces

4 Economics, security, and technology in Northeast Asia

Maneuvering between nationalist and globalist forces

Tai Ming Cheung

Introduction

Technological development and innovation is a critical but under-studied source of power, influence, and change in international relations. How states acquire and exploit their technological capabilities and the impact this has on the global system are dimly explained by international relations scholars and often treated as a residual factor in examining economic or security issues (Gilpin 2001: chap. 5).[1] For Northeast Asia, technological drivers have been central in its transformation into one of the world's most economically dynamic and prosperous regions. Japan, Taiwan, and South Korea have all successfully turned from industrial latecomers into technological front-runners, while China is aggressively catching up. Technological considerations also loom large in some of the region's most acute security problems, such as nuclear proliferation on the Korean Peninsula and military tensions in the Taiwan Strait.

States across Northeast Asia regard technological innovation and development as vital to their economic competitiveness and national security. China's latest plan charting its medium- and long-term science and technology development, for example, declared that possession of a viable indigenous technological base is "the lifeblood of the national economy and national security."[2] This sentiment is echoed in the technology strategies of other regional countries.

This chapter examines the role that technological development has played in shaping the relationship between economics and security among states in Northeast Asia over the past 60 years. Particular attention will be paid to the evolution of grand strategic thinking on technology and innovation and the impact this has had on economic development and national security, especially with regard to Japan, South Korea, and China. What are the core strategic and ideological values and interests that shape national approaches? What influence have nationalist and globalist factors had? What are the key long-term technological trends and how will they affect Northeast Asia's economic and security dynamics?

Defining techno-nationalism, techno-globalism, and techno-hybridism and their place in grand strategic thinking

A useful starting point in examining the role that technological considerations play in the economic–security nexus in Northeast Asia is to understand how the grand strategies that states pursue are forged. A state's grand strategy represents the overarching vision of how a ruling coalition coordinates and utilizes economic, military, diplomatic, technological, and other capabilities to achieve national goals (Posen 1984). Achieving such a consensus is often contentious and requires extensive deliberation among contending domestic political coalitions with diverging views as to what constitutes the state's core interests, the nature of external threats, and what are the most suitable means and ends to be pursued.

In her examination of how competing groups in industrializing states approach external cooperation and conflict, Etel Solingen argues that these domestic coalitions can be categorized into two ideal types. The first group can be labeled as "internationalists" as they are in favor of economic liberalization, the promotion of regional peace, and access to foreign capital and technology. On the opposing side are "statist-nationalists" who resist internationalization, liberalization, and peace and who support the maintenance of strong military and defense-industrial establishments by raising tensions (Solingen 1998).[3]

The degree to which these coalitions are concentrated or cartelized may be shaped to a significant extent by the nature and timing of the industrialization process of the states that they reside within. According to Jack Snyder, states such as Britain and the United States that underwent early industrialization are associated with "diffuse political elites and the development of mass democracy." Late industrializers such as Germany and Japan before World War II tended to have "immobile, concentrated elite interests and cartelized politics," while late, late industrializers like the Soviet Union are associated with a "hypercentralized political and economic system, producing a relatively united elite with relatively encompassing interests" (Snyder 1991: 55). If late industrializing states were to also face serious external security challenges, this would exacerbate the cartelization of their coalitional politics and strengthen the influence of military and autarkic groups (ibid.: 56). Very late industrializers such as China under Mao Zedong and North Korea under Kim Il-Sung and Kim Jong-Il would fit this description of regimes dominated by insular military cartels.

This coalitional framework thesis can also be applied to the technological realm where similarly aligned factions of techno-globalists compete against techno-nationalists. Within this model, a third, more centralist coalition exists in which moderate elements of these two other groups come together to advocate a techno-hybrid approach. These three schools of thought can be defined as follows (Ostry and Nelson 1995; Keller and Samuels 2003):

- techno-nationalists believe that only a state-controlled and closed-door approach to technological innovation can safeguard national security, economic competiveness, and international status. Emphasis is placed on nurturing indigenous capabilities through the adoption of highly regulated protectionist regimes that sharply restrict foreign direct investment but encourage the one-way importation of advanced technology and knowledge. Under these economic and strategic conditions, techno-nationalist cartels tend to be most assertive and hold the reins of decision-making power in late and very late industrializing countries, especially if these states face external threats to their national security. Influential domestic groups that are most often affiliated with this coalition include the military, defense, and heavy industrial sectors, and the science and technology apparatus;

- techno-globalists advocate a bottom-up market-defined approach that stresses borderless collaboration and the unrestricted flow of knowledge, technology, talent, trade, and foreign investment. Firms are the dominant drivers of the innovation process, while governments play a secondary role in supporting fundamental research and development. The backbone of this cartel is made up of the foreign affairs apparatus, commerce-related bureau-cracies, trade-oriented economic sectors, the financial sector, and firms with extensive overseas operations and foreign partnerships. Techno-globalist coalitions tend to rise to prominence as late industrializing states begin to catch up in their economic and technological development with developed front-runners, especially if they become internationally competitive. The nature of the international system is also an important driver in shaping the domestic fortunes of this coalition. Techno-globalist groups have become more prominent and influential since the 1990s as globalization has reshaped the workings of the international system;
- techno-hybridists are pragmatists who seek to integrate the dueling techno-nationalist and techno-globalist ideologies into a balanced operational model. They believe that the state and firms/markets play complementary roles either working together through public–private partnerships or occupying different components of the innovation system. State involvement should be focused toward the nurturing of basic research and development capabilities such as national laboratories and universities while firms can participate in the global marketplace, especially multinational production and innovation networks. The composition of this coalition tends to be more fluid than the techno-nationalist and techno-globalist groupings because their support for this approach is non-ideological and adaptable according to prevailing domestic and international conditions. Techno-hybridists would include groups that would benefit both from state support and engagement with the international community, such as the science, technology, and academic communities, select elements of the defense and heavy industrial bases that are extensively involved in technology transfers, and the foreign trade apparatus.

Economics, security, and technology in Northeast Asia from the 1950s to early 1990s: the era of strong techno-nationalism

For states in Northeast Asia, the competing coalitional set-up during the second half of the twentieth century was not between techno-nationalists and techno-globalists but among different subsets of techno-nationalist thinking. As the region emerged from war and foreign occupation in the late 1940s and 1950s,

Table 4.1 Defining characteristics of the three schools of technological grand strategy

	Techno-nationalism	*Techno-globalism*	*Techno-hybridism*
Dominant players	The state	Multinational firms and global markets	Balanced relationship between the state, firms, and markets
Comparative international relations theory	Realism	Liberal institutionalism	None
Innovation model	National innovation systems	Global production and innovation networks	Multiple drivers of innovation at regional, national, and global levels
Variants	Commercial or military	Commercial	Primarily commercial, but also secondary military

the focus of national policymakers was on state building and economic development. Their thinking and approaches to these priorities were framed by two common and powerful influences: nationalism and security. As Meredith Woo-Cummings has persuasively argued, the rise of the developmental state in Japan, South Korea, and Taiwan, along with China and North Korea, was decisively shaped by war, colonialism, and the fear of war (Woo-Cummings 2005). In addition, the security relationships that these countries had with their superpower benefactors, either the United States or Soviet Union, also had a profound impact. These experiences accounted for a distinctive overarching regional pattern of industrialization and technological development that was geared toward a "perpetual mobilization for war" during the Cold War (ibid.: 98).

In the technological arena, these shared security concerns—although viewed from opposing sides—led Northeast Asian states to become ardent proponents of the techno-nationalist school of grand strategic thinking in their initial stages of industrialization, especially in placing national security considerations at the very top of their development priorities. This accounted for the region-wide emphasis on the building of heavy, strategic, and technology-intensive industries.

Two distinct types of techno-nationalist grand strategies and models were adopted by Northeast Asian states during this period: commercial and military techno-nationalism. The commercial variant emphasizes the importance of technological autonomy for economic security, especially to allow homegrown vertically integrated firms to be competitive in the international marketplace. Military techno-nationalism stresses the overriding importance of military-security priorities in technological development. How states made their choices depended on the nature of their political and economic systems, whether those in power supported or opposed international engagement, and their strategic alignments within the Cold War system.

States allied with the United States and with leaderships that supported international economic liberalization such as Japan, the Republic of Korea (ROK), and Taiwan pursued the commercial techno-nationalist model (Low 2006; Samuels 2007). They were able to focus much of their attention and resources on economic development because they enjoyed security protection from an expansive U.S. forward-based military alliance system, generous U.S. military and development assistance, and trade access to the U.S. market. By contrast, Communist regimes in China and the Democratic People's Republic of Korea (DPRK) adhered to military techno-nationalist models of development because of the dominance of statist-nationalist groups that favored the building of command economies and feared attack from the United States and its regional allies.

These techno-nationalist coalitions can also be differentiated according to how assertive or accommodating they were in the pursuit of their goals. Those

Table 4.2 Key features of the military and commercial versions of the techno-nationalist development model

	Military techno-nationalist development model	*Commercial techno-nationalist development model*
Key regimes	Pre-1978 China, North Korea, pre-World War II Japan	Post-1945 Japan, South Korea, Taiwan, post-1978 China
Development priorities	Defense industrial base and heavy industries	Heavy, export-oriented and high-technology industries (iron and steel, chemicals, electronics)
Threat environment and security posture	Acute external threats, militarization of entire state	Severe external threats, significant defense outlays, heavy reliance on security protection from the United States
Orientation and nature of economy	Closed autarkic system; command-style economy	Semi-open economy with extensive trading links with Western countries; market-oriented economic structure
Science and technology drivers	Overwhelmingly state-driven	Important roles played by the state, firms, and importation of foreign knowledge and technology transfers
Technology outputs	Military equipment, heavy industrial equipment	Consumer electronics and retail goods, heavy industrial equipment

who advocated aggressive, uncompromising approaches in their technology development policies such as emphasizing complete self-reliance and focusing overtly on military priorities can be defined as strong techno-nationalists. Those who favored a more accommodationist and open posture can be labeled as pragmatic techno-nationalists.

The strong commercial techno-nationalist model of Japan and South Korea

With their successful economic take-off in the 1970s and 1980s, Japan and the ROK became role models of industrial latecomers that were able to bridge the technological gap and join the ranks of the world's leading technological powers through the pursuit of aggressive commercial techno-nationalist strategies. Techno-nationalist coalitions dominated the decision-making and policy implementation apparatuses throughout the government, national security, economic, and science and technology domains of these two countries between the 1950s to the end of the 1990s. In Japan, the key bastions of techno-nationalism throughout this period were the ruling Liberal Democratic Party, the Ministry of International Trade and Industry (MITI), the Japan Business Federation (*Keidanren*) and its defense and industrial committees, the Japan Defense Agency, and all of the country's major business and industrial conglomerates. In South Korea, military-run regimes from the 1960s through the 1990s were forceful advocates of techno-nationalist policies and they were able to establish a formidable coalitional base of support that included the entire industrial economy and newly emergent *chaebols*.

While the ROK lagged behind Japan in its technological development and national capabilities during this period, both countries pursued similar approaches in their catch-up efforts. They targeted the development of capital-intensive, technologically advanced mass manufacturing industries in which innovation was focused on incremental process refinements, foreign interaction was confined predominately to the importation of technologies and know-how, and the state and major business conglomerates played a central role in guiding this development.

Both countries had insatiable appetites for technological imports and transfers. They initially concentrated on the manufacturing and heavy industrial sectors that offered economies of scale. For Japan, the focus was on manufacturing technologies in sectors such as iron and steel, automobiles, electronics, and communications equipment (Odagiri and Goto 1993). Through intensive efforts at reverse engineering, diffusion, assimilation, and heavy investment in the development of indigenous research and development (R&D) capabilities, Japanese and ROK firms were able to master these technologies and begin to make gradual improvements. Japanese firms in particular excelled at incremental process innovation because of the high degree of integration of their R&D, production, and management systems. But a sizeable number of Japanese industries also failed to become internationally competitive despite extensive government and institutional support. They include the chemicals, civil aviation, software, and mainframe computer industries. Some of the key reasons for the poor performance of these sectors included a shortage of trained talent, inadequate R&D investment, and the misalignment between the domestic and global markets (Porter *et al.* 2000; Posen 2002).

The efforts of the ROK in catching up were more uneven. A major reason was that the country was much further behind technologically and organizationally than Japan (Shin 1996: 123–37). From this lower baseline, South Korean firms had to undertake a steep and concerted assent up the technological ladder that was extremely costly and time-consuming. When South Korean companies began to make noticeable technological advances in the 1980s and early 1990s, however, they had limited resources and had to selectively target a narrow range of areas in which to make additional progress in catching up. Moreover, the country's technological output was primarily for export as the local market was too small to absorb rising levels of production. This severely restricted the ability of different industries to coordinate and link their development with each other. For example, the semi-conductor industry grew autonomously and had little interaction with the computer or telecommunications sectors. Under these circumstances, a handful of industries that enjoyed sustained support from the country's large family-owned business conglomerates known as *chaebols* and the state, such as the DRAM, CDMA, automobile, and shipbuilding sectors, emerged to become world-class leaders in their technological areas, while the personal computer and consumer electronics industries struggled and ultimately failed in their catch-up efforts. For South Korean firms and industries that were able to narrow—and in some instances eliminate—the technology gap, some analysts credit their achievements to their ability to effectively integrate domestic and external technological resources under a strict management regime. Outsourcing of R&D and production activities both domestically and overseas was also an important route in catching up (Bae *et al.* 2002).

While Japan and the ROK were eager to acquire foreign technology, they adopted stringent protectionist policies that shut out foreign direct investment and restricted the ability of foreign companies to operate in their domestic markets or even to establish joint venture collaboration. Up until the Asian financial crisis in the late 1990s, foreign ownership and control of major Japanese and ROK firms was virtually impossible because of complex cross-shareholdings among domestic institutions. Moreover, the Japanese government set challenging domestic industrial and technological standards regimes that essentially excluded the participation of non-Japanese firms.

Institutionally, the Japanese and South Korean governments worked closely with banks and major business groups in shepherding the catch-up process among firms because they were able to effectively coordinate private activities with public policies (Shin 1996: 53–7). In Japan, MITI and *keiretsu* business groups cooperated to ensure there was adequate investment in R&D to promote long-term product and process innovation. In the ROK, the *chaebols* emerged in the 1980s to serve the same roles as the *keiretsu* and they were behind the country's technological takeoff.

While Japan and the ROK were allowed to pursue techno-nationalist policies in the civilian sphere, this did not extend into the defense arena. They were required to enter into collaborative co-production and co-development projects with the United States, as this was the only way that Washington would allow transfers of sensitive defense-related technologies to take place, especially from the 1990s as products became increasingly more complex. This technological and industrial subordination in defense was one of the costs that Tokyo and Seoul had to pay for their inclusion in the U.S. bilateral defense alliance system that provided much needed and affordable security protection in a highly volatile region. Without the dominant U.S. forward military presence in East Asia during the Cold War, Japan, the ROK, and even Taiwan would have been unable to pursue their commercial techno-nationalist models of development.

The Japanese and ROK defense industries and military establishments were far from willing to accept this defense industrial dependence relationship with the United States (Green 1995). A key tenet of Japanese grand strategy, for example, dating from the Meiji era to the present day has been military technological autonomy through the promotion of indigenous defense production, or *kokusanka* (Samuels 1994). Strenuous efforts were made by both countries to develop their own weapons systems, with mixed results. Japan and South Korea were most successful in defense electronics, armored vehicles, and warships as they were able to leverage their commercial strengths in these technologies, but they both had to rely on the United States in critical areas such as fighter aircraft, air defense systems, and missiles (Chinworth 1992: 168–80).

Defense technological and industrial cooperation between the United States and Japan and the ROK often resembled shotgun marriages between unhappy and distrustful partners as techno-nationalist sentiments ran strong and deep in the defense industries and military establishments of all of these countries. This was most vividly demonstrated in the FS-X fighter aircraft program, which was a poorly conceived and badly executed co-development project between the United States and Japan in the 1990s to produce a new combat aircraft for the Japanese Air Self-Defense Force. The United States wanted Japan to acquire an existing fighter plane, the F-16C, and undertake some limited modifications, but Japan sought to develop essentially a brand-new fighter using the F-16 as a baseline reference (Lorell 1995). The result was a long-delayed and enormously expensive program that produced the Mitsubishi F-2 fighter, which represented only a modest incremental improvement over the original U.S. version although it was refitted with Japanese avionics and technologies. But the cost of the F-2 is so high, by as much as 3–4 times compared to the F-16, that Japan has only been able to afford to buy a limited number.

Although an aggressive commercial techno-nationalist grand strategy played an instrumental role in guiding the transformation of Japan and ROK from imitative laggards to innovation front-runners in the late industrial era, this rigid and closed approach began to become a serious obstacle to continuing progress and competitiveness for these countries in the 1990s. Globalization and the emerging information technology revolution began to decisively shift the drivers responsible for economic, technological, and military development from states and national economies to multinational corporations and global production and innovation chains. Analysts argued that this meant that Japan and South Korea's techno-nationalist development model was no longer relevant. Liu Xielin pointed out that "the features of Japan and Korea's catch-up process seem outdated and in some critical ways inappropriate given recent economic, technological and social changes in the global environment" (2005: 8). The era of strong commercial techno-nationalism appeared to be over at the same time as the closing of the twentieth century.

The strong military techno-nationalist model: China and North Korea

In contrast to the commercial focus of its Northeast Asian neighbors during the Cold War era, China and the DPRK went down a development path that stressed the overriding importance of military priorities in the relationship between economics, security, and technology in their early industrialization drives. This was not surprising as both states were preoccupied with regime survival in the face of acute security threats, particularly between the 1950s and the end of the 1970s. In addition, the militaries in China and North Korea wielded extensive political and policymaking power and influence that ensured that they had priority access in resource allocations and technology and economic development plans.

The key features of the military techno-nationalist grand strategy that was adopted by China (Feigenbaum 1999)[4]—some elements of which were also pursued by the DPRK—were that:

- technological development is strategic and has implications for the relative position of the state in the global military and economic balance, or what Chinese strategists term as comprehensive national strength;
- the state must invest in critical technological sectors because of the high risks and long time cycles involved in high-technology R&D;
- the state should pursue import-substituting indigenization;
- the state must nurture an indigenous capacity to innovate;
- technology diffusion, whether through spin-offs or spin-ons, should be a central long-term goal.

From the 1950s to the end of the 1970s, China applied this grand strategy to the building of conventional and strategic defense industrial sectors that eventually overshadowed the rest of the national economy. The Chinese techno-nationalist model was known as the "Two Bombs, One Satellite" or *Liangdan Yixing* ideology (Yanqiong 2002). This referred to the defense economy's crowning success in the development of nuclear weapons and space capabilities in the 1960s and 1970s.

Another important characteristic of *Liangdan Yixing* was its overwhelming emphasis on big science, especially the undertaking of large-scale and highly complex projects. The nuclear weapons, missile, space, and nuclear submarine projects required a massive and sustained mobilization effort by the state to provide the necessary technological, financial, and engineering resources.

When Deng Xiaoping took power in 1978, one of his first tasks was to sideline the Maoist military techno-nationalist grand strategy and focus on civilian economic and technological development (Cheung 2009: chap. 3). At the same time as he rolled back the pervasive militarization of the economy and society, he adopted an economic "open door" policy and launched economic liberalization initiatives that ended the country's autarkic isolation and heralded the beginning of the building of a market economy.

During his rule between 1978 and the early 1990s, Deng did not explicitly replace the defunct military techno-nationalist model with a new strategic framework. A flexible and ad hoc approach was implemented instead, which Barry Naughton and Adam Segal have described as "purely adaptative, opportunistic policies of 'muddling through'" (2003: 186). This could be defined as techno-pragmatism. Chinese decision-makers tend to be instrumentalist in how they view and make use of nationalism, which is an imported concept (Zhao 2000). Despite the heavy emphasis on science and technology development before the 1980s, the excessive attention devoted to strategic nuclear and missile priorities meant that the country lagged well behind technologically in virtually every other civilian and military area. Consequently, the Chinese government promoted a highly opportunistic strategy focused on seeking technology imports and foreign direct investment to fill gaps that the domestic base could not meet.

A strong military techno-nationalist ideology has been the cornerstone of North Korea's national development priorities since the founding of the regime in 1948. However, between the 1950s and 1970s, the DPRK was heavily dependent on the Soviet Union and, to a much lesser extent, China for its military and technological needs, especially in the reconstruction of the country following the Korean War. From the early 1970s, a concerted effort was begun to establish a self-reliant military technological and industrial base. This initially focused on the building of conventional military science and technology and manufacturing facilities to produce tanks, warships, and aircraft, but expanded in the 1980s and 1990s to ballistic missiles, nuclear weapons, and chemical and biological warfare capabilities (So'ng-p'yo 2005). Also in the 1980s, the DPRK began to focus attention on the development of civilian science and technology capabilities, including computers and electronics (Jensen 2009).

After Kim Jong-Il assumed power in 1994, the military techno-nationalist ideology was further strengthened and elevated to become the country's overarching state doctrine through the adoption of the *Songun Chongchi* (Military-First) and *Kangsong Taeguk* (Building a Rich and Strong State) ideologies. A 2003 commentary by the North Korean newspaper *Nodong Sinmun* (21 March 2003) explained the pivotal importance of military priorities in the country's economic and technological development: "In a powerful state, the defense industry takes a leading and key position in the economy. As long as the imperialists continue to exist, the defense industry is a lifeline for the country and the nation." The obvious conclusion, the commentary noted, is that "developing the defense industry with priority while developing the light industry and agriculture simultaneously is the best way to satisfactorily ensure the people's independent and creative life while actively engaging in the fierce anti-imperialism struggle."

The advent of techno-globalism in the 1990s and techno-hybridism in the twenty-first century

A series of transformative events beginning in the late 1980s led to a far-reaching reshaping of the international order in the 1990s and called into question the continuing relevance of the techno-nationalist approach. This included the end of the Cold War, the accelerating spread of economic globalization, the advent of the information age, and the arrival of the revolution in military affairs. These developments steadily eroded the importance and reach of the state and national systems as powerful new actors and processes unbounded by national borders emerged, especially global corporations and transnational networks of production and innovation. Techno-globalism gradually found its way into the thinking of scholars, policy planners, and decision-makers across Northeast Asia to either complement or replace techno-nationalist agendas.

Techno-globalism can be compared to liberal institutionalism in which competition among states and firms is viewed as a non-zero sum game. This ideology has a number of attributes:

- allowing foreign direct investment in manufacturing and services and international mergers and acquisitions with only limited restrictions;
- the rise of global firms with horizontally integrated R&D and manufacturing facilities;
- the growth of transnational networks of production and innovation through outsourcing and modularization;
- the erosion of economic sovereignty by states, especially in the making and implementation of macro-economic policies;
- adopting open, free-trade principles that encourage capital and labor mobility and supported by low tariffs and lightly regulated regimes;
- rolling back the role of the state in science and technology development to primarily supporting basic research and encouraging firms to assume responsibility for applied and commercial R&D.

While techno-globalism is primarily focused on civilian activities, the process has also spilled over into the military arena to a limited extent. Following the end of the Cold War, close allied states in Western Europe and North America allowed their defense industries to be opened up to cross-border mergers and acquisitions with few restrictions and this led to the establishment of a handful of huge global defense and aerospace firms such as EADS and BAE in Europe and Boeing and Lockheed Martin in the United States (Bitzinger 2003; Brooks 2005). However, states in Northeast Asia and other parts of the world did not join this process and their defense and strategic sectors remain closed to foreign investment.

Singapore and Hong Kong are archetypical examples of techno-globalist regimes in East Asia. Both have market-friendly regulatory and trade systems with low tariffs, unfettered capital mobility, and transparent and non-discriminatory legal systems. This has allowed them to become hubs for the regional headquarters of multinational corporations. Their innovation systems are open and have extensive collaborations with foreign counterparts in the academic, corporate, and governmental spheres.

In the national security sphere, Singapore has pursued a techno-hybrid approach in the development of its defense economy. The Singapore government has sought to nurture an indigenous defense R&D base, but has sought to confine its activities to basic research while pushing domestic companies to engage in applied development and commercialization. In addition, Singapore's defense firms have been actively engaged in joint ventures with foreign counterparts, especially as it is heavily reliant on imports for most of its military equipment (Karniol 2006).

The wariness of Japan and South Korea toward techno-globalism

Japan and the ROK did make some limited efforts in the 1990s to relax their techno-nationalist policies and promote techno-globalist activity, but this was a carefully managed and highly selective process. Japan's MITI, for example, opened up several of its large-scale research programs to foreign participation at the end of the 1980s in areas such as intelligent manufacturing, biological research, and computing, but the overall level of external involvement in R&D was modest and proved to be the exception rather than the rule (Corning 2004). MITI and its techno-nationalist coalition allies, especially the LDP and *Keidanren*, continued to control the levers of power and they managed to keep intact Japan's techno-nationalist and economic nationalist policy frameworks.

These two countries remained committed to the techno-nationalist model until the onset of the Asian financial crisis in the late 1990s. When the crisis triggered severe economic turmoil in South Korea, the ROK government, under intense international pressure, undertook a major overhaul of its techno-nationalist regime by allowing foreign multinationals to acquire major stakes in local firms, including in the technology and industrial manufacturing sectors, and establish R&D facilities within the country. However, the South Korean authorities have continued to "use every means to retain [their] own system of technological innovation and industrial production" (Kim 2003: 87). South Korea has shifted from the strong techno-nationalist model to a limited or more pragmatic variant. The once powerful techno-nationalist alliance of government, industry, defense sector, and big business lost considerable clout and prestige as they were held responsible for many of the problems that led to the economic crisis in South Korea, paving the way for more techno-globalist and techno-hybrid minded groups to gain influence, such as private firms, universities, the financial sector, and foreign institutions.

Japan was less severely impacted by the Asian financial crisis and so was under less external pressure to take any of the market-opening steps required of its neighbor. A small number of sectors were opened up to foreign investment and participation, such as in the financial and automobile industries, but foreign firms were only allowed to acquire minority stakes. Most of the Japanese economy and its science and technology sector remained protected from the outside world. Indeed, some analysts pointed out that Japanese firms went on the offensive during the Asian financial crisis by increasing their FDI in South Korea and Southeast Asia and thereby were able to "strengthen and extend Japanese techno-nationalism and industrial policy throughout the region" (Keller and Samuels 2003: 230).

With the 2008 global economic crisis, Japan Inc. was unable to respond in the same manner and take advantage of the foreign investment opportunities available to further strengthen their overseas networks. Weakened by the prolonged anemic state of the Japanese economy and intensifying foreign competition over the past decade, Japanese firms, especially those in the manufacturing and industrial assembly sectors, could ill afford to expand their foreign investment (Iwami 2009).

In the defense technological arena, Japan's efforts to maintain its techno-nationalist policies appear to be increasingly in doubt. This is because of stagnant defense budgets; soaring defense research, development, and acquisition costs that have made the indigenous production of military equipment significantly more costly than comparable foreign hardware; strict limits on international collaboration; and a long-term ban on arms exports. This has led to a steady decline in the size of the Japanese defense industrial base over the past decade as growing numbers of Japanese firms, especially second- and third-tier subcontractors, exit this market or go bankrupt because of shrinking orders. The membership of the *Keidanren*'s Defense Production Committee, which is the chief umbrella organization of the country's defense producer associations, dropped from 84 in 1997 to 66 in 2002 (Samuels 2007: 148). This has led observers to argue that the Japanese defense techno-nationalist model is in crisis and may no longer be sustainable. The assessment of Christopher Hughes is that the domestic defense industry faces a "slow death" without major reforms and this will "undermine Japanese national technological and comprehensive strength and thus autonomy in security policy" (Hughes 2011: 452).

In contrast to the reluctance of Japan and South Korea to respond to the changing external strategic, economic, and technological landscapes in the 1990s, China was more adaptable. It had already shifted from a strong techno-nationalist ideology under Mao Zedong to a more commercial and pragmatic techno-nationalist orientation with Deng Xiaoping. Chinese economic policymakers became attracted to key elements of the Japanese and ROK technology and industrial development models. This initially focused on reverse engineering and the large-scale importation of technological and industrial capabilities during the 1980s, but broadened in the 1990s to the emulation of the Japanese *keiretsu* and Korean *chaebol* corporate models of building a small core of sprawling, highly diversified, vertically integrated state-owned firms able to compete internationally (Steinfeld 2002: 23–5; Xie and White 2004).

China's maneuvering between techno-globalism and techno-nationalism since the 1990s

China embraced key elements of techno-globalist thinking in the early 1990s by undertaking a far-reaching opening up of the national economy to foreign direct investment and rolling back state dominance of the science and technology system by allowing the participation of private and other non-state firms (Naughton and Segal 2003: 170–6). This led to massive inflows of foreign investment into the medium- and high-technology sectors by multinationals and soaring imports of technology goods by foreign and Chinese firms throughout the 1990s. In addition, large numbers of entrepreneurial domestic and foreign joint venture new technology enterprises were established or spun off from the state sector and quickly emerged to become major players in the domestic technology marketplace.

By the turn of the twenty-first century, the Chinese technology development model had become a patchwork of techno-nationalist and techno-globalist thinking stitched loosely together. These dueling sentiments came to the fore in the drafting of the country's new medium- and long-term science and technology development plan (MLP). Thousands of Chinese scientists, engineers, corporate executives, and a small number of Chinese-born foreign scholars were consulted to examine issue areas deemed to be vital to China's science and technology competitiveness, including on basic science, energy and resource science and technology, national security, and the national innovation system.[5] Heated debates took place over the fundamental orientation of the MLP. One revolved around the relationship between indigenous innovation and technology imports. Leading economists argued that China should retain its existing technological development model of attracting foreign multinationals and encouraging technology transfers to boost the country's science and technology competence. Many scientists opposed this view and insisted that China could not depend on getting core technology from other countries. The scientific community eventually prevailed and the MLP reflects the changed focus in the Chinese technology development model toward indigenous development.

The MLP was issued in 2006 and is avowedly techno-nationalistic in nature. In assessing the fundamental relationship between national security and technological development, the MLP defined this linkage in stridently realist, almost zero-term terms. The plan pointed out that the only way that China could advance against international competition was to "improve its independent innovative capabilities and master a number of core technologies, own a number of proprietary intellectual property rights, and groom internationally competitive enterprises in important fields."

One of the central concepts in the MLP is the notion of indigenous innovation (*zizhu chuangxin*). This term is viewed "by some as a regression to the self-defeating techno-nationalist notions of self-reliance from the Maoist era," although the MLP seeks to define this concept not only from an ideological viewpoint but also from a functional perspective (Cao *et al.* 2006: 40). Specifically, indigenous innovation is seen as a way to promote original innovation, re-assembling existing technologies in different ways to produce new breakthroughs, and the absorption and upgrading of imported technologies.

Although the MLP was a success for the techno-nationalist lobby, techno-globalist advocates remain vocal and influential. They continue to argue that China should take advantage of the opportunities opened up by the information technology revolution and position itself for a radically different techno-globalist development model. Liu Xielin, a technology policy scholar at the Chinese Academy of Social Sciences and adviser to the Chinese government, has written that China's development path for catching up in the twenty-first century has been fundamentally altered from the 1990s and is also significantly different from the traditional approaches taken by Japan and Korea that occurred in the late industrial age. Liu (2005) points to several developments that have caused this shift. First, the information technology revolution has dramatically changed the rules of the game for catch-up, which has given rise to new business models, products, and services. Second, modular production, or outsourcing, has become a key feature of the global economy. Modularity allows the outsourcing of design and production of components and subsystems. Third, Liu argues that global technological outsourcing provides a new channel for Chinese companies to become involved in product innovations at an earlier stage than in the previous techno-economic paradigm. Whereas innovation in the industrial era relied on absorption and adaptation, the strategy in the information age is based more on market-oriented innovation and technology outsourcing. Many leading Chinese technology firms, such as Haier and Huawei, have adopted this approach (Xie and White 2004: 13–14).

Although the enactment of the MLP may have suggested that Chinese policy-makers were retreating from their techno-globalist leanings, the evidence on the ground showed otherwise. Foreign direct investment continued to pour into the country and foreign firms were assuming growing prominence in R&D activities in China. The number of foreign-invested firms in the electronics and communications industry jumped from 350 in 1998 to more than 1,150 in 2004, while there were more than 930 foreign research and development centers in China by the end of 2006 compared to 600 in 2004, with around 200 new centers opening annually (*People's Daily Online*, 20 August 2004; OECD 2008: 268–73).

China's technology development strategy has evolved into a pragmatic and sometimes messy techno-hybrid model that incorporates both competing and complementary strands of techno-nationalist and techno-globalist thinking. With these two camps firmly entrenched and wielding extensive influence among policymakers and key state agencies, there will be occasional zigzags in technology-related policies to accommodate their different interests.[6] A prime example of such an outcome occurred in 2009 when China issued indigenous innovation procurement guidelines requesting that government agencies should only buy technology products containing domestic intellectual property. The move drew strong condemnation from foreign companies and governments who argued that the policy went against established international norms (Chao 2009).

The procurement guidelines controversy reflects a broader effort by China to promote its own home-grown technical standards within the global technology system. The setting of international technical standards has traditionally been in the hands of multinational corporations, but China has begun to raise its profile since the beginning of the twenty-first century, especially in areas such as tele-communications, digital audio and video, computer micro-processors, wireless local area network security, and Internet protocols. The MLP explicitly calls for China to "actively take part in the formulation of international standards and drive the transferring of domestic technological standards to international stand-ards." Richard Suttmeier and Yao Xiangkui argue that China's technical stand-ards strategy should be understood as a modified form of techno-nationalism, in which "technological development in support of national economic and security interests is pursued through leveraging the opportunities presented by globaliza-tion for national advantage" (Suttmeier and Xiangkui 2004: 3; Gibson 2007). How China flexes its growing technological power in this area will offer a good indicator of where the balance between techno-nationalist and techno-globalist impulses lies in its evolving techno-hybrid framework.

Another important new state-directed technology development initiative was unveiled in 2010 that offers insights into China's techno-hybrid grand strategy. This is the development of a batch of so-called strategic emerging industries (SEI) or *Zhanluexing Xinxing Chanye*. This policy appears to be updating elements of the MLP to the changed realities of the international economic and technological order in the aftermath of the 2008–2009 global economic crisis. Seven sectors were selected for additional state support to accelerate their devel-opment. Some of these areas were already included in the MLP, such as high-end equipment manufacturing, information technology, and advanced materials, but alternative energy and new-energy vehicles were sectors that were picked for the first time.

Of more potential significance is that the SEI initiative appears to represent a shift from the techno-nationalist framework toward a more cooperative techno-globalist oriented approach. One of the new guiding principles is an emphasis on expanding international cooperation in all these seven sectors in order to "make better use of global S&T achievements" and allow Chinese firms to compete more effectively in external markets (*Xinhua Domestic Service*, 31 May 2011). Another difference from the MLP is that the SEI is aimed primarily at developing technological capabilities for social and economic goals, such as tackling environmental pollution and nurturing sustainable energy resources, while there is limited attention paid to national security considerations. Of the seven indus-tries, only the high-end equipment manufacturing and advanced materials would also directly benefit the defense sector. This shows that the Chinese authorities are willing to pursue a number of innovation models that are adaptable and suit the specific needs and circumstances of different technology and industrial sectors.

Chinese technology strategy in the national security arena has also witnessed major changes since the 1990s with the end of the Cold War and the advent of the revolution in military affairs. The beginning of the information age in the early 1990s forced the Chinese military and defense industrial establishments to critically re-examine their development strategies. Mechanization was the central goal of modernization efforts in the industrial era through the development and acquisition of conventional weapons systems such as tanks, warships, and aircraft. But with the emergence of a new information-based techno-military paradigm, debate switched to how to adapt to these far-reaching changes (Ji 2004).

Military chiefs and defense industrialists have been urged to come up with new approaches to meet this paradigm shift. At the 16th Communist Party Congress in 2002, the country's senior leadership proclaimed that the first 20 years of the twenty-first century would be a period of "important strategic opportunities" that would allow China to make rapid advances in its goal of building a prosperous society (Suettinger 2004).[7] The People's Liberation Army (PLA) and the defense economy were required to "firmly seize this period of strategic opportunities" and leapfrog ahead in their military modernization efforts (Zhaoyin 2003). Chinese President and Commander-in-Chief Jiang Zemin called for the fulfillment of the "dual task of building mechanization and informationization" of the country's armed forces.[8] This meant that the building of information systems and systems integration technology would be accorded the same priority as the development of conventional weapons systems.

Finding ways to catch up and leap-frog ahead have become central tenets in this search for a new military development model. This is because a key assumption framing this debate is that the new information paradigm offers a unique chance to leap ahead and significantly narrow the military technological gap with the world's advanced military powers (Ji 2004: 104–6). However, if this window of opportunity is not decisively grasped, some military strategists warn, "the gap between China and military powers may widen… and we may find ourselves in a passive position in future military struggles" (*Liaowang*, 14 July 2003: 21–4).

While Chinese leaders urge the PLA and the defense economy to catch up with the world's technological leaders as quickly as possible, defense planners are more cautious and do not envisage developing the mix of capabilities required to be an advanced military information power until at least the middle of the twenty-first century at the earliest (*Hong Kong Wen Wei Po*, 14 March 2005). These assets include command, control, communications, computers, intelligence, surveillance, and reconnaissance (C4ISR) systems, sophisticated electronic warfare systems, and integrated command automation networks. As an interim goal though, the PLA will seek to equip and connect its mechanized platforms with sensors, navigational positioning systems, infrared detectors, computers, and other devices that would allow them to conduct network-enabled operations within the 2020 timeframe (Yujin 2003: 6).

These military requirements represent an unprecedented technological challenge for the defense scientific and industrial communities. Their ability to adequately fulfill these needs will depend crucially on the nature of the developmental catch-up models they adopt. For the defense industry, the evidence from the structural and organizational reforms that have taken place since the late

1990s indicates that it will follow a path similar to that taken by Japan and Korea with the building of a closed developmental model spearheaded by an elite of vertically integrated companies. These 10 or 11 defense corporations are huge vertically integrated behemoths that have a near-monopoly control of the domestic defense market.

However, reliance on these conglomerates has risks. First, the track record of technological innovation among these firms is mixed. Second, their institutional cultures are deeply rooted in the legacy of the central planning system. Third, their overwhelming focus is on industrial-era practices and processes, and much of their industrial equipment and plants are not suitable to develop or manufacture the military products of the information age, such as electronic components, software, and precision-guided munitions. The authorities have sought to introduce a modicum of competition and outsourcing into this closed apparatus, especially through the establishment of a dual-use system. However, this only applies to non-critical products and technologies and will not include technological projects intended for frontline combat use.

Under this closed, vertically integrated, developmental model, the prospects for achieving major gains in technological catching up by the defense economy may be limited. The general pattern of innovation under this model, as shown by the Japanese and Korean experiences, is incremental in nature, which suggests that any technological advancement would be gradual and deliberate in nature. The more open and vertically disintegrated developmental catch-up model that is favored by the fledging dual-use economy may offer a better recipe for success in narrowing the technology gap. The information and communications technology (ICT) sector, which is a central player in the building of military information-technology capabilities, has embraced this alternative approach that allows for greater market-oriented innovation and the ability of firms to learn and absorb from global technology outsourcing, not only in manufacturing but also increasingly in R&D work. Chinese firms such as Huawei, ZTE, and Datang have emerged to become market leaders in the ICT sector in China while at the same time making inroads into global markets.

While these two alternative catch-up models operate along separate trajectories, growing interaction and convergence between the defense economy and dual-use economy are gradually leading to the emergence of yet another development path. This is a semi-open hybrid model in which the defense economy selectively opens itself up to the domestic civilian economy for investment and joint partnerships, and makes use of the dual-use economy as an intermediate conduit for cooperation with foreign firms. Although this will be primarily with Chinese firms, it could also extend to local subsidiaries of foreign companies.

This hybrid approach began to take root at the end of the 1990s. The defense economy has been eager to tap into the domestic and foreign capital markets to raise funds and form strategic partnerships with leading foreign defense companies and it has sought to pursue this strategy through the listing of its converted civilian portions of its major defense conglomerates. How to balance these opposing techno-national and techno-globalist tendencies will be a major long-term challenge for the Chinese leadership. While the Chinese leadership in the post-1979 reform era has made the opening up of its economy to the outside world a core pillar of its policies, there has been an inherent caution over excessive foreign dependence, especially in strategic areas related to national security and technology.

Taiwan offers another example of a state that has embraced a techno-hybrid approach in its technology development. Keller and Samuels (2003: 12) refer to Taiwan as the "paradigmatic example of the technohybrid regime", in which the formula is "not quite liberal" yet "not quite mercantile." Taiwan has encouraged the forging of close linkages and mutual dependence between its leading technology companies and foreign multinationals through foreign direct investment and the seamless integration of Taiwanese firms into global production and innovation systems through outsourcing. At the same time, there has been a strong emphasis by the Taiwanese government on building robust domestic innovation capabilities such as state-backed research institutes that act as hubs for the diffusion of R&D resources and knowledge and the nurturing of university–industry partnerships (Chang and Shih 2004). This hybrid model has been critical to the global success of Taiwan's electronics and semi-conductor industries.

Future prospects for technological change in Northeast Asia and its impact on the security–economic nexus

The gales of technological progress that have already had such a profound impact on Northeast Asia will only intensify in the coming decades. How states respond and adapt to these changes will determine whether they will keep abreast or get left behind in the ongoing race for technological leadership. Regimes such as Japan and, to a lesser extent, South Korea, that continue to adhere to outdated techno-nationalist notions of self-sufficiency and closed doors are likely to struggle compared to those with more flexible techno-globalist and techno-hybrid approaches, of which China and Taiwan are prime examples.

In peering at the long-term horizon, a couple of technological trends are worthy of examination for their implications for Northeast Asia's economic and security dynamics. The first issue is Northeast Asia's changing place and role in the global technology hierarchy. The transition from the late industrial era to the information age since the 1990s has heralded a transformation in the nature of technological globalization. One of the principal developments during the 1990s and the early years of the twenty-first century, especially in East Asia, was the rise of global production networks, in which multinational firms relocated or outsourced their manufacturing requirements to lower-cost areas elsewhere in the world.

In the past decade, a new emerging trend has been the formation of global innovation networks (GINs) that "integrate dispersed engineering, product development, and research activities across geographic borders." There has been debate as to whether multinationals in the United States, Europe, and Japan would allow their innovation activities to be expanded abroad or kept within their national borders because of their strategic importance. Recent research on the global electronics industry, which often is a harbinger of change for the rest of the high-technology economy, indicates that the rise of GINs is rapidly taking place and will lead to far-reaching structural changes to the geography of innovation and production in the high-technology sector within the next decade (Ernst 2009). Dieter Ernst offers some distinct features of the new global technology order shaped by the arrival of the GINs:

• while GINs originated in the United States, Europe, and Japan, they have now expanded into less developed regions, especially across Asia. China, Korea, Taiwan, and India have become leading hubs of this reconfigured geography of offshore innovation;[9]
• this new global technology order cannot simply be left to market forces. Governments, especially from catch-up economies, have a critical role to play to ensure their countries reap the benefits of this globalization and are not left behind.

Although competition for global technology leadership is intense and requires access to extensive resources and a robust R&D base, many Northeast Asian states have invested heavily in these areas and are well-placed to continue to move up the innovation ladder. Some of the less developed countries such as China have to overcome critical bottlenecks such as improving intellectual property protection, so they are likely to require more time to make progress. But the prospects appear strong that the rest of Northeast Asia will join Japan within the next one to two decades and become a new pole of advanced innovation in the global technology order.

The second major long-term trend is China's effort to become a world-class technological leader. The stated goal of the country's leadership is to catch up technologically by 2020 and this has led to a concerted mobilization of the country's burgeoning economic, political, organizational, military, and scientific resources to meet the challenge. While the 2020 target maybe overly ambitious to overcome the still-wide gulf in innovation infrastructure and capabilities with the United States, Europe, and Japan, China is making major strides and could catch up in a few select areas.

China's eventual emergence as a technological powerhouse, especially in defense-related sectors, has profound implications for regional and global security. While China's overall military technological capabilities still lag behind the United States by at least one to two generations, this gap will gradually narrow so that China may be in position to begin challenging U.S. military technological dominance in a few select strategic areas in the next couple of decades. This includes outer space, the maritime commons, and the digital domain. Technology-related frictions have already been growing between the United States and China in the past few years, especially in cyber-security. Of even more near-term concern is the impact on the military situation in the Taiwan Strait. The PLA's sustained build-up of its military and technological capabilities against Taiwan over the past 15 years has seriously affected the ability of the United States to militarily intervene in the event that an armed conflict were to take place between China and Taiwan.

Moreover, China's intensive development of asymmetric military capabilities aimed at deterring the ability of the United States to freely project its military power in the Asia-Pacific region has caused the Pentagon to quickly come up with technological and doctrinal responses to prevent the permanent loss of the dominant military presence that it has enjoyed in this region since the end of World War II. A new defense strategy issued by the U.S. Defense Department in January 2012 pointed out that the U.S. military is being challenged by sophisticated adversaries using asymmetric capabilities such as electronic and cyber warfare, ballistic and cruise missiles, advanced air defenses, and mining (U.S. Department of Defense 2012, 4–5). China was highlighted as one of these states pursuing such capabilities. In response, the U.S. military is developing a new air-sea battle doctrine to thwart these anti-access and area denial environments, including the development of a new stealth bomber, improving missile defenses, enhancing the resilience of its space-based assets, and maintaining a strong naval presence in the Asia-Pacific region, centered on its aircraft carriers and basing more warships in the region.

These developments point to an intensifying military technological action–reaction dynamic between the United States and China that may become the new superpower arms race. This has far-reaching and potentially destabilizing consequences for regional security. Other countries in the region, especially the likes of Japan, Taiwan, South Korea, India, and even states in Southeast Asia, are being drawn into the spiraling arms dynamic as they try to keep pace with the improvements being pursued by the United States and China or risk falling far behind and leaving themselves vulnerable. The security-technology landscape in Northeast Asia and across the Asia-Pacific region is in the midst of profound upheaval and what emerges over the next one to two decades promises to be very different from the situation today.

Notes

1. For a useful discussion see Herrera (2006). More attention has been devoted to technological change in the field of international political economy.
2. State Council of the People's Republic of China, Medium- and Long-Term Science and Technology Development Plan (2006–2020), available at <http://www.most.gov.cn/kjgh/>.
3. See also Narizny (2007) who puts forward a similar argument but uses the cases of the United States and Great Britain in the nineteenth and twentieth centuries.
4. Feigenbaum further points out that closely related to this integrative economic-security developmental approach is the importance of organizational flexibility.
5. For background to the drafting of the MLP see Cao *et al.* (2006) and Xin and Yidong (2006). See also Schwaag Serger and Breidne (2007) and Xin and Jia (2007).
6. State entities that are most supportive of techno-nationalist approaches include the National Development and Reform Commission, the Ministry of Industry and Information Technology, and the People's Liberation Army. Organizations that are more techno-globalist in orientation include the Ministries of Commerce and Foreign Affairs.

7. Also see http://news.xinhuanet.com/english/2002-11/18/content_633685.htm.
8. See Xu and Zhai (2002: 6).
9. Ernst defines the global hierarchy of innovation as follows: top tier comprising centers of excellence located in the United States, Japan, and the European Community; second tier of advanced locations in Israel, Taiwan, Ireland, and South Korea; a third tier of catch-up regions such as Beijing, the Yangtze and Pearl river deltas in China, and Bangalore, Chennai, Hyderabad, and Delhi in India; and a fourth "new frontiers'" tier in lower-tier cities in China and India as well in Vietnam and Eastern Europe.

References

Bae, Yong-Ho, Sungsoo Song, Mi-Jung Um, Dae-Hee Lee, and Michael Hobday. 2002. *Case Study of Technological Innovation of Korean Firms*. Seoul: Science and Technology Policy Institute, November.

Bitzinger, Richard. 2003. *Towards a Brave New Arms Industry? Adelphi Paper* No. 356. London: International Institute for Strategic Studies.

Brooks, Stephen G. 2005. *Producing Security: Multinational Corporations, Globalization, and the Changing Calculus of Conflict*. Princeton, NJ: Princeton University Press.

Cao, Cong, Richard P. Suttmeier, and Denis Fred Simon. 2006. China's 15-Year Science and Technology Plan. *Physics Today* (December): 38–43.

Chang, Pao-Long and Hsin-Yu Shih. 2004. The Innovation Systems of Taiwan and China: A Comparative Analysis. *Technovation* 24: 529–39.

Chao, Loretta. 2009. China's Curbs on Tech Purchases Draw Ire; U.S. Government, Dozens of Global Industry Groups Speak against Push for State Agencies to Buy "Indigenous Innovation." *Wall Street Journal*, 11 December.

Cheung, Tai Ming. 2009. *Fortifying China*. Ithaca, NY: Cornell University Press.

Chinworth, Michael W. 1992. *Inside Japan's Defense*. Washington, DC: Brassey's.

Corning, Gregory. 2004. *Japan and the Politics of Techno-globalism*. Armonk, NY: M.E. Sharpe.

Ernst, Dieter. 2009. *A New Geography of Knowledge in the Electronics Industry? Asia's Role in Global Innovation Networks*. Policy Studies No. 5. Honolulu, HI: East-West Center.

Feigenbaum, Evan. 1999. Soldiers, Weapons and Chinese Development Strategy: The Mao Era Military in China's Economic and Institutional Debate. *China Quarterly* 158(June): 285–313.

Gibson, Christopher S. 2007. Technology Standards: New Technical Barriers to Trade? In *The Standards Edge: The Golden Means*, Sherrie Bolin, ed. Ann Arbor, MI: Bolin Group.

Gilpin, Robert. 2001. *Global Political Economy*. Princeton, NJ: Princeton University Press.

Green, Michael. 1995. *Arming Japan: Defense Production, Alliance Politics, and the Postwar Search for Autonomy*. New York: Columbia University Press.

Herrera, Geoffrey. 2006. *Technology and International Transformation*. Albany, NY: State University of New York Press.

Hughes, Christopher. 2011. The Slow Death of Japanese Techno-nationalism? Emerging Comparative Lessons for China's Defense Production. *Journal of Strategic Studies* 34 (3): 451–79.

Iwami, Motoko. 2009. Japanese FDI: Recent Development and Outlook. *Japan Institute for Overseas Investment Bulletin* No. 15.

Jensen, Rian. 2009. *State over Society: Science and Technology Policy in North Korea. U.S.-Korea Working Paper Series*, SAIS, Johns Hopkins University, August.

Ji,You. 2004. Learning and Catching Up: China's Revolution in Military Affairs Initiative. In *The Information Revolution in Military Affairs in Asia*, Emily Goldman and Thomas Mahnken, eds. New York: Palgrave Macmillan.

Karniol, Robert. 2006. Singapore: Defence Ecosystem. *Jane's Defence Weekly* 15 February, available at: http://www.dso.org.sg/data/JDW_Feb15_Defence_Ecosystem_210220061215.pdf.

Keller, William W. and Richard J. Samuels. 2003. Innovation and the Asian Economies. In *Crisis and Innovation in Asian Technology*, William W. Keller and Richard J. Samuels, eds. Cambridge: Cambridge University Press.

Kim, Linsu. 2003. Crisis, Reform, and National Innovation in South Korea. In *Crisis and Innovation in Asian Technology*, William W. Keller and Richard J. Samuels, eds. Cambridge: Cambridge University Press.

Liu, Xielin. 2005. *China's Development Model: An Alternative Strategy for Technological Catch-up*. Working paper, Hitotsubashi University, 22 March.

Lorell, Mark. 1995. *Troubled Partnership: A History of U.S.–Japan Collaboration on the FS-X Fighter*. Santa Monica, CA: RAND Corporation.

Low, Morris. 2006. Displaying the Future: Techno-nationalism and the Rise of the Consumer in Postwar Japan. *History and Technology* 19 (3): 197–209.

Narizny, Kevin. 2007. *The Political Economy of Grand Strategy*. Ithaca, NY: Cornell University Press.

Naughton, Barry and Adam Segal. 2003. China: In Search of a Workable Model. In *Crisis and Innovation in Asian Technology*, William W. Keller and Richard J. Samuels, eds. Cambridge: Cambridge University Press.

Odagiri, Hiroyuki and Akira Goto. 1993. The Japanese System of Innovation: Past, Present and Future. In *National Innovation Systems*, RichardNelson, ed. Oxford: Oxford University Press.

OECD. 2008. *OECD Reviews of Innovation Policy: China*. Paris: Organization for Economic Cooperation and Development.

Ostry, Sylvia and Richard Nelson. 1995. *Techno-nationalism and Techno-globalism: Conflict and Cooperation*. Washington, DC: Brookings Institution.

Porter, Michael E., Hirotaka Takeuchi, and Mariko Sakakibara. 2000. *Can Japan Compete?* London: Macmillan.

Posen, Adam S. 2002. Japan. In *Technological Innovation and Economic Performance*, Benn Steil, David G. Victor, and Richard R. Nelson, eds. Princeton, NJ: Princeton University Press.

Posen, Barry. 1984. *The Sources of Military Doctrine*. Ithaca, NY: Cornell University Press.

Samuels, Richard. 1994. *Rich Nation, Strong Nation: National Security and the Technological Transformation of Japan*. Ithaca, NY: Cornell University Press.

——. 2007. *Securing Japan: Tokyo's Grand Strategy and the Future of East Asia*. Ithaca, NY: Cornell University Press.

Schwaag Serger, Sylvia and Magnus Breidne. 2007. China's Fifteen-year Plan for Science and Technology. *Asia Policy* 4 (July): 135–64.

Shin, Jang-Sup. 1996. *The Economics of the Latecomers*. London: Routledge.

Snyder, Jack. 1991. *Myths of Empire: Domestic Politics and International Ambition*. Ithaca, NY: Cornell University Press.

So'ng-p'yo, Hong. 2005. North Korea's Military Science and Technology. *Kunsa Nontan* 29 April.

Solingen, Etel. 1998. *Regional Orders at Century's Dawn: Global and Domestic Influences on Grand Strategy*. Princeton, NJ: Princeton University Press.

Steinfeld, Edward S. 2002. *Chinese Enterprise Development and the Challenge of Global Integration. MIT Special Working Paper Series*, January.

Suettinger, Robert L. 2004. China's Foreign Policy Leadership: Testing Time. *China Leadership Monitor* 9 (winter).

Suttmeier, Richard P. and Xiangkui, Yao. 2004. *China's Post-WTO Technology Policy: Standards, Software, and the Changing Nature of Techno-nationalism. National Bureau of Asian Research Special Report* No.7, May.

U.S. Department of Defense. 2012. *Sustaining U.S. Global Leadership: Priorities for Twenty-first Century Defense*. January.

Woo-Cummings, Meredith. 2005. Back to Basics: Ideology, Nationalism, and Asian Values in East Asia. In *Economic Nationalism in a Globalizing World*, Eric Helleiner and Andreas Pickel, eds. Ithaca, NY: Cornell University Press.

Xie, Wei and Steven White. 2004. *From Imitation to Creation? The Critical yet Uncertain Paradigm Shift for Chinese Firms*. INSEAD working paper. Available at <http://ged.insead.edu/fichiersti/inseadwp2004/2004-07.pdf>.

Xin, Hao and Gong Yidong. 2006. China Bets Big on Big Science. *Science* 16 March: 1548–9.

Xin, Hao and Jia Hepeng. 2007. China Supersizes its Science. *Science* 9 March: 1354–6.

Xu, Xiaoyan and Zhai Tongzheng. 2002. Hasten Informationization Building within Our Forces. *Jiefangjun Bao*, 10 December.

Yanqiong, Liu. 2002. Liangdan Yixing Gongcheng De Chenggong Jingyan Yu Qishi [The Experience and Enlightenment from the Success of the Two Bombs and One Satellite Project]. Master's thesis, National Defense Science and Technology University.

Yujin, Wu. 2003. Explore Effective Ways of Securing Leap Forward in Armaments Development. *Jiefangjun Bao* 30 September.

Zhao, Suisheng. 2000. Chinese Nationalism and its International Orientations. *Political Science Quarterly* 115 (1): 1–33.

Zhaoyin, Zhang. 2003. Firmly Seize the Period of Important Strategic Opportunities to Promote Leap-type Development. *Jiefangjun Bao* 25 February.

5 Bolstering economic interdependence despite bullying memories in Northeast Asia

Jong Kun Choi

Introduction

Within the broad literature of international relations, the relationship between economic interdependence and security remains controversial (Ripsman and Blandchard 1996/97). What we know is only that among trading states economic interdependence seems to affect security links. Yet we do not know how important these economic ties are in shaping security behavior and to what extent and how economic links affect states' behaviors. The argument that economic interdependence is a catalyst for peace relies largely on a rationalist perspective that, as long as states benefit from trading, they will not go to war (Barbieri and Schneider 1999; Mansfield and Pollins 2001; Russet and Oneal 2001). At the same time, we also know that power transition, nuclear proliferation, long-range missiles, defiant dictators, non-democracy, historical and territorial disputes, arms races, national division, nationalism, and a lack of multilateral cooperative platforms may increase the probability of conflicts and full-scale wars among states (Ikenberry and Moon 2008). And no other region has such vibrant conflictual elements clouding regional dynamics in the twenty-first century than does Northeast Asia (Lake and Morgan 1997; Solingen 1998; Lemke 2002; Choi and Moon 2010).[1]

Northeast Asia suffers regional instability because of North Korea's nuclear and missile ventures of the last 20 years, never-ending historical quarrels between the regional states, and the lack of pan-regional institutions that could work as a platform to induce more institutionalized cooperation. Korea, China, and Japan remain at loggerheads over history and territory despite their geographical proximity and shared historical backgrounds. The Senkakus/Diaoyutai islands, a group of uninhabited rocky outcroppings in the East China Sea between Okinawa and Taiwan, are the usual source of territorial conflicts between Beijing and Tokyo, as recently demonstrated in September 2010. A similar situation exists for Tokyo and Seoul over Dokdo Island in the East Sea. Both sets of islands have become icons of potential regional flashpoints with the capacity to trigger a spiral of disputatious memories that in turn unleash a grand showcase of hostile nationalism in each capital city. Moreover, the region may also become the forefront of conflictual great power politics spurred by a power transition between the

United States and China in the foreseeable future (Friedberg 1993/94: 7; Mosher 2000; Mearsheimer 2001; Pyle 2007; Hughes 2009). The recent sinking of the *Cheonan*, South Korea's naval vessel, in March 2010, revealed the underlying strategic rivalry over the Korean Peninsula between Washington and Beijing (Yan 2010). While Seoul's northern policy has remained anything but a traditional engagement policy since 2008, inter-Korean relations have thus far not signaled any positive directions. The prospects for resumption of the Six Party Talks are as improbable as they have ever been since the talks began. Equally problematic are the chances for resolving North Korea's nuclear program. In short, one may say that optimism for Northeast Asia's immediate future is not particularly well placed.

Despite such turbulent regional dynamics, the region has experienced what Stein Tonneson labeled "relative peace" as the result of the region's dramatically reduced number and low intensity of armed conflicts. And such relative peace despite many factors threatening security has recently attracted the scholarly attention of international relations specialists (Jervis 2002; Ross 2003; Choi 2006; Solingen 2007; Tonneson 2009). Northeast Asia has not experienced inter-state military conflicts since the end of the Korean War, whereas since 1989 alone there have been major wars in Europe, South Asia, Africa, and the Middle East. Contending theories of international relations offer a number of potential explanatory variables for this phenomenon. Realists would attribute the low level of conflict to the delicate balance of power that exists between a continental China and a maritime United States with its hub-and-spoke alliance (Ross 2003). And the realists may be right that the United States is playing a decisive role in the relative peace in Northeast Asia. At the same time, the balance of power in Northeast Asia has not eliminated the indigenous conflictual factors contributing to regional instability, such as historical animosities and nuclear proliferation by North Korea. And certainly, the democratic peace theory put forth by the liberal school of IR specialists has yet to prove applicable to Northeast Asia, as the region still consists of divergent regime types.

Against such a backdrop, this chapter approaches Northeast Asia's lack of overt state-to-state shooting conflicts from a different angle by focusing on the most distinctively positive and robust aspect of Northeast Asia; that is, economic interdependence (Pempel 2005; Shambaugh 2006; Calder and Fukuyama 2008). In the face of the many lingering conflictual elements still present in Northeast Asia, the region's deepening economic ties remain one of the few positive configurations potentially contributing to regional stability. The region consists of three major trading states deriving its economic growth and development from integrating with the world market (Rosecrance 1986). The region has become the leading economic global power house, pioneering cutting-edge information technologies, setting new management standards for entrepreneurship, and maintaining high economic growth rates. South Korea, Japan, and China account for 16 percent of world GDP and 15 percent of global trade (IMF 2008).

If economic prosperity sustained by economic interdependence constitutes one major portion of the regional dynamics, the existence of lingering memory politics stands as an important pillar. Perhaps memory politics may fuel intrinsic regional instability. As differing memories among South Korea, Japan, and China have caused their implicit misperception about each other's intentions in territorial disputes, military modernization and diplomatic standoffs, I believe that the historical memory issue essentially defines the genesis of Northeast Asia's unique regional identity—weak institutionalization, potentially hostile nationalism, and relatively low regional trust and sense of common community. These historical animosities continue to define important regional interactions, impeding progressive improvement in the regional order (Manning and Stern 1994; Christensen 2002). The point is that the region still possesses ideational elements that contribute to instability even in the face of growing economic interdependence.

Northeast Asia did in fact suffer a series of diplomatic crises during the Koizumi era. Prime Minister Koizumi's recurrent visits to the Yasukuni shrine, governmental approval of certain Japanese history textbooks downplaying Japan's militaristic past against its neighbors, and Japan's persistent territorial claims to sovereignty over Dokdo all ruffled the region. South Korea and China were on the same page in criticizing what they saw as Japan's nationalistic nostalgia and its justification of the country's behavior in the early twentieth century. The first five years of the twenty-first century (2001–06) became a litmus test case for examining the impact of economic interdependence on Northeast Asia's regional order. By closely examining this period, we can gain better insights as to where the region is headed—toward irreconcilable relationships rooted in past animosities or toward cooperation and mutual benefits through deepening economic interdependence.

The region has a Janus-faced reality. Thus, we need to inquire as to how historical memory and economic interdependence play out with each other. Whether or not deepening economic ties are likely to have a positive impact on inter-state cooperation should be subject to an empirical inquiry. On the other hand, the existence of historical conflicts should not be assumed as a variable that will always spawn conflict. The relevant questions are: what will happen when the benefits of economic interdependence meet the scars of historical memory? How has economic interdependence constrained regional state behaviors over historically conflictual issues that might otherwise damage regional stability? If the deepening economic interdependence is an irresistible structural configuration of Northeast Asia, it should have behavioral impacts that work toward mitigating conflictual behaviors fueled by emotional agendas rooted in nationalistic identities. In this vein, Northeast Asia is an ideal domain for observation, as the three core states—South Korea, Japan, and China—share the benefits of economic interdependence while quarreling over differing memories of their recent and remote historical interactions. If states demonstrate evidence that they do not want to give up the beneficial economic interdependence among them even in the face of historical legacies that are negative, then economic interdependence can be said to have a pacific effect on regional security. All in all, states must consider economic interdependence when dealing with their trading partners over conflictual issues.

Lingering historical disputes in Northeast Asia

The unique aspect of the Northeast Asian history dispute is that South Korea's and China's perceptions that Japan has neo-imperial intentions are confirmed when Japan makes territorial claims over what they believe to be their territory. In 2006, the textbook issue became more explosive when it was linked with Japan's claim over South Korea's Dokdo islands. Moreover, on 23 February of that year, Takano Toshiyuki, Japan's ambassador to South Korea, at the Korean Press Center, also expressed the view that "historically Takeshima is Japanese territory," which provoked public outrage in South Korea (*Chosun Ilbo*, 24 February 2006). On 16 March, the Shimane Prefectural Assembly enacted a "Takeshima Day" ordinance to celebrate the 100th anniversary of Takeshima's incorporation into Japan, overriding South Korea's explicit protest. In the midst of these events, the Japanese Ministry of Education announced that a highly controversial textbook had passed the screening by the ministry's Committee for Re-writing History Textbooks on 5 April 2006. This came on top of similar authorizations in 2001 and 2005 of history textbooks that unprecedentedly covered up the records of Japan's wartime atrocities, again despite China and South Korea's explicit diplomatic warnings (Hamada 2002). The right-wing history textbook approved in 2006 failed to mention that Japan had invaded China in 1932, that the Japanese Army had carried out large-scale civilian massacres in Nanjing in 1937, and that tens of thousands of Asian women were forced into sexual slavery by imperial Japanese forces in the 1930s and 1940s (Egelko 2001; French 2001). In addition, these history textbooks distorted the facts of atrocities committed by Japanese troops, especially on the Korean Peninsula from 1910 to 1945 and in China during the 14 years of occupation from 1931. For example, one passage regularly referred to the 1937 Nanking massacre, in which Chinese historians believe up to 300,000 people perished, as but "an incident" (*South China Morning Post*, 2005). Former Prime Minister Koizumi's repeated visits to the Yasukuni Shrine during his tenure also exacerbated tensions in the region (Daiki 2005). South Korea and China argued that repeated apologies made by prime ministers Murayama in 1995, Obuchi in 1998, and Koizumi in 2005, all of which expressed a "heartfelt apology" and "deep remorse," appeared meaningless in the face of Japan's educational policy on history textbooks and persistent visits by politicians to the Yasukuni Shrine.

These cases were perceived in both South Korea and China as the result of Japan's failure to accept its wartime responsibility. South Korea and China appeared to be on the same page; they saw events in the mid-2000s as reflecting Japan's nostalgia and justification for its aggression in the early twentieth century. The crux of the history dispute in Northeast Asia is that China and South Korea see a discrepancy between Japan's verbal apologies and its actual behavior (Kingston 2001: 45–8, 140–3). South Korea and China agree that the content of history textbooks is a reflection of how a county presents its own history for the purpose of educating its own future generations. In both South Korea and China, these various historical issues remind them of the unresolved heritage of Japanese colonialism.

Table 5.1 Visits to Yasukuni by Japanese prime ministers in the post-Cold War period

Prime minister	Tenure	Visit to Yasukuni	Date
Kaifu	Aug 89–Nov 91	None	
Miyazawa	Nov 91–Aug 93	Once	November 1992 (undisclosed)
Hosokawa	Aug 93–Apr 94	None	
Hata	Apr 94–Jun 94	None	
Murayama	Jun 94–Jan 96	None	
Hashimoto	Jan 96–Jun 98	Once	July 1996 (on his birthday)
Obuchi	Jul 98–Apr 00	None	
Mori	Apr 00–Apr 01	None	
Koizumi	Apr 01–2006	Five	13 August 2001; 21 April 2002; 14 January 2003; 1 January 2004; 17 October 2005

The Japanese government argued, in response, that South Korea and China should recognize and give more weight to Japan's pacific behavior during the postwar era. Regarding the Yasukuni Shrine, some local supporters argue that visits to the shrine (see Table 5.1) symbolize Japan's bid for peace by mourning those who sacrificed their lives during the war (*Korea Herald*, 21 June 2005). Koizumi occasionally counter-criticized the opposition from neighboring states by expressing doubts as to how visits to Yasukuni violate the Constitution and emphasizing that he was merely paying his respects to those who died in the war, "with the conviction that we must never wage a war again" (*New York Times*, 17 October 2005: A7). He characterized South Korea's and China's criticisms as "temporary confrontations and differences of opinion" (*South China Morning Post*, 2005), asserting that "Other countries should not interfere with the way countries pay tribute to the war dead" (*Dong-A Ilbo*, 2005). Moreover, the Japanese government occasionally criticized the governments of China and South Korea by pointing out that "Every day they [Chinese and South Korean citizens] are reminded of the brutalities in the war. They don't know or appreciate Japan's efforts to become a peaceful nation after the war" (K. Ide, spokesperson of the Japanese Embassy to the People's Republic of China, quoted in *South China Morning Post*, 7 April 2005: 10) and "South Korea and China are the only two countries in the world problematizing Koizumi's visit to the Yasukuni Shrine" (*Dong-A Ilbo*, 25 January 2006).

Regarding the history textbook issue, Japan argued that if draft textbooks submitted by publishing companies to the Ministry of Education fulfill certain criteria, the government could not prevent their publication because of freedom of speech. Japanese right-wingers claimed that Japan had its own sovereign right to interpret and teach its own history. Japan's then Foreign Minister Asō Tarō stated that "Japan may not have to pay much attention to South Korea and China's warning about Japan's isolation because it is simply not true" (*Chosun Ilbo*, 27 November 2005).

The recurrence of acrimonious relations, especially between Japan, on the one hand, and China and South Korea, on the other, has been a familiar theme in the regional IR literature as the decisive factor in the lack of cross-national trust and the failure to forge any multilateral institution in the region akin to the European Union (Dosch and Mons 2000; Hayes 2001; Lampton 2001; Mahbubani 2001; Capie and Evans 2002). The prevailing argument is that the failure of the regional states to resolve their historical disputes contributes to the pessimistic outlook for regional cooperation. Regarding Sino–Japanese relations, for example, the lack of trust rooted in history has bedeviled other aspects of their relationship, such as mutual suspicions that each is enhancing its military capabilities, differences over the Taiwan issue, and Japan's alliance with the United States. The emotional elements perpetuated the recurring ebbs and flows in regional cooperation. However, as the next section will demonstrate, another reality of Northeast's regional order involves deepening economic interdependence, which I believe is as real as historical disputes are in constituting the regional order of Northeast Asia.

Deepening economic interdependence in Northeast Asia?

The expansion of the EU and the launch of NAFTA have changed the landscape of global trade. The consequent economic integration based on regional boundaries has contributed to a boosting of intra-regional trade and the enhancement of intra-regional interdependence. Furthermore, pressures for regional integration have increased even more following the global financial crisis of 2008, as trading states can no longer rely as heavily on consumers in the United States or Europe. In this vein, this section aims to measure the intensity of economic interdependence among South Korea, Japan, and China and make comparative analyses vis-à-vis other economic blocs. From this, we can infer that economic interdependence is an ongoing process with certain directionality, which will allow us to construct a more accurate picture of regional realities.

Economic interdependence among these three Northeast Asian states is rapidly increasing relative to their earlier trade with each other. Northeast Asia is not a formal economic bloc institutionalized by any type of free trade agreement. Northeast Asia's intra-regional trade is far less intense than the EU and NAFTA. As Table 5.2 indicates, the intra-regional trade of the EU has averaged 61.3 percent since 2000 while NAFTA has averaged about 44 percent. These two economic blocs have maintained intensive intra-regional trade empowered by free trade agreements and institutional safety nets. On the other hand, Northeast Asia's intra-regional trade has become substantially larger than MERCOSUR since 2000 and is as intense as ASEAN despite the absence of any formal trading institutionalization. Moreover, intra-regional trade for China, Japan, and Korea has also increased in importance relative to their own trade over the past two decades. In 1991, intra-regional trade represented only a modest 13.9 percent of the total exports of the three countries. By 1995, it had risen to 18.6 percent and further rose to 23.7 percent in 2005. In other words, Northeast Asia's intra-regional trade increased by 70.5 percent (13.9 to 23.7) over the last 14 years,

Table 5.2 Intra-regional trade ratio (percent)

Year	ASEAN	EU	MERCOSUR	NAFTA	NEA
1991	17.5	59.6	12.8	38.9	13.9
1992	17.7	60.1	16.0	39.7	14.0
1993	18.4	55.3	18.8	41.0	16.1
1994	20.0	55.8	19.4	43.0	17.5
1995	20.4(7)*	61.7(15)*	19.2	42.0	18.6
1996	20.6	60.9	21.2	43.4	19.0
1997	21.2(9)*	54.8	22.4	44.4	18.6
1998	20.9	55.9	23.0	45.7	17.4
1999	21.8(10)*	62.0	19.8	46.8	19.2
2000	22.7	60.0	19.9	46.8	20.3
2001	22.2	59.5	17.9	46.5	21.2
2002	22.7	59.9	13.9	45.9	22.4
2003	24.4	60.6	14.8	44.8	23.7
2004	24.4	65.6(25)*	15.2	43.7	24.1
2005	24.9	64.2	15.4	43.6	23.7

Source: IMF, *Direction of Trade Statistics* and IMF, *Direction of Trade Statistics History*.
Note: *Numbers in parenthesis indicate changes in the number of member states.

while the EU grew only 7.7 percent (59.6 to 64.2) and NAFTA, 12 percent (38.9 to 43.6) during the same period. This indicates that South Korea, Japan, and China's trading intensities have increased substantially faster than the other formal economic blocs and their trading interdependence has become strengthened without any formal agreements.

Northeast Asian states are fundamentally trading states (Amsden 1989; Chan 1990). They have sustained their economic development by reliance on export-oriented strategies. Engaging in such trading transactions with foreign states has been vital to the realization of their national interest. Figure 5.1 illustrates the growth of trilateral trade volume in Northeast Asia. In 2008, the volume of Northeast Asian intra-regional trade tripled from eight years earlier, expanding to US$ 524.6 billion in 2008 from US$ 166.8 billion in 2000. Two noticeable facts are observed. First, while the proportion of Japan's exports in the Northeast Asian intra-regional trade was reduced from 43.9 percent in 2009 to 40.4 percent in 2008, China's exports increased from 32.7 percent to 36.8 percent. Second, Sino–Korea trade (US$ 168.3 billion) has become larger than Korea–Japan trade (US$ 89.3 billion). Sino–Korea trade significantly expanded about 540 percent while Korea–Japan trade rose 170 percent and Sino–Japanese trade grew by 320 percent. China as a rising power tends to enjoy trade surpluses with the rest of the world but suffers trade deficits with its neighboring states. In 2000, Japan was the center of Northeast Asian intra-regional trade. However, China in 2008 emerged as the center of the trilateral trade as Sino–Korea trade increased to 31 percent of the intra-regional trade while Korea–Japan trade decreased to 18 percent in 2008. From this, it is clear that China, rather than Japan, is emerging as the hub of intra-regional trade.

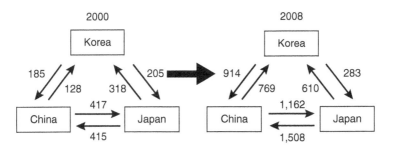

Figure 5.1 Change in trilateral trade volume.
Source: IMF, Direction of Trade Statistics and IMF, Direction of Trade Statistics History.

Measuring the trade ties among Northeast Asian states on the basis of the trade intensity index[2] also indicates the region's greater economic interdependence. Based on that index, trade among China, Japan, and Korea is considerably greater than what should be expected based on their geographical proximity and relative size in world trade. As seen in Figure 5.2a, South Korea's trade intensity with China and Japan is larger than its trade intensity with the United States and the EU. South Korea's trading intensity with China and Japan remains at the top while that with the United States continues to decrease and that with the EU is almost stagnant. This means that South Korea's trading interdependence has gravitated toward its regional trading partners. In Figure 5.2b, Japan's trading intensity with South Korea and China remains preeminent while that with the United States has been declining to the point where it now matches the relatively low levels of the EU. This also means that South Korea and China have become the most interdependent trading partners with Japan. The same pattern appears for China in Figure 5.2c, as it is enjoying a much higher trade intensity with South Korea and Japan than with the EU or the United States. China's trading pattern has become more intra-regional, mostly concentrating its trading interdependence with its Northeast Asian partners. In particular, China and Korea remarkably increased their trade intensity from 1993 to 2001. These three powerful engines of the global economy have become interlocked and are producing a very condensed "natural" trading zone without the formalized arrangements that are critical to each state's economic development (Choi 2006).

As the economic relationship among South Korea, Japan, and China has been undergoing this deepening interdependence, national trading profiles have been dramatically changing as the consequence of strengthening intra-industry interdependence. In other words, the trading relationships within Northeast Asia have become more complementary to each state's comparative advantages, resulting in more intensive production networks and supply chains. For example, China's industrial composition of intra-regional trade underwent a dramatic change from an orientation toward raw materials and light industry to one reliant on heavy industry. As Table 5.3 indicates, China's intra-regional trade saw a decrease in

a. South Korea's trading intensity with major trading partners

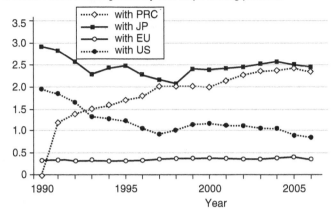

b. Japan's trading intensity with major trading partners

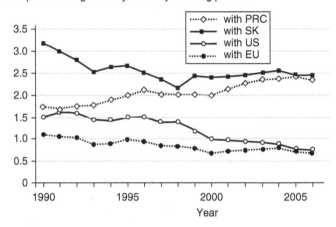

c. China's trading intensity with major trading partners

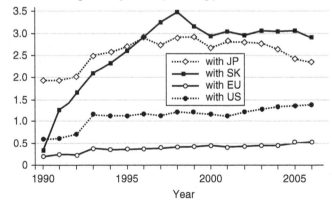

Figure 5.2 Intra-regional trading intensity of Northeast Asia.

Source: Computed from IMF, Direction of Trade Statistics and IMF, Direction of Trade Statistics History.

Table 5.3 Industrial composition of Northeast Asian intra-regional trade (percent)

	2000			2007		
	Korea	*China*	*Japan*	*Korea*	*China*	*Japan*
Raw materials	1.8	8.7	0.3	0.50	4.0	0.3
Light-industry products	17.4	44.0	6.6	5.10	25.2	3.2
Heavy-industry products	78.0	39.6	88.1	92.40	61.9	86.8
Others	2.8	7.7	4.9	2.05	9.0	9.7

Source: OECD STAN bilateral trade database.

raw material exports to 4.0 percent in 2007 from 8.7 percent in 2000, while light and heavy industry products now make up 87.1 percent of China's intra-regional trade. While Japan's heavy industrial products maintained above 85 percent for the last 7 years, South Korea's heavy industry composition for the Northeast Asian intra-regional trade increased to 92.4 percent in 2007 from 78 percent in 2000. This demonstrates two important changes in the trade patterns in Northeast Asia. First, South Korea has emerged as an important importing state for China's light industrial products. South Korea used to enjoy a trade surplus of US$ 200 million with China in light industrial products in 2000 but subsequently recorded a trade deficit of US$ 9.6 billion. Second, Korea and Japan enjoy dominant roles in heavy industrial products within Northeast Asian intra-regional trade, even as China has increased its export of heavy industrial products to 62 percent. From this we can infer that the three states are intensely linked up with each other in terms of industrial production networks. This is confirmed by Table 5.4.

Table 5.4 indicates the contents of intra-regional trade among the three states, which allows us to infer the comparative advantage of particular export industries. Textiles and clothing were China's top export items, accounting for 33.4 percent of the intra-regional export composition in 2000. By 2007, electrical equipment had become the largest commodity of China's export to its neighboring states, accounting for 33.2 percent while textiles and clothing decreased to 18.7 percent. For South Korea, the strongest growth for its intra-regional trade commodity was also electrical equipment, which accounted for 43.7 percent in 2007, up sharply from 30 percent in 2000. On the other hand, Japan's electrical equipment fell from 38.2 percent in 2000 to 30.5 percent in 2007 while chemicals, steel, and automobiles increased its portion. As confirmed from Table 5.4, these three Northeast Asian states heavily trade medium- to high-tech products with each other. In Northeast Asian production networks, Korea mainly exports capital and core parts and components to China, and China uses them to process or assemble into final products that are then exported back to Korea or other economies, a relationship which greatly improves the level of China–Korea intra-industry trade.

Table 5.4 Commodity composition of Northeast Asian intra-regional trade (percent)

	2000			2007		
	Korea	China	Japan	Korea	China	Japan
Textiles-clothing	12.3	33.4	4.8	3.4	18.70	2.0
Steel	6.4	2.1	7.7	5.0	5.50	8.5
Chemicals	31.2	6.7	17.5	27.3	9.15	20.0
Machineries	5.2	2.9	16.7	7.6	6.30	16.0
Electrical equipment	30.0	23.7	38.2	43.7	33.20	30.5
Automobiles	1.0	0.4	3.6	3.4	1.30	6.0
Ships	0.0	0.1	0.1	0.1	0.10	0.7
Others	14.0	30.8	11.3	9.4	25.70	16.4

Source: OECD STAN bilateral trade database.

Figure 5.3 also reveals that trade interdependence has deepened as intra-regional trade has become heavily concentrated on parts and components, up sharply from 2000. In other words, the export competiveness of each Northeast Asian state has become highly dependent upon the price and quality of parts and components in other Northeast Asian states. Significant changes in the composition of trade commodities suggest that economic interdependence among these three states is becoming irreversible and increasingly sensitive to one another.

This is particularly important in estimating the nature of Northeast Asian economic interdependence since a higher percentage of parts and components export for intra-regional trade means that Northeast Asia has now evolved into a region with a built-in production network of intensive horizontal and vertical

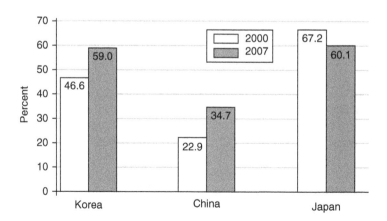

Figure 5.3 Percent of parts and components exports for intra-regional trade.
Source: Korea International Trade Association database, OECD STAN Bilateral Trade database.

intra-industry trade. Production networks bring about a large amount of parts and components trade. Many of the imported parts and components are processed or assembled into final products, then re-exported. In addition, due to domestic value added, they are increasingly enhancing vertical intra-industry trade. Still other parts and components are similar in production technology and quality, while they differ in properties such as type or color, and thus could be categorized as horizontal intra-industry trade. Hence, theoretically speaking, parts and components trade arising from these strengthened regional production networks is greatly improving the level of intra-industry trade.

The economic growth of the Northeast Asian states has generally been fueled by the growth of industries (such as electronics, machineries, and automobiles) that require a particularly large number of parts and components in the final exported products. Such developmental trends naturally promote the creation of regional production networks as each producer seeks to secure the best priced parts and components produced anywhere. This naturally drives multinational firms to fragment production throughout a region, in this case, Northeast Asia. What's unique in Northeast Asia has been the strong presence of conscious national efforts to promote export expansion together with a trade liberalization strategy. The natural inclination of multinational firms to maximize their competitiveness has meshed with the regional states' export drives, thus generating the conspicuous volume of trilateral trade in parts and components that we see across major export industries of each state in Northeast Asia (Capannelli and Filippini 2009).

Deepening economic interdependence among South Korea, Japan, and China is nothing new. It is real. The magnitude of bilateral and trilateral trade and investment flows among these three states is large and strong. Each state's economic growth affects that of the others within Northeast Asia. Moreover, the direct and positive linkage of each state's major export industries through intra-industry production networks has tightened the linkages across the economy of Northeast Asia, turning it into something similar to a singular production community. As the analysis above indicates, the regional expansion of economic prosperity has been the structural consequence of common economic growth patterns that have relied on intra-regional production networks, conscious efforts by each government to maintain export-driven development along with the synergetic effects of the market, and national economic policies. In other words, the vertical and horizontal interdependence of Northeast Asia has enhanced the sensitivity and vulnerability of each state in the region. And as many studies have shown, as states become economically interdependent through trade relations their deepening linkages become ever more costly to break (Cooper 1968; Waltz 1970; Keohane and Nye 1977). Northeast Asia has become indisputably a regional community of precisely such economic interdependence.

Trilateral interactions in the midst of memory conflicts

An ironic aspect of relations between Japan, Korea, and China during the years of intensive historical disputes from 2001 to 2006 was their heightened trilateral cooperation, especially in the conspicuous efforts to construct a regional economic environment under which the growing trilateral economic interdependence could stay on course. Thus despite the diplomatic turmoil over historical memories, the regional states continued to meet on the sidelines of the ASEAN Plus Three summits from the third summit in 2001 onward, and in the process actually formulated tangible action plans to further implement agreements made by their respective heads of states. In this way, trilateral cooperation expanded, evolving from declaratory and ceremonial gestures to more tangible and issue-specific actions plans aimed at managing the deepening economic interdependence within Northeast Asia (Table 5.5).

While there were intensified exchanges of verbal invectives on the historical matters fueled by Japan's authorization of the right-wing history textbooks and Koizumi's visits to Yasukuni, substantial progress in detailing economic interdependence was made in various areas among South Korea, Japan, and China at the third summit in Brunei in November 2001. The three agreed to create an annual tripartite economic ministerial meeting in order to enhance cooperation in trade, prevent trade conflicts, and support China's entry into the WTO. In essence, they agreed that governmental-level cooperation and coordination in trade areas was necessary at a regional level as regional interdependence had become more intensified. At the fourth summit in 2002, in response to Chinese Premier Zhu's proposal to form a study group to analyze the feasibility of a free trade zone encompassing South Korea, China, and Japan, the three states launched a "Working Group on Free Trade Agreements." The group was made up of each state's government-funded think tanks and aimed at developing road maps for intra-regional economic integration. In the same vein, the three also agreed to promote intra-regional cooperation in the areas of telecommunication, human resource development, and environmental protection. At the fourth summit in Phnom Penh in 2002, the need for a peaceful solution to North Korea's nuclear problem was agreed to as essential for Northeast Asia's regional stability, showing China's gradual willingness to promote trilateral cooperation not only in economic but also in security matters. Initially, China had been reluctant to include this issue for fear of alienating North Korea. The shift also came in the midst of strained Sino–Japan relations over differences in the interpretation of wartime history and the expansion of the U.S.–Japan defense cooperation guidelines. However, as all three states shared a common fear that a nuclear armed and/or collapsing North Korea could destabilize the region and thereby disrupt the deepening economic interdependence, the issue of North Korea was finally raised trilaterally for discussion and agreement.

At the fifth summit in Bali in 2003, in response to South Korea and China's initiatives, the three states issued their Joint Declaration on the Promotion of Tripartite Cooperation. The declaration called for trilateral cooperation and actual action plans in 14 areas such as trade and investment, information technology, and environmental protection. This was to concretize what had been agreed to in previous years and confirmed the need for governmental-level cooperation. Moreover, in the declaration, the three states confirmed their commitment to a peaceful resolution of the North Korean nuclear issue and the denuclearization of

Table 5.5 Chronology of Northeast Asian summits and historical disputes

	Northeast Asian states' summit agreements	*Historical disputes*
2001 Brunei	Northeast Asia Business Forum Northeast Asian Economic Minister Meeting Joint IT ventures Cooperation on environment Cultural exchange	Japan's claim on Dokdo by Governor of Shinema Prefecture Koizumi visit to Yasukuni, 13 August Approval of right-wing history textbook
2002 Phnom Penh	Working groups on free trade agreements Peaceful solution to North Korea's nuclear program Cooperation with ASEAN	Koizumi visit to Yasukuni, 21 April
2003 Bali	Joint Declaration on the Promotion of Tripartite Cooperation Seek future-oriented and comprehensive relationship based on mutual trust, respect, and reciprocity Expand and encourage the role of NGOs and scholars in promoting tripartite cooperation Strengthen coordination and support the process of ASEAN integration for stability and prosperity in the region	Koizumi visit to Yasukuni, 14 January
2004 Vientiane	Action strategy for cooperation among the three countries calling for strengthening joint efforts to start governmental-level talks on a new trilateral investment treaty and to assist a joint study on a trilateral FTA Reference to security issues for the peaceful denuclearization of the Korean Peninsula through the Six Party Talks	Koizumi visit to Yasukuni, 1 January
2005 Kuala Lumpur	Cancelled due to the history dispute	Resolution on Dokdo by Shinema Prefecture Council, 13 March Koizumi visit to Yasukuni, 17 October Re-approval of right-wing history textbook

Source: Compiled by author from *Kyodo News Service, New York Times,* and *Chosun Ilbo* .

the Korean Peninsula. In this vein, the Three Party Committee made up of governmental officials was installed to study, plan, and execute cooperative activities. At its first meeting in June 2004, the foreign ministers of South Korea, China, and Japan formulated specific action strategies outlining measures to implement trilateral cooperation in the 14 principal areas in the declaration. At the sixth summit in November 2004, the heads of three states released an action strategy for trilateral cooperation, which called for strengthening joint efforts to start governmental talks on a new trilateral investment treaty and to pursue a joint study on a possible trilateral FTA.

A break in state-to-state cooperation came at the 2005 meeting when the three failed to meet as a result of the dispute caused by the publication in Japan of the right-wing history textbook and Koizumi's persistent visits to Yasukuni. Cui Tiankai, the head of the Chinese Foreign Ministry's Asian Affairs Department, announced that China would boycott the tripartite summit meeting, the bilateral China–Japan summit, and the foreign ministerial meeting in Kuala Lumpur, stating that "the Japanese decision to continue visiting Tokyo's Yasukuni shrine made a meeting with Mr. Wen out of the question" (McGregor 2005). In short, the history dispute finally stalled tripartite cooperation that had been going forward within the framework of the ASEAN Plus Three. China and South Korea had their own summits but boycotted bilateral meetings with Japan until Prime Minister Koizumi left office.

From the above discussion, it seems as if the history disputes did not affect Northeast Asian cooperation until 2005. What is clear is that declarations made in the last four meetings did not include these problematic historical issues, which were always mentioned in official documents involving bilateral relations. However, the history dispute in 2005 finally led China and South Korea to declare that they would not hold the summits with Japan as long as Koizumi remained as prime minister.

However, for the six years in question, two distinct observations can be made. First, China's gradual commitment to trilateral cooperation increased substantially. If China's regional strategy in early 1990s was prudent, careful, and incremental, its regional strategy in the twenty-first century became more active, multilateral, and confident. This coincides with their national strategy to seek a more stable regional environment as their economic development continued. Moreover, China was clearly not willing to forgo its economic relations with Japan simply over the history dispute. While boycotting the ASEAN Plus Three summits, the leaders of China and Japan had meetings on the sidelines of other international conferences at the ministerial level. Japanese Foreign Minister Kawaguchi, for example, made formal visits to China five times between April 2002 and September 2004. On top of the historical issues, the Chinese government proposed repeatedly to hold annual strategic talks at the foreign vice-ministerial level. The regional political leaders who had criticized one another on the history dispute actually continued to meet so as to continue their discussions about cooperation in key functional issues. And following the dust-up in 2005, dialogue resumed even more conspicuously.

During Prime Minister Abe's visit to Beijing, China and Japan confirmed that "interdependence has deepened, and Japan–China relations have become one of the most important bilateral relations for both countries." They agreed that promoting a positive Sino–Japan relationship was critical to the stability and development of Northeast Asia (Japanese Ministry of Foreign Affairs 2006). In December 2007, at the first China–Japan high-level economic dialogue, both sides discussed in detail the various macroeconomic issues pertaining to trade and investment in light of the growing interdependence of the two economies and agreed to promote bilateral private sector economic exchanges. Obviously, the two sides acknowledged that "their economies are in a 'win-win' relationship," as Japan acknowledged the "positive effects of Chinese economic development" (Japanese Ministry of Foreign Affairs 2007). In 2008, at the Sino–Japanese summit, both sides agreed to concretize their prior agreements by expanding and detailing cooperation in "trade, investment, information and communication technology, finance, food and product safety, protection of intellectual property rights, the business environment, agriculture, forestry and fisheries industries, transport and tourism, water, and healthcare" (Japanese Ministry of Foreign Affairs 2008).

Second, the history dispute and rising nationalism garnered the headlines from 2001 to 2005 along with mutual accusations and demand for apologies; however, progress toward more cooperative regional interaction has continued. Each state's strategic goals prevented the history disputes from spilling over and affecting the more substantial economic issues. South Korea and Japan conspicuously endeavored to reap the benefits of economic interdependence in the midst of the historical disputes. In 2001, when Japan authorized history textbooks that went further than any earlier books in covering up the records of Japan's wartime atrocities, both governments explicitly confirmed the vital importance of the bilateral economic relationship: "for the Republic of Korea, Japan is our second largest trading partner and the Republic of Korea is the third largest trading partner for Japan" (Japanese Ministry of Foreign Affairs 2002). The expanding bilateral economic relationship superseded the historical disputes. In 2003, the two governments took one more step to acknowledge "the importance of industrial cooperation" to rely on industrial complementarities to enhance their mutual export competitiveness in times of expanding bilateral trade (Japanese Ministry of Foreign Affairs 2003). South Korean President Roh emphasized in his speech to the Japanese Diet that, despite the need for the regional states to express their unpalatable sense of despair over their differing memories, they needed also to acknowledge the indisputable benefits of economic interdependence in the region. The leaders knew that the historical disputes should not become so dominant as to force them to forgo the economic benefits of cooperation, which had produced unprecedented trilateral economic cooperation in Northeast Asia through both bilateral trade and investment.

In essence, Northeast Asian regional interactions have evolved so that they are now quite complex, multi-layered, and inter-sectorial; no single negative element is likely to disturb the path of regional cooperation. On the other hand, although we have seen the strengthening of the Chinese–South Korean relations, there was something of a deterioration in bilateral relations between Japan and South Korea, and Japan and China, particularly toward the end of the Koizumi years. And yet, even then, we saw no dramatic and conflictual behaviors involving China or South Korea vis-à-vis Japan. This coincides with both states' functional strategy emphasizing regional stability as a basis for incubating regional economic integration. In other words, even as the history dispute became intensified and emotional reactions boiled up in domestic politics (largely as anti-Japanese nationalism), South Korea and China diplomatically demanded apologies from Japan, but showed no punitive behaviors and retained selectively cooperative behavior toward Japan, all in the service of maintaining and enhancing their economic interdependence. The governments of South Korea and China also tried to cool down the public outrage while continuing to cooperate with Japan on critically selective issues that affect their respective national interests. This all suggests that the history dispute in the region is unlikely to be a determining factor that could shift the momentum of regional cooperation.

Conclusion

History disputes in Northeast Asia are essentially memory disputes derived from each state's different recognition of historical events reflecting differing images of self and other. These have generated emotional outrage in South Korea and China, both of whose images of Japan remain dominated by the memories of subjugation. This emotional outrage has been expressed in the streets of major cities in South Korea and China through massive anti-Japanese demonstrations. At the level of state interactions in Northeast Asia, in contrast, deepening economic interdependence across Northeast Asia has encouraged leaders to work to maintain these ever-closer economic relations. This deepening economic interdependence and its role in enhancing the national interests of all three states may explain better why trilateral cooperation has continued and expanded despite the chronic historical conflicts (Alagappa 2002).

Nevertheless, South Korea's and China's skepticism about Japan is not shallow. Their collective memory constitutes an essential element in their respective national identities (He 2004; Suh *et al.* 2004; Kang 2007). Therefore these will not quickly go away. And the memories of subjugation are too often refreshed by the actions of Japanese leadership. As long as Japan maintains its current position on Yasukuni shrine visits, Dokdo, history textbooks, and history issues generally, the shadow of the past will continue to dim the lights of Northeast Asian integration. Ultimately these problems come down to the central issue of nationalism in the era of globalization. As rational and future oriented as the regional states are, they are also obsessed with their competing interpretations of history, especially regarding Japan's imperial expansion during the first 40 years or so of the twentieth century. Historical animosity undoubtedly constitutes one major aspect of Northeast Asian regional order. This is an ongoing issue and will not be resolved for some time. Moreover, what and how each state remembers, and chooses not to forget, issues of past history will essentially define each state's collective identity. But at the same time, the history dispute is by no means the whole picture of Northeast Asia and therefore not as determining as it sometimes seems.

As the data above suggest, the benefits of economic interdependence may sustain the incentive for regional cooperation in Northeast Asia as states place higher values on regional trade and investment as the most promising routes to fulfill their own economic development. Increased transnational activities, including cross-national border trade, investments, telecommunications, and travel will foster more stable international relations in the region. Growing economic interdependence may dampen the negative effects generated by differing historical memories, although such interdependence may not completely erase the scars of the past. The weight of historical memory is by no means light. However the reason why the burden of such disputes has not yet deteriorated and turned back the progressive development of the regional order in Northeast Asia is because of the power of patient rationality created by the awareness of the mutual benefits derived from economic interdependence.

Economic complementarities are causing speedy and cohesive economic integration across Northeast Asia. In this way, historical rivals who have a strong sense of resentment or distrust could begin to cooperate out of economic rationality. Intra-regional economic interdependence is an important platform and a useful tool for policymakers, assisting them in counterbalancing the regional vulnerability that emerges from lingering history and territorial disputes. Central to a progressive regional order is the need for regional states to consciously envision an optimistic future in which intra-regional economic interdependence becomes a key component in achieving domestic developmental goals.

As regional interaction becomes more multilayered, unresolved memory issues may receive more political and media attention as hindering progressive and stable regional order creation. However, the three states of Northeast Asia have fewer incentives to permit their regional interaction, which has so far been very beneficial and productive, to be hemmed in by what most regional leaders are coming to perceive as non-solvable issues. Bilateral cooperation may slow down, but it does not mean that it will be reversed. Non-governmental and market-driven interactions will sustain the cooperative regional order. As Northeast Asian states commonly realize the necessity of maintaining economic interdependence in their own national interest, they are likely to prevent historical memory issues from dominating their regional political agendas.

Notes

1. Northeast Asia is defined as a region consisting of the Korean Peninsula, China, and Japan.
2. The trade intensity index is the ratio of trade shares of a county/region to the share of world trade with a partner. The index is a uniform export share that informs whether or not a region or a state exports more to a given destination than the world does on average. Values greater than 1 indicate an intense trade relationship. Therefore, the larger the value of the trade intensity index is, the stronger the trade links are between two

trading states. It is calculated by the following formula: $\dfrac{X_{ij}}{X_i} \div \dfrac{M_j}{M_w}$ where X_{ij} are the exports of country I to country J; X_i are the total exports of country I; M_j are the total imports of country J; and M_w are global imports.

References

Acharya, Amitav. 2009. *Whose Ideas Matter: Agency and Power in Asian Regionalism.* Ithaca, NY: Cornell University Press.

Alagappa, Muthiah. 2002. *Asian Security Order.* Stanford, CA: Stanford University Press.

Amsden, A.H. 1989. *Asia's Next Giant: South Korea and Late Industrialization.* Oxford: Oxford University Press.

Barbieri, Katherine and Gerald Schneider. 1999. Globalization and Peace: Assessing New Directions in the Study of Trade and Conflict. *Journal of Peace Research* 36: 387–404.

Calder, Kent and Francis Fukuyama. 2008. *East Asian Regionalism: Prospects for Regional Stability.* Baltimore, MD: Johns Hopkins University Press.

Capannelli, Giovanni and Carlo Filippini. 2009. *East Asian and European Economic Integration: A Comparative Analysis. Asian Development Bank Working Paper Series on Regional Economic Integration.*

Capie, D. and P. Evans. 2002. *The Asia-Pacific Security Lexicon.* Singapore: Institute of Asian Studies.

Chan, Steve. 1990. *East Asian Dynamism: Growth, Order, and Security in the Pacific Region.* Boulder, CO: Westview Press.

Choi, Jong Kun. 2006. Predictions of Tragedy versus Tragedy of Predictions in Northeast Asian Security. *Korean Journal of Defense Analysis* 18: 7–33.

Choi, Jong Kun and Chung-in Moon. 2010. Understanding Northeast Asian Regional Dynamics: Inventory Checking and New Discourses on Power, Interests, and Identity. *International Relations of the Asia Pacific* 10: 343–72.

Christensen, T.J. 2002. China, the U.S.–Japan Alliance, and the Security Dilemma in East Asia. *International Security* 23: 49–80.

Cooper, Richard. 1968. *The Economics of Interdependence.* New York: McGraw-Hill.

Daiki, S. 2005. The Yasukuni Shrine Dispute and the Politics of Identity in Japan. *Asian Survey* 45 (2): 197–215.

Dosch, J. and M. Mons, eds. 2000. *International Relations in the Asia-Pacific: New Patterns of Power, Interest, and Cooperation.* New York: St. Martin's Press.

Egelko, B. 2001. World War II Reparations: Asian Sex Slaves Hope New Law Will Aid in Fight for Redress. *San Francisco Chronicle* 1 July: A8.

French, H. 2001. Japan's Refusal to Revise Textbooks Angers its Neighbors. *New York Times* 9 July: A3.

Friedberg, A.L. 1993/94. Ripe for Rivalry: Prospects for Peace in a Multipolar Asia. *International Security* 18 (3): 5–33.

Hamada, Tomoko. 2002. Contended Memories of the Imperial Sun: History Textbook Controversy in Japan. *American Asian Review* 20 (4): 1–38.

Hayes, L. 2001. *Japan and the Security of Asia.* Oxford, Lanham, MD: Lexington Books.

He, B. 2004. Transnational Civil Society and the National Identity Question in East Asia. *Global Governance* 10: 227–46.

Hughes, Christopher W. 2009. *Japan's Remilitarization.* London: International Institute for Strategic Studies.

Ikenberry, G.J. and C.I. Moon. 2008. *The United States and Northeast Asia: Debates, Issues, and New Order*. Lanham, MD: Rowman & Littlefield.

International Monetary Fund (IMF). 2008. *Direction of Trade Statistics*. Washington, DC: IMF.

Japanese Ministry of Foreign Affairs. 2002. ROK–Japan Summit Joint Press Conference. President Kim's opening statement, 22 March. Available at: <http://www.mofa.go.jp/region/asia-paci/korea/pv0306/pdfs/joint.html>.

———. 2003. Building the Foundations of ROK–Japan Cooperation: Towards an Age of Peace and Prosperity in Northeast Asia. ROK–Japan Summit Joint Statement, 7 June. Available at: <http://www.mofa.go.jp/region/asia-paci/korea/pv0306/pdfs/joint.html>.

———. 2006. China–Japan Joint Press Statement. Beijing, 8 October. Available at: <http://www.mofa.go.jp/region/asia-paci/china/joint0610.html>.

———. 2007. First China–Japan High Level Economic Dialogue Press Communiqué. Tokyo, 1 December. Available at: <http://www.mofa.go.jp/region/asia-paci/china/dialogue0712.html>.

———. 2008. PRC–Japan Summit Joint Statement. Tokyo, 7 May. Available at: <http://www.mofa.go.jp/region/asia-paci/china/joint0805.html>.

Jervis, Robert. 2002. Theories of War in an Era of Leading-power Peace. *American Journal of Political Science* 96: 4–7.

Kang, D.C. 2007. *China Rising: Peace, Power, and Order in East Asia*. New York: Columbia University Press.

Keohane, Robert and Joseph Nye, Jr. 1977. *Power and Interdependence: World Politics in Transition*. Boston, MA: Little Brown.

Kingston, J. 2001. *Japan's Transformation, 1952–2000*. Harlow: Pearson.

Lake, David and Pat Morgan. 1997. *Regional Orders: Building Security in a New World*. University Park, PA: Pennsylvania State Press.

Lampton, D. 2001. *Major Power Relations in Northeast Asia: Win-win or Zero Sum Game?* Tokyo: Japan Center for International Exchange.

Lemke, Douglas. 2002. *Regions of War and Peace*. Cambridge: Cambridge University Press.

McGregor, Richard. 2005. Divisions Undermine East Asia Summit. *The Financial Times* 1 December.

Mahbubani, K. 2001. *Can Asians Think?* Toronto: Key Porter Books.

Manning, R.A. and P. Stern. 1994. The Myth of the Pacific Community. *Foreign Affairs* 73 (6): 79–93.

Mansfield, Edward D. and Brian M. Pollins. 2001. The Study of Interdependence and Conflict: Recent Advances, Open Questions, and Directions for Future Research. *Journal of Conflict Resolution* 45: 834–59.

Mearsheimer, J.J. 2001. *The Tragedy of Great Power Politics*. New York: W.W. Norton.

Moon, C.I. and S.W. Suh. 2007. Burdens of the Past: Overcoming History, the Politics of Identity, and Nationalism in Asia. *Global Asia* 2: 33–49.

Mosher, Steven W. 2000. *Hegemon: China's Plan to Dominate Asia and the World*. San Francisco, CA: Encounter Book.

Pempel, T.J. 2005. *Remapping East Asia: The Construction of a Region*. Ithaca, NY: Cornell University Press.

Pyle, Kenneth B. 2007. *Japan Rising: The Resurgence of Japanese Power and Purpose*. New York: The Century Foundation.

Ripsman, Norin M. and Jean-Marc F. Blandchard. 1996/97. Commercial Liberalism under Fire: Evidence from 1914 and 1936. *Security Studies* 6: 4–50.

Rosecrance, Richard. 1986. *The Rise of the Trading State: Commerce and Conquest in the Modern World*. New York: Basic Books.

Ross, Robert. 2003. The U.S.–China Peace: Great Power Politics, Sphere of Influence and the Peace of East Asia. *Journal of East Asian Studies* 3: 351–75.

Russet, Bruce and John R. Oneal. 2001. *Triangulating Peace: Democracy, Interdependence and International Organizations*. New York: W.W. Norton.

Shambaugh, David. 2006. Asia in Transition: The Evolving Regional Order. *Current History* 105: 153–9.

Solingen, E. 1998. *Regional Orders at Century's Dawn: Global and Domestic Influences on Grand Strategy*. Princeton, NJ: Princeton University Press.

———. 2007. Pax Asiatica versus Bella Levantina: The Foundations of War and Peace in East Asia and the Middle East. *American Political Science Review* 101: 757–80.

Suh, J.J., P.J. Katzenstein and A. Carson. 2004. *Rethinking Security in East Asia*. Stanford, CA: Stanford University Press.

Tonneson, Stein. 2009. What is it that Best Explains the East Asian Peace 1979? A Call for a Research Agenda. *Asian Perspective* 33: 111–36.

Yan, Xuetong. 2010. The Instability of China–U.S. Relations. *The Chinese Journal of International Politics* 3: 263–92.

Waltz, Kenneth N. 1970. The Myth of Interdependence. In Charles P. Kindleberger, ed. *The International Cooperation*. Cambridge, MA: MIT Press.

6 Northeast Asia after the global financial crisis

Power shift, competition, and cooperation in the global and regional arenas

Mie Oba

Introduction

The most recent global financial crisis broke out in August 2007 with the collapse of the subprime mortgage market in the United States. The crisis led to economic declines not only in the United States but also in other developed economies such as Japan and Europe, as well as in developing economies within East Asia and other regions. The situation deteriorated after September 2008, following the default of Lehman Brothers and the government rescue of the insurance firm American International Group (AIG). Economic turmoil in Greece and its request in April 2010 for International Monetary Fund (IMF) financial support have worsened the economic downturn in Europe, evoking pessimistic prospects for the world economy. The crisis has had severe impacts both globally and regionally. For East Asian countries, however, the current economic crisis is really their "second crisis" following the Asian financial crisis in 1997. And both crises have been intimately linked to East Asian conceptions of security and national vulnerability.

The current financial crisis and the earlier Asian financial crisis show that states and economies all over the world are tightly interconnected by financial globalization. In such a world of globalization, economic troubles in one country easily spread to other countries and can quickly damage their economies as well. Such turmoil in any state's economic and financial system can undermine its very existence. Therefore, any economic crisis that cuts across national borders can be perceived by the affected countries as a "security" crisis rather than being simply an "economic" crisis. The economic downturn that began in 2007 and the near-collapse of the global financial system certainly warrant being treated as critical threats to "national security" for a number of countries throughout the world.

One of the remarkable results brought about by the latest global financial crisis is that it revealed a shift in the global balance of power, a shift that had already begun years before. Emerging countries were able to extend their political leverage in the aftermath of the crisis, because the developed economies of the United States, Europe, and Japan were in severe decline while evaluations of the potential for developing economies rose substantially. Among these emerging countries, the rise of China and India in the international sphere and their enhanced political leverage were particularly remarkable.

This shift of power strongly affected the political and economic landscape in East Asia. China and its rising regional influence stand out all the more clearly in contrast with Japan, which formerly had the second-largest economy in the world and had demonstrated extensive economic and political leverage throughout most of the post-WWII era. China's economic success and its increasing influence across East Asia have been major topics of discussion since the 1990s, during which time Japan has decreased in political significance due to its seemingly permanent economic stagnation since the collapse of the economic bubble in the early 1990s. Both Japan and China have come out of the most recent economic crisis with strong positive positions that are not only regional but also global in scope.[1] So have most of the other East Asian economies. Their rapid collective recoveries point to the rise of East Asia as the most dynamic region in the world economy. However, the ascendance of China plus the seemingly permanent economic stagnation in Japan also underscore the shift in relative power between Japan and China within East Asia and the world. Some analysts argue that the global economic crisis has not changed East Asia's fundamental strategic balance, which is determined by U.S. supremacy in its tight alliance with Japan, even though China is rising rapidly in absolute terms both regionally and globally.[2] It is true that China is not replacing the United States as the regional hegemon at present, while Japan continues to support the United States as its primary ally. However, the financial crisis altered the paradigm in the Asia-Pacific in ways that reflect a much deeper shift in global power and in the structure of the global economy. The crisis was vividly emblematic of the power transition that was long underway in the global economic sphere.

It should not go unnoticed that regional financial cooperation schemes established after the Asian financial crisis in 1997—such as the Chiang Mai Initiative (CMI), Asian Bond Market Initiative (ABMI), and Asian Bond Fund (ABF)—now play a role in responding to the global financial crisis. It is unclear whether these schemes directly functioned as "buffers" for East Asian countries during the worst of the financial crisis in 2007–09. Their scale and mandate may not have been sufficiently effective in the current circumstances. However, these schemes represent an enduring orientation toward greater regional financial governance in East Asia.

This chapter examines how the global economic and financial crisis has transformed both the political and economic landscapes in Northeast Asia, focusing on changes in the power structure within the global arena and on conflicts and cooperation within the region. The shift of power globally—with the rise of emerging countries relative to the decline of developed countries—has been particularly salient within Northeast Asia particularly because of the clear-cut alteration of previous power relationships between emerging power China and declining power Japan. The United States, also a diminishing global power particularly in relative economic muscle, is an additional key player in this region.

From a regional perspective, therefore, responses by Northeast Asian countries to the 2007–09 financial crisis have brought about a new phase of development, not only within the region but also on the broader East Asian, as well as global scenes.

The next section examines how the global economic and financial crisis upended the economic situation across East Asia. The third section examines how the global economic governance system has been reformed in response to the demands of emerging countries, including China. Our focus is on the upgrading of the G20 and reform of the IMF. The fourth section clarifies how China and Japan responded to the 2007–09 crisis and how various measures taken by these two countries are affecting the rest of the region as well as the world at large. The fifth section clarifies the implications of the promotion of regional financial cooperation schemes in East Asia with respect to integration and perceptions of power in the region. A final section examines certain prospects for the region following the global financial crisis.

Two crises and their impact in East Asia

Impacts on the East Asian economics

Both the Asian financial crisis and the more recent global financial crisis clearly demonstrate how easily economic upheaval within one country can spill beyond national borders. Rapidly advancing and deepening financial globalization contributed greatly to the geographical sweep of these catastrophes. However, the two crises were different in several important respects. In particular, the Asian financial crisis was a "local" crisis that transformed the previous "East Asian miracle" into an "East Asian meltdown." The crisis of 2007–09 has shaken economies all over the world by rattling the global financial system to its core.

The IMF, the U.S. government, the World Bank, and the Japanese Ministry of Finance (MOF) clashed over the origins of the Asian financial crisis and consequently the best response to it.[3] The MOF insisted that excessive capital liquidity had been the cause, citing the large amounts of foreign currency-dominated short-term capital that had flowed into East Asia in the run-up to the crisis (Eisuke 1988). This inflow of capital resulted in high ratios of short-term external debt while foreign-exchange reserves were insufficient to meet the exploding debt. The sudden capital outflow that resulted in 1997 had created the currency crisis.

The IMF and U.S. government in contrast focused on the institutional vulnerabilities within the economic, financial, and political structures, the corporate system, and the labor market in the affected East Asian countries. According to this argument, responsibility for the collapse lay with weak banking sectors, poor assessment and management of financial risks, unwise maintenance of relatively fixed exchange rates, poor quality investment of foreign capital, inadequate government involvement in the private sector, and lack of transparency in corporate and fiscal accounting, including poor provision of important financial and economic data.

Disagreement concerning the origins of the Asian crisis led logically to alternative views on rescue policies for the most severely damaged countries. Regardless, it was clear to all that the deepening globalization and the resulting defects in the economies on the periphery of globalization had engendered the Asian financial crisis.

In contrast, the 2008 crisis was caused by flaws in the core structure of the world economy. In particular, many analysts traced the crisis to "global imbalances," meaning overdependence of the world economy on the U.S. market and dollar, caused by the overly large capital inflows to the U.S. market from other areas of the world, including from East Asia. Masahiro Kawai, referring to an IMF report, identified three key contributors to the most recent crisis: 1) a lack of effective financial regulation and supervision; 2) the failure of monetary policy to address the buildup of systemic risk; and 3) a weak global financial architecture.[4] In short, the global financial crisis in his analysis came from structural imperfections in the world economy and/or deficiencies in the biggest global power, the United States.

These two crises also differed in the depths of damage they inflicted on East Asia. The Asian financial crisis severely hit both financial and other sectors in some East Asian countries, though the damaged economies typically experienced a V-shaped recovery after 1999 (World Bank 2000). Authoritarian regimes that had been sustained by booming economic development were shaken or brought down in the aftermath of the crisis. One collective message delivered to East Asian governments was that economic challenges could present existential security threats to regime stability that were at least as potent as hard security threats. In contrast, the impact of the 2008 crisis on East Asia's financial sector was contained because of improved fundamentals and limited exposure to subprime assets. For example, when the situation deteriorated rapidly across the globe following the "Lehman shock" in September 2008, Japan's financial sector was largely unaffected because of its limited exposure to the toxic assets that were so detrimental in the United States and Europe (Asian Development Bank 2009: 11). Limited exposure to subprime mortgages and similar assets underscored the fact that investors in East Asia were risk-averse, investing instead in U.S. treasury securities and agency-related bonds. Meanwhile, investors in Europe, where the financial sector was severely damaged by the crisis, were more like American risk-takers with large holdings in riskier stocks and corporate bonds in the United States (Shirai 2009a: 28).

The turmoil in the United States and Europe challenged East Asia by causing a sharp reduction in exports to these markets, leading the manufacturing sectors in East Asia to suffer a serious blow which in turn slowed economic growth in most East Asian countries. Economic growth for the region as a whole slowed to 6.6 percent in 2008 from 10.4 percent in 2007. Growth in the Republic of Korea (ROK) was cut in half, falling to 2.5 percent in 2008 from 5 percent in 2007. Southeast Asia's growth dropped to 4.3 percent in 2008 from 6.4 percent in 2007 (Asian Development Bank 2009: 5–6). China's growth pulled back from the rapid 13 percent level in 2007 to 9 percent in 2008, China's lowest rate since 2002. As for Japan, its growth rate fell from 2.4 percent in 2007 to 0.6 percent in 2008, driven by sharp declines in exports and gross capital formation (ibid.: 11). However, these declines in growth rates reflected the combined effects of the global economic downturn, policy tightening to curb inflation, and natural disasters in 2008 (ibid.: 161).

Lessons from the Asian financial crisis

From a long-term point of view, the robustness of East Asian economies in 2008–09 was partly the result of lessons learned from the Asian financial crisis. After 1997, East Asian countries faced economic, social, and political turmoil. That period of crisis catalyzed system reforms and policy cooperation aimed at stabilizing the macroeconomic and financial environments.

Prior to 1997, East Asian countries had adopted a virtual dollar peg. This monetary system invited capital inflows that were unreasonable and which became one of the important factors engendering the financial crisis. After the crisis, many East Asian countries changed their exchange and monetary policies. Korea, Thailand, and Indonesia switched to floating exchange rates and, at the same time, introduced inflation targeting. The Philippines increased the flexibility of its exchange rate system. Unlike these countries, Malaysia introduced capital outflow regulations, and China maintained its virtual dollar peg. However, East Asia achieved near-transparency in monetary policy and looked forward to the stabilization of market expectations.

Before the Asian financial crisis, reserves of foreign currency were insufficient for short-term debt balances, and current account deficits were common. During the crisis, as funds flowed out rapidly, it was impossible to maintain stable exchange rates. Therefore, after the crisis, each East Asian country reduced its short-term foreign debt and accumulated foreign currency reserves. As a result, most East Asian countries held little in the way of subprime mortgages and other high-risk securitized paper when the global crisis struck, thereby limiting the effect of the U.S.–European deterioration on the financial sector in East Asia.[5]

The Asian financial crisis also generated awareness of the necessity for buffers against global hot money. These included enhanced foreign reserves and the formulation of a regional financial governance system with the creation of the CMI, the Asian Development Bank Institute (ADBI), and other regional monetary cooperation mechanisms. The progress of these schemes is examined later in this chapter.

Recovery in East Asia following the 2008 global crisis

East Asian economies, with the exception of Japan's, have, since 2009, begun to show signs of recovery from the global financial crisis. Within the Association of Southeast Asian Nations (ASEAN), growth in GDP for five economies—Indonesia, Malaysia, Philippines, Singapore, and Thailand—in the second quarter in 2009 rose 10 percent compared to the previous quarter (*Nikkei Shinbun*,

28 August 2009). Although the GDP growth in most East Asian countries remained slow, the ADB's Asian Development Outlook 2010 anticipated brighter prospects as global recovery seemed to be underway (ibid.: 27), pointing out that "developing Asia [including the East Asian economies] was the first region to emerge from the global turmoil" (ibid.: 2).[6] The IMF's World Economic Outlook April 2010 (IMF 2010: 47) declared that "Asia is staging a vigorous and balanced recovery." The report also said that output growth in 2009 in almost all Asian countries was stronger than predicted in the preceding World Economic Outlook, with the notable exception of Japan (ibid.). Domestic demand in Japan has been weak for several reasons, including long-term deflation, continued excess capacity, and a weak labor market. Japan's exports have helped support a tentative recovery. However, continued appreciation by the yen has undermined the contributions of exports to growth. Moreover, exports have failed to stimulate the expansion of domestic demand by very much (ibid.: 50).

Several reasons for Asia's "V-shaped" recovery can be pointed out. First, active and speedy implementation of stimulus measures by each government in East Asia contributed to the region's rapid comeback. Second, strong domestic demand in India and China—which are emerging as leading powers in terms of population, market scale, and rapid development—supported recovery elsewhere in the region. China's GDP growth in 2009 reached 8.7 percent, which exceeded the government target for that year (Asian Development Bank 2010: 8; IMF 2010: 48). Third, expanding domestic demand in these two countries, but especially in China, has had positive effects on development in other East Asian economies, particularly for exporters of commodities and capital goods. In other words, the expansion of exports from other East Asian economies to China's huge market has contributed further to regional recovery.

It should be noted that the U.S. economy and its recovery remain critical for East Asia. The U.S. economy began to show signs of a stimulus-driven recovery, and East Asian exports to the U.S. market have improved since the middle of 2009. The U.S. financial market remains attractive, as shown by fund inflows from Asia and the Middle East after 2008 even as the crisis worsened.[7] But a serious slowdown in the U.S. recovery will surely have profound and negative effects on East Asia. If the United States has seen a reduction in its global economic weight, the country still remains a critical investor and export market vital to East Asia's continued growth.

Transformation of global economic governance and implications for Northeast Asia

Shifting power and the transformation of global economic governance

As mentioned earlier, the global economic and financial crisis revealed the shift that was already in progress in the global balance of power before the crisis arrived. Among emerging countries, the rising economic success and political influence of China and India had become increasingly difficult to ignore. The shift of power from advanced countries like the United States, European nations, and Japan toward emerging countries has become even more noticeable since the 2008 crisis.

The global financial crisis spurred reforms of economic governance aimed at managing and stabilizing the world financial system. The existing system put the bulk of the responsibility for world economic governance on key global organizations such as the IMF, the World Bank, the Bank for International Settlements (BIS), the Financial Stability Board, and G7/G8. The dollar-centered monetary system, in which the U.S. dollar functions as a key currency, has continued even after the collapse of the Bretton Woods system in the early 1970s. Since the outbreak of the crisis, reform measures in the financial field have reflected the shift of global power, most notably in the enhanced status of the G20 as well as reform of the IMF.[8]

Changes in the balance of power, as emerging countries, and particularly China, gain more influence, have affected the political and economic landscape in East Asia as well as the region's position in the global arena.

The rise of the G20

The G20 was created in response to the Asian financial crisis but also in recognition that key emerging countries were inadequately represented in the core of global economic discussion and governance. The G20 was launched when finance ministers and central bank governors from 19 countries and the European Union (EU) as well as representatives from four international financial organizations (the IMF, the International Monetary and Financial Committee, and the development committees of the IMF and the World Bank) met in Berlin in December 1999.[9] Significantly, the membership included both developed countries (G8 members, ROK, and Australia) and developing countries that had shown expanding leverage and power, including China, India, Indonesia, Brazil, Argentina, Russia, Saudi Arabia, South Africa, and Turkey.

After the first G20 conference, finance ministers and central bank governors continued to meet annually, but the G20's position in global economic governance remained largely peripheral. After the financial crisis broke in September 2008 with its serious impact not only on the developed countries, but also on fast-developing countries in Latin America, Central Europe, and Africa (*New York Times*, 24 October 2008), the G20 gained enhanced status as an appropriate forum for discussion of global economic and financial issues.

Against the backdrop of the deteriorating world economy, an extraordinary meeting of G20 finance ministers and central bank governors took place in Sao Paulo in October 2008 soon after the G7 meeting. The first G20 summit was held in Washington, DC, in November 2008. At that first summit, leaders showed their determination to "enhance our cooperation and work together to restore global growth and achieve needed reforms in the world's financial systems."[10] In addition, the leaders declared that "the Bretton Woods Institutions must be comprehensively reformed so that they can more adequately reflect changing economic weights in the world economy and be more responsive to future challenges." Further, they affirmed that "emerging and developing economies should have greater voice and representation in these institutions."[11] The first G20 meeting thus demonstrated the rising status of the G20 as the platform that would best allow emerging countries to gain a greater voice in global economic and financial affairs (Barrionuevo 2008). Moreover, the declaration adopted at the third G20 summit in Pittsburgh during September 2009 designated the G20 as "the premier forum" for international economic cooperation.[12]

The upgraded status of the G20 and the enhancement of its role demonstrate the new trend away from global management exclusively by developed countries, usually G7 members. Their power and resources are no longer sufficient to allow them to exercise effective economic governance and stabilization of financial markets worldwide. Few now have sufficient resources to manage the global financial system or to come to the aid of other countries damaged by economic crisis in a major way. Many analysts have pointed out that the new prominence of the G20 reflects the growing leverage that developing countries now exercise in global governance. In particular, among the developing countries, China now has extensive financial resources and has demonstrated its strong commitment to reform the international governance system. For example, Premier Wen Jiabao stated that China would contribute to reform through active engagement in the G20 and other multilateral forums, in order to support and defend developing countries' interests (*Nikkei Shinbun*, 6 March 2010).

Acceleration of IMF reform

Discussion in the G20 about the influence and representation of developing countries soon led to reforms in the IMF quota system. Japan has long appealed for enhanced quota shares for the Asian countries (Shirai 2009b: 3). China, as a dynamic emerging power, has joined the attempt to promote this shift.

At the second G20 summit, held in London in April 2009, leaders reconfirmed the large-scale IMF quota reforms that had previously been approved in April 2008. They also agreed to encourage further quota and voice reform in the direction of raising the overall weight for emerging countries, while also calling on the IMF to move up the schedule for review of quotas.[13] The third G20 summit, held in Pittsburgh, agreed to shift at least 5 percent of votes from overrepresented countries to underrepresented countries, mainly emerging countries, with the use of the current quota formula.[14] This call was endorsed by the International Monetary and Financial Committee (IMFC) in October 2009.[15] Such a shift in vote shares would change the distribution of voting power between developed countries and others from the current 60:40 to 55:45, a clear response to the strong request of emerging countries to expand their voice in the IMF (Kawai 2009: 19).

The establishment of the Financial Stability Board (FSB) further transformed economic governance in the same direction. The meeting of G20 financial ministers in November 2008 noted the necessity of expanding the membership of the

Financial Stability Forum (FSF) to include developing countries.[16] The G20 London summit agreed to establish the FSB as a successor to the FSF, with representation including all G20 countries, FSF members, Spain, and the European Commission, to coordinate and monitor progress in strengthening financial regulation.

China, Japan, and the global financial crisis

China as "contributor" as well as "challenger"

Through the global financial crisis, China emerged as one of the main powers with the wherewithal to shape the global economic and political landscape. Endowed with a large population, China has grown rapidly in economic size and financial power, and these factors provide a robust foundation for its strength. Success in economic development since the 1990s has enhanced China's political leverage both regionally and globally. As the 2008 global financial crisis enhanced perceptions that U.S. power was in decline, China came simultaneously to be seen as a potential new power that could pull the world economy into prosperity. China had accumulated huge foreign reserves, totaling approximately US$ 3 trillion, with approximately 70 percent of it denominated in U.S. dollars. As the global financial crisis spread, these foreign assets came to be regarded as evidence of China's potential to shape the prospects of the world economy. Moreover, large-scale economic stimulus measures, hammered out by the Chinese government to deal with the crisis, further contributed to expectations for Chinese global economic leadership.

In accordance with such expectations that it would take a role in stabilizing the world economic and financial situation and lead post-crisis development globally, the Chinese government conducted active economic and financial diplomacy in the global arena and demonstrated its positive stance on contributing to revitalization not only of its domestic economy but of the global economy as well.

In early October 2008 the Chinese government announced an economic stimulus package worth 4 trillion yuan (about US$ 570 billion), composed of relaxed credit conditions, tax cuts, and a massive infrastructural spending program.[17] Although this stimulus package was aimed directly at expanding domestic demand, it also met the expectation that China would do its part to pull the world economy out of recession, rather than relying solely on European and American markets, which clearly could no longer bring about a strong recovery solely through consumer spending (Shirai 2009b: 7). In June 2009, the Chinese authorities signaled their intention to invest up to US$ 50 billion in notes issued by the IMF.[18] As mentioned in the previous section, China also took on a larger role in the movement to reform global economic governance, proposing various reforms of the global currency system, a topic which will be examined next. These attitudes demonstrated China's intention to be an "active contributor" as well as a "challenger" to the global economic governance system.

Reform of the dollar-centered monetary system?

In a March 2009 paper published on the bank's website, Zhou Xiaochuan, the chairman of the People's Bank of China, proposed that the world consider using IMF Special Drawing Rights (SDRs) as the world reserve currency instead of U.S. dollars.[19] The SDR is an IMF-created asset based on the exchange rates of four key currencies. Zhou underscored the "inherent weakness of the current international monetary system" and the necessity of "reestablishment of a new and widely accepted reserve currency with a stable valuation benchmark" for the long run. The SDR, he said, "has features and potential to act as a super-sovereign reserve currency." In this context, he proposed four specific measures: 1) setting up a settlement system between the SDR and other currencies; 2) actively promoting the use of the SDR in international trade, commodities pricing, international investment, and corporate bookkeeping; 3) creating financial assets denominated in the SDR; and 4) further improving the evaluation and allocation of the SDR.World leaders were shocked by this proposal, especially policymakers in the United States, who were strongly opposed. In a press conference, President Obama emphasized that the U.S. dollar was "extraordinarily strong" and that the U.S. economy was regarded as "the strongest economy", "with the most stable political system in the world," and he denied the necessity of any such global currency (White House 2009). Quite obviously, the U.S. government was concerned that assets denominated in U.S. dollars might be rapidly sold if the value of the dollar fell due to this proposal not to mention the longer-term impact such a shift would have on U.S. financial power as exercised through dollar diplomacy (Shirai 2009b: 6).

Zhou's proposal was also included in a suggestion from the Kremlin as well as from an expert panel of the United Nations on international finance/economic reform. The proposal from China (which continued to buy dollars regardless) stimulated discussion on reform of the current monetary system. However, prospects for the realization of Zhou's idea were already dubious when it was being proposed. Implementation of his idea would have required support from developed countries, especially the United States, because of the strength of its influence in the IMF, which issues the SDRs. Indeed, the United States still retains a virtual veto in decisions on such important matters.

In reality, China's attitude toward actually using the SDR as the world reserve currency seems ambivalent. If the value of the dollar were to fall, Chinese assets overseas would also decrease, so it is doubtful that a change in the international currency would automatically be beneficial to China. Zhou recognized in his paper that development of a new international reserve currency would take a long time.

Despite its lack of immediate feasibility, Chinese authorities argued that Zhou's proposal called attention to the desirability of reforming the current financial and monetary system. Barry Eichengreen has concluded that Zhou's paper was a signal intended to convey "China's unhappiness with prevailing arrangements and remind other countries," in particular members of the G20, "that China expected to actively participate in discussions of international monetary reform and to advocate a rules-based multilateral system" (Eichengreen 2009). Zhou's proposal had the definite impact of prompting discussion on economic governance reform and according to Shirai, Zhou's proposal functioned as an impetus to expand SDRs in the second G20 summit (2009b: 1).

Increased internationalization of the renminbi

Along with China's rising leverage in the global economic scene, an increase in the valuation of the renminbi began to be strongly requested by several countries, especially the United States. The Obama administration shelved this issue initially because the priority in U.S. policy was to overcome the global financial crisis (*Nikkei Shinbun*, 16 March 2010). However, since the fall of 2009, the policy on the renminbi has shifted, though the United States also continues to emphasize the maintenance of cooperative relations with China. In February 2010, President Obama harshly criticized what he argued was China's manipulation of the renminbi. Interested members of the U.S. Senate and House of Representatives also pressed the administration on the renminbi many times, insisting that low exchange rates undermined the competitiveness of U.S. industries both domestically and overseas.

The Chinese government took a reluctant and sometimes ambivalent attitude toward the revaluation of the renminbi. This divided attitude was caused in part by conflict surrounding who would win and who would lose in a revaluation. The Ministry of Commerce strongly opposed revaluation because it would decrease the competitiveness of Chinese export industries. The Ministry of Foreign Affairs claimed the issue was "politicized" and insisted that the fourth G20 summit in Toronto, in June 2010, not deal with this issue (*Nikkei Shinbun*, 18 June 2010).

Eventually, however, the People's Bank of China announced that it would allow greater flexibility in the exchange rate for the renminbi, which would lead it to appreciate gradually against the dollar (People's Bank of China 2010). The People's Bank of China stated a day after the announcement of the new policy that any appreciation in the renminbi's value would be gradual (*New York Times*, 20 June 2010). Chinese decision-makers tried to avoid discussing the renminbi issue at the fourth G20 summit and have continued to maintain a cautious attitude. Nevertheless, this decision was epoch-making, in that the change in currency policy took place despite internal disagreement.

The Chinese government and People's Bank of China are simultaneously promoting internationalization of the renminbi (*China View*, 25 December 2008). The renminbi was already being used in border trade with neighboring countries, such as Vietnam, Laos, Myanmar, Central Asian countries, and Russia. In addition, owing to the increase in tourism from China, the renminbi came to circulate along with local currencies in Hong Kong and Macao. Given this reality, the Chinese government launched the yuan settlement pilot program on 24 December 2008, facilitating trade in designated regions, including Guangdong, the Pearl River delta area, the Hong Kong–Macao area, Guangxi Zhuangzu Autonomous

Region, Yunnan, and the ASEAN countries (*China View*, 25 December 2008; Seki 2008). Moreover, in June 2010, the People's Bank of China announced that the yuan settlement pilot program in foreign trade would eventually be expanded to cover the entire world, and added 18 provinces and municipalities to the program.[20] Furthermore, after the global financial crisis broke out, the People's Bank of China concluded bilateral swap arrangements on a yuan basis with the central banks of the ROK, Hong Kong, Malaysia, Belarus, Indonesia, Argentina, Brazil, and Singapore (Shirai 2009b: 6; *China Daily*, 23 July 2010). These measures are representative of China's active movement to enhance the internationalization of the renminbi.

Japan: an agonized and old economic power

As a member of the G7/G8, Japan worked out various measures to support the world financial system and global economy in response to the global crisis. Any financial incentives to do so were bolstered by a Japanese desire to retain some of its political and diplomatic influence across the region and to offset perceptions of Japan's declining economic significance. Specifically, the government made contributions to reinforce the IMF while the Japan Bank for International Cooperation (JBIC) provided financial support in Asia. Despite these efforts, however, huge budget deficits and slow economic growth have weakened Japan's influence on the international stage.

The Japanese government also announced plans for various forms of assistance to the IMF and within Asia despite the fact that the Japanese economy was itself struggling, especially in its exports, due to the shrinking U.S. market. In other words, Japan attempted both to contribute to global recovery while simultaneously attempting to revitalize its own economy. At the November 2008 summit of the G20, Taro Aso, then prime minister of Japan, announced his country's willingness to lend up to US$ 100 billion to the IMF to help overcome the global crisis.[21] The loan represented a substantial contribution to the multilateral effort to ensure that the IMF had adequate financial resources. The IMF and the Japanese government signed an agreement on this commitment in February 2009.[22]

In addition, in November 2008, Japan's Minister of Finance Shoichi Nakagawa and World Bank Group President Robert B. Zoellick agreed to establish the Bank Recapitalization Fund (BRF) under the auspices of the JBIC and the International Finance Corporation (IFC). The BRF seeks to recapitalize major local banks in developing countries by making equity contributions or giving subordinate loans to strengthen the capital base of local banks and thus help to stabilize the financial systems in each country.[23] The JBIC signed agreements with the IFC to provide loans and equity capital to the IFC Recapitalization (Equity) Fund and the IFC Recapitalization (Subordinated Debt) Fund. According to the agreements, the JBIC will contribute US$ 2 billion, while the IFC will contribute US$ 1 billion.[24]

Moreover, Prime Minister Aso announced on January 2008 at the Davos conference that Japan was ready to provide Official Development Assistance (ODA) loans and grants of not less than 1.5 trillion yen (US$ 17 billion) to support Asian countries.[25] About three months later, the Japanese government expanded its ODA commitment to 2 trillion yen (US$ 20 billion). This ODA plan was meant to "bolster the important role of Asia in contributing to world growth as 'a center of growth open to the world'" (Ministry of Economy and Trade 2009).

On 14 March 2009, Finance Minister Kaoru Yosano announced the Leading Investment to Future Environment (LIFE) Initiative, the goal of which was to implement the principle, decided at the G7 meeting of financial ministers and central bank governors in Rome in February 2009, "that fiscal policy measures should be 'frontloaded and quickly executed' in response to the ongoing and severe global economic downturn" and that these measures should "address long-term goals in infrastructure sectors in developing countries."[26]

Prime Minister Aso announced that Japan would make a further contribution of up to US$ 22 billion over a two-year period to support trade finance, over and above its normal contribution of around US$ 220 billion a year, when G20 leaders at the second summit (London) agreed to support trade finance through the Export Credit Agencies (ECAs) and International Finance Institutions (IFIs) (Ministry of Finance 2009; Shirai 2009b: 7).

The amount of Japan's financial assistance to the IMF and to developing countries, especially in Asia, is not small. However, Japan's leverage in the global arena seems to be declining because its own economy has been sluggish and its budget deficit has become enormous, a striking contrast to the economic dynamism of China.

Japan has been pressed by other countries to achieve fiscal consolidation and economic growth through domestic demand. The fourth G20 summit announced that developed countries "have committed to fiscal plans that will at least halve deficits by 2013 and stabilize or reduce government debt-to-GDP ratios by 2016,"[27] with an exception being made for Japan, which was not asked to accomplish the same targets because of its huge fiscal deficit. Instead, Japan was expected to develop a clear fiscal consolidation plan, announced by the Kan administration; Japan will halve the GDP deficit by 2015 and pull the fiscal balance into the black by 2020. The reason G20 members allowed Japan to aim for more modest targets was that they expected demand-led development in the Japanese domestic economy, which in turn would lead to the reduction of government deficits (*Nikkei Shinbun*, 29 June 2010).

Japan's strong yen has undermined the country's export industries. Consequently, those export-oriented industries, which led Japanese economic growth in the past, have pressed for a depreciation of the yen. However, the announcement at the end of 2009 of a New Growth Strategy showed that the Hatoyama administration and some Japanese elites were trying to transform the structure of the Japanese economy into one based on domestic demand. Reinforcing this position were voices from overseas calling for the continuation of a strong yen, because governments in the United States, Europe, and East Asia wanted to boost exports from their own countries. Under pressure from overseas and due to its own economic downturn, Japan is now confronting pressure to decide between 1) support for export-oriented development; and 2) support for domestic demand. To date that debate has not been resolved.

Post-crises development of the regional financial system

The Asian financial crisis and the development of regional financial cooperation

Japan, China, and most other Asian countries worked to advance regional financial cooperation in East Asia after the 1997 financial crisis and to construct a more robust regional financial system. Japan, China, the ROK, and ASEAN countries achieved some measure of regional financial cooperation under the ASEAN Plus 3 framework and the creation of the CMI and ABMI.[28]

Japanese activity in promoting regional financial cooperation was remarkable. In August 1997, at the height of the crisis, the Ministry of Finance had proposed establishing a US$ 100 billion Asian Monetary Fund (AMF). The U.S. government was strongly opposed because of fears that such an AMF would undermine the role of the IMF and might be too lax in imposing conditions on the crisis economies. The Chinese government also opposed the idea because it was reluctant to enhance Japanese leadership in the region.[29] Following the rejection of the initial AMF proposal, Japan announced the New Miyazawa Initiative, making US$ 30 billion available to crisis-hit countries in Asia. Implementation of the New Miyazawa Initiative led to the establishment of a regional network of foreign currency swaps, known as the Chiang Mai Initiative, which was agreed upon at the ASEAN Plus 3 financial ministers meeting in May 2000.

China also adopted several policies to help the recovery. In the initial shock of the crisis, the Chinese government feared that the damage would spread and destabilize its vulnerable banking system. The Chinese government, however, acted in a responsible and stabilizing manner by not devaluating its currency and instead offering packages of aid and low-interest loans to Thailand, Indonesia, and South Korea despite rejecting the Japan-led AMF proposal (Shambaugh 2004–05: 68). Many specialists in Chinese foreign relations have argued that these policies showed that China was beginning to behave as a "responsible great power." Although the total amount of bailout packages to Asian countries was only US$ 4 billion (Lampton 2001: 222), Chinese leadership in the efforts to revitalize regional economies should not be underestimated.

Regional financial cooperation schemes after the global financial crisis

The regional financial cooperation schemes under ASEAN Plus 3 have seen steady progress. At the height of the 2008 financial crisis, East Asian countries responded individually by adopting economic stimulus measures and participating in international forums, such as the G20, IMF, and others. However, the global crisis did not generate the same level of enthusiasm for regional financial cooperation among East Asian countries as had the 1997 crisis.

The 11th ASEAN Plus 3 finance ministers meeting in Madrid in May 2008 reached an agreement toward attainment of CMI Multilateralization (CMIM).[30] The special ASEAN Plus 3 finance ministers meeting in Phuket in February 2009 considered the contagion of the economic crisis and agreed to adopt concrete policy measures to ensure regional market stability and to foster market confidence. In this context, they decided to increase the size of the CMIM from US\$ 80 billion to US\$ 120 billion.[31] The ASEAN Plus 3 finance ministers and central bank governors and the monetary authority of Hong Kong signed the CMIM agreement in December 2009.[32] Financial contributions by China and Japan to the CMIM were equal, at US\$ 38.4 billion each (32 percent of total contributions), making it clear that neither would occupy a dominant position.

The CMIM regional financial scheme remained linked to the IMF framework. A crisis-affected member requesting short-term liquidity support could immediately get financial assistance for the first 20 percent of the bilateral swap amount, but the remaining 80 percent would be provided under an IMF program.[33] This so-called IMF link was established to avoid any moral hazard of making loans "too easy" for the borrowing countries. East Asian countries tried to reduce the extent of this dependence on the IMF through the so-called IMF delink, a system for enhancing surveillance of the regional economy. The 13th ASEAN Plus 3 finance ministers meeting gave its approval, and a new surveillance system was established as the ASEAN Plus 3 Macroeconomic Research Office (AMRO).[34] AMRO is expected to facilitate prompt activation of the CMIM, which starting in early 2011 can be independent of the IMF.

As for the ABMI, another financial cooperation scheme of ASEAN Plus 3, the finance ministers meeting in May 2009 endorsed the establishment of the Credit Guarantee and Investment Mechanism (CGIM) with initial capital of US\$ 500 million to support the issuance of local currency-denominated corporate bonds within the region.

It is important to note that trilateral cooperation among China, Japan, and the ROK was active in response to the global financial crisis, a point that is congruent with the findings of Iida (Chapter 9, this volume) as well. The ninth trilateral finance ministers meeting in Washington, DC, in particular, agreed on specific measures, including strengthening policy dialogues among the three countries, enhancing financial cooperation, and increasing the size of bilateral currency swap arrangements among the three countries.[35]

Conclusion

The Asian financial crisis in 1997 delivered a serious blow to some East Asian economies telegraphing the message that existential security threats could come as powerfully from the economic sphere as from the military. As a result, it brought reform and transformation of economic and financial policies that ultimately spawned a fast recovery and the development of a robust economic structure that worked as a buffer against future challenges. It also generated regional awareness and a collective willingness to construct a regional governance system, including several financial cooperation schemes. At that time, Japan took the initiative to rescue neighbors in Northeast and East Asia and to construct regional assistance schemes, even though its own economy was sluggish. Japan's initiative was rebuffed however, adding to perceptions that it was no longer the automatic leader of the region. After the crisis had passed, East Asia emerged as the center of global development. East Asian countries continued to develop, not least through exports to the U.S. market, even as intra-Asian trade was reducing overall U.S. importance as a final market for many countries' specific exports. And within East Asia, it was clearly China that was now leading the region's economic dynamism.

The global financial crisis, on the other hand, damaged almost all economies in the world. This crisis underscored the shift in global economic power, and particularly the rising power of emerging countries. The global financial crisis generated new forms of global economic governance, particularly by enhancing the relative positions of China and other developing economies while simultaneously reducing the influence of Japan. Both Japan and China remain key players in the global arena, and both tried to contribute to the recovery of the world economy with concrete measures. At the same time, competition between China and Japan in the global and regional arenas has become visible. After the global financial crisis, however, the rising political leverage of China became undeniable. Meanwhile, regional financial cooperation schemes in East Asia as well as in Northeast Asia have continued beyond the crises that spawned them, though their scales of operation and mandates remain somewhat limited. Yet, such Northeast Asian cooperation in finance and economics exists in the context of continued competition as well.

That competition is not limited to the economic and financial spheres: there it continues to be manifest in such areas as the competition for markets, the search for secure energy supplies, and efforts to use economic assistance as a diplomatic tool. Furthermore, as China's economic weight globally as well as within East Asia has risen, so has the willingness of the Chinese leadership to invest more heavily in building up China's military and security capabilities. As well, particularly in the first two years following the Lehman Crisis, Chinese leaders began engaging in what many other countries perceived to be a new security aggressiveness. Close support for North Korea despite the latter's nuclear programs and military provocations; conflicts with Japan over the Senkaku Islands; declarations that disputed territories in the South China Sea constituted 'core interests' for China, and the like, all triggered worries that the economic–security nexus in China would mean that a stronger economy would catalyze a more hard-line security posture.

In reaction, a number of countries in East Asia, including Japan, the ROK, the Philippines, Singapore, and Indonesia, enhanced their security ties to the United States, moves that have been warmly welcomed by the Pentagon and the Obama administration. And despite Japan's increased economic interdependence with China, particularly after the Asian financial crisis, the country has continued to view China's new prowess as a challenge to its own economic and political leverage.

Thus, East Asia collectively has emerged from the two crises much stronger and more financially integrated, giving it added regional weight in global economics and financial diplomacy which in turn enhances the region's shared diplomatic and security stature. China has been at the core of this growing leverage. At the same time, there is no evidence at all that East Asia's growing economic strength, nor its enhanced economic interdependence, is automatically eradicating longstanding political rivalries. These may well soften with time, closer economic interdependence, and more systematic participation in schemes of regional cooperation. But plenty of evidence suggests that the latest global economic crisis has also stimulated new competition and security challenges that partly offset the collective rise in East Asia's global economic strength and cooperation.

Notes

1. As for both Japan's and China's policies after the outbreak of the crisis, see Shirai (2009a).
2. For example, Green and Schrage (2009).
3. For further detail, see Rapkin and Strand (1996–97); Higgott (1998).
4. For these arguments on the origins of the global economic and financial crisis, see Kawai (2009: 2–6).
5. Naikaku-fu (Cabinet Office of Japan), Sekai-Keizai no Choryu, 2010 I, May 2010, 2-4-6.
6. "Developing Asia" in this report refers to 44 developing member countries of the Asian Development Bank (ADB) and Brunei.
7. Naikaku-fu (Cabinet Office of Japan), Sekai-Keizai no Choryu, 2010 I, 1-1-5.
8. For an analysis of the development of the G20 and its meaning for the change of global governance, see Cooper (2010).
9. Press Release, G20 Financial and Central Bank Governors Meeting, 15–16 December 1999, Berlin, Germany, available at: <http://www.mof.go.jp/english/if/if029.htm#01>.
10. G20 summit, Declaration, Summit on Financial Markets and the World Economy, 15 November 2008.
11. Ibid.
12. G20 Summit, Leaders' Statement, Pittsburgh Summit, 24–25 September 2009.
13. G20, Leaders Statement, London Summit, 2 April 2009, paragraph 20. The leaders called on the IMF to complete the review by January 2011.
14. G20, Leaders' Statement, Pittsburgh Summit, 24–25 September 2009.
15. IMF, "IMF Quota" fact sheet, 11 March 2010, available at: <http://www.imf.org/external/np/exr/facts/quotas.htm>.
16. G20 Meeting of Ministers and Governors, Communiqué, São Paulo, Brazil, 8–9 November 2008, available at: <http://www.mof.go.jp/english/if/g20_081109.pdf>.
17. "China's 4 trillion yuan stimulus to boost economy, domestic demand," www.chinaview.cn, available at: <http://news.xinhuanet.com/english/2008-11/09/content_10331324.htm>.
18. IMF Press Release No. 09/204, 9 June 2009.
19. See Zhou Xiaochuan, "Reform the International Monetary System," 23 March 2009, available at: <http://www.pbc.gov.cn/english/detail.asp?col=6500&id=178>, and the transcript of a press briefing by International Monetary Fund First Deputy Managing Director John Lipsky on Steps to Reform IMF Financing Facilities, 24 March 2009, available at: <http://www.imf.org/external/np/tr/2009/tr032409.htm>.
20. "China Expands Yuan Settlement Pilot Program," available at: <http://www.china-embassy.org/eng/zgyw/t710873.htm>. The 18 provinces include Beijing, Tianjin, Inner Mongolia, Liaoning, Jiangsu, Zhejiang, Fujian, Shandong, Hubei, Guangxi Zhuang Autonomous Region, Hainan, Chongqing, Yunnan, Sichuan, Jilin, Heilongjiang, Tibet, and Xinjiang Uygur Autonomous Region.

21. IMF Press Release No.08/284, 14 November 2008, available at: <http://www.imf.
    org/external/np/sec/pr/2008/pr08284.htm>, and IMF, "Borrowing Agreement with the
    Government of Japan, Prepared by the Finance Department and the Legal Department,"
    10 February 2009: 1.
22. IMF Press Release No.09/32, 13 February 2009.
23. *JBIC Today*, January 2009: 4.
24. JBIC Press Release NR/2008-67, 2 February 2009, available at: <http://www.jbic.
    go.jp/en/about/press/2008/0202-01/index.html>.
25. "My Prescriptions for Reviving the World Economy," special address by H.E.
    Mr. Taro Aso, Prime Minister of Japan, on the occasion of the Annual Meeting of World
    Economic Forum, Congress Center, Davos, Switzerland, 31 January 2009, available
    at: <http://www.kantei.go.jp/foreign/asospeech/2009/01/31davos_e.html>.
26. Japan Finance Corporation, Establishing Leading Investment to Future Environment
    (LIFE) Initiative, 23 March 2009, available at: <http://www.jbic.go.jp/en/about/news/
    2008/0323-01/index.html>.
27. G20, Declaration of G20 Toronto Summit, Toronto, Canada, 26–27 June 2010, para-
    graph 10, available at: <http://www.mofa.go.jp/policy/economy/g20_summit/2010–1/
    pdfs/declaration_1006.pdf>.
28. As for a comprehensive analysis of the development of financial cooperation in East
    Asia after the Asian financial crisis, see Grimes (2009).
29. For more detail on this process, see Higgott (1998); Amyx (2002).
30. The Joint Ministerial Statement of the 11th ASEAN Plus 3 Finance Ministers' Meeting,
    4 May 2008, Madrid, Spain, paragraph 6.
31. Joint Media Statement: Action Plan to Restore Economic and Financial Stability of the
    Asian Region, ASEAN Plus 3 Finance Ministers' Meeting, 22 February 2009, Phuket,
    Thailand.
32. Joint Press Release, The Establishment of Chiang Mai Initiative Multilateralization,
    28 December 2009, available at: <http://www.mof.go.jp/english/if/091228press_
    release.pdf>.
33. For a brief explanation of the linkage between the CMI and the IMF, see Kawai (2009: 21).
34. Joint Ministerial Statement of the 13th ASEAN Plus 3 Financial Ministers' Meeting,
    2 May 2010, Tashkent, Uzbekistan, paragraph 9, available at: <http://www.mof.go.jp/
    english/if/as3_100502.pdf>.
35. The 9th Trilateral Financial Ministers' Meeting, Joint Message, Washington, DC,
    14 November 2008, available at: <http://www.mof.go.jp/english/if/080504joint_
    message.pdf>.

References

Amyx, Jennifer. 2002. *Moving beyond Bilateralism? Japan and the Asian Monetary Fund.*
    Pacific Economic Paper No. 331, September.
Asian Development Bank. 2009. *Asian Development Outlook 2009: Rebalancing Asia's*
    Growth. Manila: ADB.
_____. 2010. *Asian Development Outlook 2010: Macroeconomic Management beyond*
    the Crisis. Manila: ADB.
Barrionuevo, Alexei. 2008. Demand for a Say on a Way Out of Crisis. *New York Times*,
    10 November.
Cooper, Andrew F. 2010. The G20 as an Improvised Crisis Committee and/or a Contested
    "Steering Committee" for the World. *International Affairs* 86 (3): 741–57.
Eichengreen, Barry. 2009. The Dollar Dilemma. *Foreign Affairs* 88 (5): 53–68.
Eisuke, Sakakibara. 1988. *Kokusai-kinyu no Genba*. Kyoto: PHP publisher.

Green, Michael J. and Steven Schrage. 2009. It's not just the Economy, Stupid: Asia's Strategic Dangers from the Financial Crisis. *PacNet Newsletter* 22 (25 March): 25.

Grimes, William W. 2009. *Currency and Contest in East Asia: The Great Power Politics of Financial Regionalism*. Ithaca, NY: Cornell University Press.

Higgott, Richard. 1998. The Asian Economic Crisis: A Study in the Politics of Resentment. *New Political Economy* 3 (3): 333–57.

IMF. 2010. *World Economic Outlook 2010*. April. Washington, DC: IMF.

Kawai, Masahiro. 2009. *Reform of the International Financial Architecture: An Asian Perspective. ADBI Working Paper Series* No. 167, November. Tokyo: Asian Development Bank Institute.

Lampton, David M. 2001. *The Making of Chinese Foreign and Security Policy in the Era of Reform*. Stanford, CA: Stanford University Press.

Ministry of Economy and Trade. Trade and Economic Cooperation Bureau. 2009. Japan's Support for Trade Finance and ODA, 3 April, available at: <http://www.meti.go.jp/english/press/data/20090403_02.html>.

Ministry of Finance. 2009. Japan's Initiative of Trade Finance, 2 April, available at: <http://www.mof.go.jp/english/if/jbic_090402.pdf>.

People's Bank of China. 2010. Further Reform the RMB Exchange Regime and Enhance the Renminbi Exchange Rate Flexibility, available at: <http://www.pbc.gov.cn/english//detail.asp?col=6400&ID=1488>.

Rapkin, David P. and Jonathan R. Strand. 1996–97. The U.S. and Japan in the Bretton Woods Institutions: Sharing or Contesting Leadership? *International Journal* 52 (2): 265–96.

Seki, Shiyu. 2008. Honkakuka suru Jinmingen no kokusaika heno mosaku [China's Trials for the Realization of the Internationalization of the Renminbi], available at: <http://www.rieti.go.jp/users/china-tr/jp/ssqs/090406-1ssqs.htm>.

Shambaugh, David. 2004–05. China Engages Asia: Reshaping the Regional Order. *International Security* 29 (3): 64–99.

Shirai, Sayuri. 2009a. *The Impact of the U.S. Subprime Mortgage Crisis on the World and East Asia: Through Analyses of Cross-border Capital Movements*. ERIA Discussion Paper Series, April. Jakarta: Economic Research Institute for ASEAN and East Asia (ERIA).

Shirai, Sayuri. 2009b. Sekai-Keizai-kiki to Keizai Gaiko [Global Economic Crisis and Economic Diplomacy]. *Kaigai Jijo* June: 2–13.

White House. 2009. News Conference by the President, 24 March, available at: <http://www.whitehouse.gov/the_press_office/News-Conference-by-the-President-3-24-2009/>.

World Bank. 2000. *East Asia: Recovery and Beyond*. Washington, DC: World Bank.

Part 3

Northeast Asian structures for economic cooperation and conflict management

7 Security implications of free trade agreements for South Korea

Min Gyo Koo

Introduction

South Korea's perceptions and approaches concerning the trade–security nexus have changed over time. From one perspective, South Korea's trade and security are more connected to each other than ever before against the backdrop of fluid geo-strategic and geo-economic conditions surrounding the Korean Peninsula. As is true of other countries in the region, South Korea has actively pursued free trade agreements (FTAs) for a variety of strategic and diplomatic purposes, from confidence-building among countries with little contact with one another, to winning diplomatic points over regional rivals, to establishing an international legal personality, to locking extra-regional powers—such as the United States and the European Union (EU)—into the region. If we look beneath the surface, the postwar South Korean trade–security nexus has undergone significant changes, especially over the past two decades.

For a long time during the Cold War period, security considerations under the hub-and-spokes alliance system backed by American hegemony overshadowed South Korea's commercial interests. The Cold War regional order heavily constrained South Korean perceptions of the trade–security nexus as well as the idea of the region to which the country belonged. Hostile geo-strategic circumstances and historical animosities created a strong security and geographic bias that favored strong extra-regional ties to the United States both economically and strategically but with weak intra-regional linkages to their Asian neighbors. During the Cold War period, South Korea's security concerns predisposed policymakers to conceive of "the region" primarily as the "Asia-Pacific." However, two external shocks in the 1990s—the end of the Cold War and the Asian financial crisis—reversed that earlier bias, placing trade policy at the front of the trade–security nexus. At the same time, "Northeast Asia" came to replace the "Asia-Pacific" as a dominant regional conception in South Korea (Kim 2010). During this period, the United States pursued an aggressive trade policy aimed at opening specific foreign markets under the threat of closing U.S. markets, further accelerating the ease with which South Korea came to see trade and security as more separated arenas. South Korea realized that it needed to diversify its export markets in the face of growing market-opening pressure from the United States.

This trend became more obvious in the aftermath of the Asian financial crisis. For many East Asian countries including South Korea, the United States was no longer a benign, far-sighted hegemon willing to provide both economic and military public goods free of charge.

More recently, things have changed once again with a growing tendency in favor of embedding trade within security. Moreover, with the rise of China and the decline of America's ability as the ultimate regional power broker, South Korea has also begun looking further west to the vast "Asian" region consisting of Northeast Asia, Southeast Asia, Central Asia, and South Asia as part of its overall foreign policy orientation. The complex balance of power and interests in this region no longer allows for a single pacesetter, thus motivating a number of powers to consider sharing (and competing for) the regional leadership and influence through multilateral forums such as the ASEAN Plus Three (APT), ASEAN Plus Six (APS), and the ASEAN Plus Eight (APE).

Both at the bilateral and multilateral levels, South Korea has sought to play a balancer role among its giant neighbors but to date it has achieved only limited success. South Korea faces gigantic challenges ahead. And it might find itself in a more favorable position to implement its Asian initiative than China, Japan, or the United States because it bears few of the historical burdens and political suspicions than its larger counterparts. Yet in many respects, its big neighbors remain ahead of South Korea in winning the trust and support of the countries in the region.

This chapter examines South Korea's changing approach to the trade–security nexus both chronologically and geographically. The main goal is to access its contemporary efforts at connecting trade and security in a larger regional setting than in the past. The next section examines how South Korea's trade–security nexus has evolved under U.S. hegemony, stressing that the United States still serves as a powerful shaper of South Korea's foreign policy. The third section explores South Korea's initiative to engage Asia through bilateral FTAs. It highlights South Korea's goal of hedging against the rise of China and the decline of the United States by a more active embrace of its Asian neighbors through trade. The fourth section investigates South Korea's still mixed efforts to connect its economic and strategic interests in more broad-based regional forums. The final section draws conclusions and policy implications.

South Korea's trade–security nexus under U.S. hegemony

As aptly illustrated in the lead chapter by Pempel, the trade–security nexus is not always an easy relationship to define. This conceptual difficulty notwithstanding, there is a growing body of literature on "security-embedded" or "securitized" FTAs in East Asia.[1] From this perspective, it would indeed be surprising if countries sought such agreements devoid of political security calculations and if such agreements had no international political-security consequences.

The most obvious example of this can be found in the United States, where FTAs with its Asia-Pacific trading partners have been used to reinforce strategic relationships. This trend in U.S. trade policy gained added momentum in the wake of the September 11 attacks when the George W. Bush administration turned to FTAs as a way to buttress U.S. relations with key friends and allies in the region. During its tenure, the Bush administration put into effect FTAs with Jordan, Chile, Singapore, Australia, and Morocco, and completed free trade deals with Costa Rica, the Dominican Republic, El Salvador, Guatemala, Honduras, Nicaragua, Peru, Panama, Colombia, and South Korea. The United States also launched negotiations with Thailand in 2004 and with Malaysia in 2006. Further to the security linkage, New Zealand was excluded from FTA consideration because of its longstanding refusal to welcome U.S. vessels that might be carrying nuclear weapons. And the signing of the final agreement with Chile was delayed because that nation had failed to give clear support to the U.S.–British resolution authorizing war with Iraq in 2003. The Bush administration also turned aside a Taiwanese request for an FTA because such an accord would jeopardize Sino–U.S. strategic relations. Albeit with less enthusiasm in the aftermath of the 2008–09 economic crisis, the Obama administration continues to make efforts to cement ties with America's strategically important trading partners (Chan 2005; Destler 2005: 299–300; Koo 2011: 49–50).

Many in East Asia have also sought to use FTAs in the service of wider foreign policy objectives. The FTA between China and ASEAN is a good example of a security-embedded trade deal among East Asian countries.

The economic–security nexus is further complicated by institutional activities. Thus, in order to mitigate concerns about its hegemonic ambition and abrasive foreign policies, China has chosen to use not only purely security forums like the ASEAN Regional Forum and the Shanghai Cooperation Organization, but also economic and other soft institutional mechanisms, some prominent examples of which include the 2002 Code of Conduct in the South China Sea and the 2003 Treaty of Amity and Cooperation with ASEAN, the APT, the East Asia Summit (EAS), as well as FTAs with its trading partners both within and outside the region (Shambaugh 2004; Goldstein 2005; Yahuda 2005; Kwei 2006).

For most of the Cold War period, the trade–security nexus of South Korea was determined by its relationship with the United States. That marked the first of three different phases in which policy has moved, from securitization to de-securitization to re-securitization of economic relations (Koo 2011). The key player in all three phases has been the United States, but recently, South Korea has taken a more proactive role.

During the first phase, under the hub-and-spokes system during the Cold War period, security and strategic considerations overshadowed South Korea's commercial interests.[2] Realist calculations prevailed with security considerations overshadowing, if not totally supplanting, South Korea's trade policy—which itself was heavily dependent on the United States.[3] The hostile geostrategic atmosphere shaped the unique institutional pathways through which South Korea managed its economic and strategic ties with its allies. Central was a combination of U.S.–centric bilateral and multilateral arrangements. In pursuit of security-embedded economic stability, South Korea agreed to the system that offered it access to the U.S. market in return for a bilateral security alliance with the United States. The bilateral security ties with South Korea were part of a larger deployment of substantial U.S. military forces stationed in Japan, the Philippines, South Vietnam, and Guam which collectively served as the backbone of America's hub-and-spokes strategy to contain communist forces in the region (Cumings 1997; Calder 2004; Aggarwal and Koo 2008; Pempel 2008; Moon and Rhyu 2010).

The 1990s saw a reversal of this pattern as the United States became less committed to South Korean security as well as to the East Asian region as a whole (Moon and Rhyu 2010: 443–8). This sudden shift in Washington's calculations put greater and more pointed market-opening pressure on America's East Asian allies, most of which had economic policies that focused on rapid growth through import protection, industrial policy, and export promotion. Absent the Soviet threat, America was free to give greater priority to the promotion of its longstanding belief in the fair trade idea, which held that no countries should assist their own industries or interfere with consumer market preferences to a greater extent than is done in the United States. The Clinton administration adopted an aggressive approach to prying open East Asia's traditionally protected markets. Although U.S. alliance relations remained fundamentally intact, the relatively new American separation of trade and security policy was clearly manifested in a series of prominent trade disputes between Washington and its East Asian allies (Tyson 1990; Irwin 1997; Conti 1998).

The difficulties facing the American economy accelerated this shift in the immediate post-Cold War period. The United States had remained competitive and committed to open trade until the late 1970s. However, the second oil shock of 1979 revealed that American manufacturers were unprepared for the dramatic shift in market demands resulting from the move toward high energy efficiency. The congressional response produced a wave of explicit protection for America's industries, voluntary export restraints by foreign manufacturers, voluntary import expansion by foreign countries, and local content legislation (Destler 2005: 77–9).

The United States saw a dramatic increase in industrial petitions under the new legislative initiative against unfair trade practices by foreign manufacturers. Initially, the major target of the U.S. fair trade policy was Japan, but as the trade imbalance with South Korea worsened in the late 1980s, the United States also became concerned about what it claimed were South Korea's unfair trade practices. The Clinton administration invoked provisions of the Super 301 clause in October 1997 to secure a meaningful opening of the Korean market, listing South Korea's auto market as a "Priority Foreign Country" practicing discrimination, the result of which is likely to increase U.S. auto exports, either directly or through the establishment of a beneficial precedent (Stevenson 1997). During this period, much of the United States Trade Representative's (USTR) energy was directed to what was labeled "aggressive unilateralism:" negotiations aimed at opening specific foreign markets under the threat of closing U.S. markets (Bhagwati and Patrick 1991). In many respects, the 1990s were the heyday of fair trade ideas in U.S. trade policy circles, which in turn accelerated the separation of economics and security (Goldstein 1988; Sohn and Koo 2011).

Yet again, under the Bush administration's first USTR Robert Zoellick, U.S. trade policy changed dramatically under the rubric of "competitive liberalization," in which global, regional, and bilateral trade negotiations would complement and reinforce each other. Zoellick had long seen such agreements as having geopolitical significance. His view clearly found resonance in the Bush White House (Zoellick 2001; White House 2002). The audience for this re-securitization—America's trading partners—was quickly made aware of the salience of the relationship between the two closely related but discrete domains of policy and the accompanying expectation that they respond. During the Bush administration, America's trading partners were explicitly considered in ways that connected security with economic cooperation (Koo 2011: 48–9).

The United States–Korea Free Trade Agreement (KORUS FTA) clearly demonstrates how countries can utilize trade negotiations in the simultaneous pursuit of economic benefits and strategic interests. In addition to the goal of maximizing the gains from trade and investment, South Korea sought to hedge against the growing strategic uncertainties in Northeast Asia by cementing its economic ties with the United States. South Korea wanted the United States to be more engaged in Asia, if only to check the rising power of China and hedge against American abandonment. To South Korea, an FTA with the United States offered a double-edged sword. Despite potential economic risks, South Korea sought to bind the United States economically while simultaneously hedging against Chinese predation or the possibility of Chinese economic domination (Sohn and Koo 2011: 12–15).

For its own part, the United States realized that an FTA with South Korea would give it a strong foothold in the maintenance of a strategic and economic presence in the region increasingly dominated by its sometime competitor and other times partner, China. China was capitalizing on U.S. policy drift by stepping into the void left by America's increasing disengagement in Asia. For the United States, Japan was naturally the first choice as a security-embedded FTA partner. However, Japan showed tepid interest in such a proposal because U.S. tariff rates on Japanese exports were already very low, while Japan's politically powerful agricultural sector was vehemently opposed to such a trade deal. In addition, the Koizumi administration successfully forged an integrated bilateral alliance with the Bush administration, making an FTA with the United States for strategic purposes less attractive. Hence the KORUS FTA provided U.S. strategists with a credible alternative to an FTA with Japan (Sohn and Koo 2011: 9–12).

Engaging Asia bilaterally through FTAs

As Sohn and Koo (2011) point out, South Korea has considered security as one of the most important motives for entering an FTA negotiation with the United States in 2006, while it expected also to reap significant economic benefits from the agreement thanks to growing competition with its Asian neighbors in the U.S. market. At the same time, South Korea has made a conscious effort to improve its political and economic relations with Asia so that the KORUS FTA would not irritate its Asian neighbors, especially China (Moon and Rhyu 2010). South Korea's simultaneous approach to the United States and Asia shows the country's changing perception about the trade–security nexus. For example, during his visit to Indonesia in March 2009, South Korea's incumbent President Lee Myung-bak launched an ambitious diplomatic endeavor, dubbed the "New Asia Initiative," that envisions South Korea as a regional leader able to speak for Asian countries in the international community. Yet President Lee is not the first Korean leader with such ambitious regionalist goals vis-à-vis Asian neighbors. Comparison with his two late predecessors, Kim Dae-jung and Roh Moo-hyun, provides a perspective (Koo 2009b).

President Kim Dae-jung (1998–2003) pursued an ambitious initiative to make South Korea a regional hub for transportation and international business. He also launched a dramatic policy shift as part of his strategic goals for regional cooperation. At the first APT summit meeting in Kuala Lumpur in December 1997, he made public South Korea's aspiration to become a hub country within East Asia by playing a balancer role between regional powers.[4] During the 1999 APT summit, Kim also proposed the establishment of an expert panel, the East Asia Vision Group (EAVG), as the first step in forging a regional cooperation mechanism and developing the APT into a more permanent regional institution.[5] As long as both China and Japan were eager for enhanced regional ties, President Kim could play the role of visionary for an East Asian community and serve as a bridge between the two longstanding rivals. Beyond the relatively warm Sino–Japanese relations at the turn of the new millennium, Kim's Sunshine Policy, which culminated in the June 2000 inter-Korean summit, created a great deal of diplomatic capital for South Korea, allowing it to actively address the delicate issues of peace and stability in the region (Aggarwal and Koo 2008; Koo 2009b).

Kim's policy ideas inspired his successor, President Roh Moo-hyun (2003–08). Upon his inauguration in February 2003, Roh launched an ambitious initiative aimed at creating a peaceful and prosperous Northeast Asia. He created a presidential committee to explore making Korea a hub for Northeast Asian business. Goals included the creation of financial and logistic hubs, and the promotion of cooperation in the areas of business, energy, and transportation. At the same time, Roh launched the "Northeast Asian Cooperation Initiative for Peace and Prosperity," designed to carry out his vision of a new regional order based on mutual trust and cooperation (Presidential Committee on Northeast Asian Cooperation 2004). Despite Roh's wishes to serve as an honest broker between China and Japan and between the United States and China, he encountered unfriendly regional geopolitics from the outset due to the ever-expanding global war on terror and growing tensions between China and Japan over maritime sovereignty, energy, history textbooks, Taiwan, and the like. In addition, the simultaneous political leadership changes in the United States, China, Japan, and South Korea put unpredictable pressure on East Asian regionalism.[6] None of the great powers surrounding the Korean Peninsula thus showed much support for Roh's regionalist ventures, which resulted in their gaining far less diplomatic and moral attraction than those of his predecessor Kim (Aggarwal and Koo 2008; Koo 2009b).

President Roh was unable to further pursue his regionalist vision after he was immediately pegged by his domestic opponents and foreign observers as being excessively naïve and ideological. Beleaguered at home and abroad, Roh switched gears and began advocating bilateral FTAs as alternative instruments in the service of his foreign and economic policy goals. The policy shift toward FTAs under President Kim marked a dramatic departure from South Korea's prior mercantilist policies. Yet, it was not until President Roh entered office in 2003 that the road map for FTAs and detailed action plans for its multi-track FTA strategy were completed. In contrast to its rather peripheral status on President Kim's economic and strategic agenda, the FTA policy became a core element of President Roh's economic policy reforms and regional vision. At first glance, it appears that Roh inherited his predecessor Kim's economic and foreign policy agenda. If we look beneath the surface, however, Roh further expanded on that agenda by completing a road map for South Korea's multi-track FTAs and adopting comprehensive side payments to adversely affected groups (Koo 2010: 112–18).

Set against this background, the accelerating pace of South Korea's bilateral FTA initiative has been remarkable in its speed and scope. Over the past decade, South Korea has successfully concluded FTAs with Chile (2003), Singapore (2004), the European Free Trade Association (EFTA, 2005), the ASEAN (2006), the United States (2007), India (2009), Peru (2010), and the European Union (2010). In addition to FTA negotiations initiated under the Roh administration with Canada, Japan, the Gulf Cooperation Council (GCC), and Mexico, the incumbent Lee administration has begun formal negotiations or will begin informal discussions with Australia, New Zealand, Turkey, Columbia, Russia, and China with an aim to establish South Korea as a hub country for a global FTA network.

Engaging Asia multilaterally and its limits

As noted above, President Lee's New Asia Initiative envisions South Korea as a regional leader that speaks for Asian countries in the international community. If successfully implemented, the new initiative will not only expand the country's foreign policy focus from Northeast Asia to the broader Asian region, but it will also extend the scope of cooperation from economics to security, culture, energy, and other sectors. As President Roh was unable to further pursue his regionalist vision as originally planned, President Lee has faced similar challenges due to limited support from the major powers as well as from his domestic constituents. At the same time, however, the shifting political-economic dynamic in Asia has created diplomatic space for Lee to maneuver within. If South Korea is to pursue an Asia-first policy, it must also strengthen economic and strategic relations that go beyond FTAs.

The Lee administration has thus attempted to lessen its diplomatic deficit within Asia by more active engagement with the region at the multilateral level.

The principal candidates have been Southeast Asian countries. Over the past five years, ASEAN has emerged as South Korea's third largest trading partner after China and the EU, while South Korea's investment in ASEAN soared from US$ 500 million to US$ 3.6 billion, thus making ASEAN South Korea's second biggest investment target, after the United States. As the two sides marked the 20th anniversary of the Korean–ASEAN Dialogue Partnership, ASEAN has pressed for even more cooperation through Lee's New Asia Initiative. South Korea and ASEAN completed their Framework Agreement on Comprehensive Economic Cooperation with the signing of the ASEAN–Korea Investment Agreement in June 2009. To enhance cooperation in economic development, South Korea also plans to triple its official development assistance to ASEAN by the year 2015. Yet, South Korea can, and should, do more than that. South Korea's major trading partners—including the United States, China, and Japan—have already concluded or will conclude FTAs with individual ASEAN member countries (Koo 2009b).[7]

The Lee administration has also sought a greater role in key multilateral, catch-all forums for regional issues including trade, finance, investment, currency, energy, nuclear power, and human security. Most notably, the 1997–98 Asian Financial Crisis fostered the rise of APT; the region-wide economic difficulties greatly strengthened perceptions of mutual economic interdependence and vulnerability in Asia as well as resentment against the West and the United States.[8] The first significant concrete product of APT was the Chiang Mai Initiative (CMI), which was agreed to in Thailand in May 2000. CMI was proposed by Japan and accepted cautiously by China, which, along with the United States, had opposed Japan's more sweeping earlier proposal for an Asian Monetary Fund (Moore 2007: 49–50; Ravenhill 2008: 46).[9] The CMI has since offered an opportunity for regional financial collaboration that has simultaneously reduced Asian dependence on the U.S. dollar for financial reserves, currency baskets, and international transactions.[10]

APT members have attempted to increase their cooperation, most recently at the 13th APT Summit in Hanoi in October 2010. The summit reaffirmed the APT process as a main vehicle to achieve the long-term goal of building an East Asian community and recognized the mutually reinforcing and complementary roles of the APT process and such regional forums as the EAS and the ASEAN Regional Forum. Aside from economic cooperation, the summit meeting highlighted the ongoing need for cooperation, and some progress, in the areas of non-traditional security such as transportation safety, food security, pandemic disease protection, energy supply, the rights of women and children, and natural disaster recovery.[11] Ironically, however, the summit meeting worsened rather than improved the traditional security situation since the hosting country, Vietnam, along with several other ASEAN member countries, exchanged in hostile rhetoric with China vis-à-vis the disputed South China Sea.

The inherent weakness of the APT process has clearly been demonstrated by its expanded version, that is, the APS (and more broadly the EAS). It was Japan who initially proposed the APS framework as an expanded East Asian regional concept despite the existence of APT.[12] The APS proposal evolved into the launch of the EAS in 2005. From one perspective, the EAVG's proposal that the annual summit meeting of the thirteen member countries be transformed into an East Asian summit was realized more swiftly than its protagonists initially envisaged. Yet, the creation of the EAS seriously aggravated inter-state rivalry within the region (Webber 2010: 318).

Most APT states do not advocate any form of distinctive pan-East Asian regionalism; rather, most gravitate toward an Asia-Pacific perspective. Only Malaysia and China appear to be promoting more exclusive forms of East Asian regionalism. Within the APT, China has been aggressively pushing a strong China–ASEAN axis, whereas Japan has sought to balance China's efforts and step up its political and economic cooperative profile in the region, in part by pressing for the EAS. The additional plus three countries—Australia, New Zealand, and India—were admitted to the EAS, while China and other supporters of a narrower conception of the EAS were assured that the APT would remain the primary vehicle for promoting closer cooperation in the region. In theory, the larger membership may expand both the security and economic interest of the members. In practice, however, the dilution of common purpose has served no members thus far (Cook 2008: 296, 303).

The essentially unresolved issues of EAS membership and the relationship of competing forums—the APT, the APS, and the APE (including the United States and Russia)—indicate divergent views on China's regional role and the complex economic–security implications for its neighbors. To China, the APT offers an ideal institutional platform to raise its profile and image in the region, as it imposes few economic and political costs, while presenting an opportunity to diffuse concerns about the China threat. Although committed to cooperation within the APT framework, Japan prefers more expansive regional forums (such as the EAS) as opposed to advancing the cause of exclusive regional integration, primarily due to its strategic opposition to Chinese leadership. In a similar vein, South Korea has welcomed the APT as the basis for an increasingly institutionalized regional body for economic, political, and security cooperation. Despite its growing economic interdependence with China, however, South Korea's ultimate political and economic reliance on the United States ensures South Korea's continued Asia-Pacific orientation. Finally, the APT provides a welcome opportunity for ASEAN to improve its credentials as a core, albeit soft, leader for East Asian regionalism. But with respect to the EAS, ASEAN is divided, leaving Malaysia almost isolated in its opposition (Hund 2003: 394–5, 400–3, 406).[13]

A tangle of regional institutions now competes for attention and resources. The APS framework (and more broadly the EAS) continues to coexist with the APT to the point that East Asian regionalism is likely to become more polarized before it gets integrated. Central to East Asia's integration is a close and cooperative Sino–Japanese relationship, particularly as the role of the United States as a hegemonic broker between the two regional giants continues to wane. It is remarkable that Japan and China managed, as they did, to agree to limited monetary cooperation through the CMI in an attempt to ward off any repetition of the

Asian financial crisis. The two countries have also forged closer investment and trade ties, currently making them the most important economic partners for one another. In general, however, political wariness and rivalry continue to characterize postwar Sino–Japanese relations. Diplomacy continues to fail to ease deep mutual suspicions. The so-called "cold politics and hot economics" (*seirei keinetsu* in Japanese or *zhengleng jingre* in Chinese) has thus become a defining feature of their bilateral relations (Koo 2009a).

To summarize, mini-lateral institutions—in addition to bilateral FTAs—have been important venues for South Korea in recent years to improve strategic and economic ties with its Asian neighbors. Compared to the case of bilateral FTAs, however, South Korea's preferences for such forums are neither visible nor vocal because existing mini-lateral institutions pursue much broader and more abstract goals. As in the case of bilateral FTAs, policy elites have driven South Korea's move toward mini-lateralism. However, their identities around, and interests in, legally binding mini-lateral institutions are ambiguous at best. As a result, South Korea prefers soft rules and informally structured mini-lateral institutions. Under these circumstances, it is uncertain whether South Korea's highly ambitious New Asia Initiative will work. The path to this new policy initiative is likely to be a bumpy one.

Conclusion

In an effort to understand the shifting dynamics between trade and security as perceived, and carried out, by South Korea, this chapter focused on the role of external shocks—most notably the end of the Cold War and the Asian financial crisis—and South Korea's multi-track response to geostrategic uncertainties as a result of the rise of China and the decline of the United States.

South Korea has pursued a variety of strategic and diplomatic goals through FTAs. From one perspective, South Korea's trade and security policies could not be more connected than at present. If we look beneath the surface, however, the postwar Korean trade–security nexus has undergone significant changes with the longstanding subordination of trade policy to security during the Cold War period subsequently being weakened, if not completely severed. It is a myth to believe that South Korea's economic relations have always been tightly securitized under the postwar hub-and-spokes system. Rather, the country's trade–security nexus has undergone three distinct phases, moving from securitization to de-securitization to re-securitization, although the last phase of re-securitization is still evolving and lacks a strong sense of direction. For a long time during the Cold War period, security considerations overshadowed commercial interests under the hub-and-spoke alliance of the San Francisco system. Yet, the end of the Cold War and the Asian financial crisis reversed that trend in the 1990s, with trade policy taking a greater priority in the trade–security nexus. In the second decade of a new millennium, the trade–security nexus has been changing again in favor of embedding trade in security. South Korea's engagement in Asia through bilateral FTAs as well as through multilateral forums such as the APT, the APS, and the EAS prove the point, although it is not clear how strongly this pattern will continue in the face of the global economic downturn that started with America's subprime mortgage crisis in 2008.

The findings of this chapter also have significant implications for the future of Asian economic and security regionalism. Despite the many positive developments for the past few decades, many still hold that the Asian region remains largely inhospitable soil in which to cultivate multilateral institutions. Most East Asian countries still stick to the notion of Westphalian sovereignty and non-interference. Yet, there has been a spate of scholarly attempts at creating future scenarios as to how regional and trans-regional Asian institutions in economics and security might evolve. However, insufficient efforts have been made to systematically link the dynamic interaction of key powers with broader institutions in both the economic and security areas. For instance, it is not enough to claim that "the emerging regional security architecture will be firmly grounded in national self-reliance, with strong and important bilateral connections, and a gradually thickening but still very thin veneer of multilateralism" (Ball 2000: 143). Instead, we must explore the conditions under which these linkages are likely to evolve into broader institutions as well as the conditions under which they might undermine global institutions if they are not firmly nested in those institutions. This chapter indicates that economic regionalism is likely to provide a positive context for regional security institution-building, rather than the other way around. At the same time, the security context remains critical for the future of regional economic institutions.

Finally, South Korea's dream of becoming a leading player on the East Asian chess board will not be realized unless the country is more willing to provide public goods. The provision of public goods does not have to involve the direct transfer of resources from South Korea to the rest of Asia. It can be made available through multiple FTAs. It is uncertain whether South Korea's highly ambitious New Asia Initiative will work. This new policy initiative is likely to face many future bumps in the road. Without consolidating domestic and international support, President Lee and his policy cohorts face an uphill battle to achieve their foreign policy objectives.

Notes

1. Higgott (2004) defines securitization as a process in which "an issue is framed as a security problem." Rather than existing in two parallel policy areas, economic policy is subsumed or subjugated within the wider context of the U.S. security agenda (ibid.: 3). According to Buzan *et al.* (1998: 23), securitization "is the move that takes... [foreign economic policy]... beyond the established rules of the game and frame the issue as either a special kind of politics or as above politics." See Solís and Katada (2007), Capling (2008), Mochizuki (2009), Moon and Rhyu (2010), Pempel (2008, 2010), Koo (2011), and Sohn and Koo (2011).
2. Calder (2004: 138–40) outlines the key defining features of the San Francisco system as: 1) a dense network of bilateral security alliances; 2) an absence of multilateral security structures; 3) strong asymmetry in alliance relations, both in security and economics; 4) special precedence to Japan; and 5) liberal trade access to American markets, coupled with relatively limited development assistance.

3. A realist view argues that state actors under anarchy must worry that others will gain more from cooperation than they will, and that those relative gains might later be turned into military advantage. Under these circumstances, states may choose to trade predominantly with allies in order to avoid granting the gains from trade to adversaries (Grieco 1990; Gowa 1995).

4. The APT proposal was first discussed in the mid-1990s in preparation of the inaugural ASEAN–Europe Meeting (ASEM). European countries could coordinate their participation relatively easily through the EU, but East Asian counterparts lacked such an institutional arrangement. ASEAN thus asked Japan, South Korea, and China to participate in a preliminary ministerial meeting, which took place in 1995. The ministerial meeting was later supplemented by a summit meeting in Kuala Lumpur on the occasion of the annual ASEAN leaders' meeting in December 1997. After a second leaders' meeting, a year later, the group agreed to make the dialogue an annual affair. Since 1999, the scope of the dialogue has expanded to include separate ministerial meetings under the rubric of APT rather than simply as preparation sessions for the ASEM meeting (Stubbs 2002).

5. The EAVG also studied a joint surveillance mechanism for short-term capital movements and an early financial warning system. The group later proposed the establishment of an East Asian Monetary Fund and a regional exchange-rate coordination mechanism, with the long-term goal of creating a common currency area. Other recommendations included upgrading the annual APT meetings to an East Asian Summit and the establishment of the East Asian Free Trade Area (Moon 2005).

6. U.S. President George W. Bush and Japanese Prime Minister Junichiro Koizumi entered office in 2001. Hu Jintao and Roh Moo-hyun were elected presidents of the People's Republic of China and the Republic of Korea, respectively, in 2003. All four of these leaders were characterized as defiant and dogmatic—rather than pragmatic—in their foreign policy orientation, thus often causing diplomatic spats with one another.

7. The South Korean government has made conscious efforts to mitigate the negative perception of South Korea as an "economic animal." Asia can benefit significantly in the short run from South Korean capital and technology exports, but might suffer in the long run if South Korea followed in the footsteps of Japan from the past two decades. Many observers of Japanese business penetration in Southeast Asia have noted that the once-benevolent Japan as a "lead goose" became a "stingier bird," which was only concerned about replicating its domestic system of hierarchical and potentially exploitative *keiretsu* networking in the region as a whole, thus allowing "embraced development" to give way to "captive development" (Hatch and Yamamura 1996).

8. The APT replicates ASEAN's norms of consensual decision-making and mutual non-interference in member states' domestic affairs. It has remained a consultative organ, in which the participating members exchange views on a wide range of issues, but without making any binding policy commitments. Nevertheless, the web of relations among the thirteen member countries has developed steadily since its first summit meeting in 1997. Not only heads of government, but also finance, economics, and foreign ministers, central bank governors, and senior government officials in related domains have started meeting regularly to address a wide range of issues ranging from monetary, economic, social, security and technological, and cultural (Webber 2001: 340–5).

9. The CMI aims to establish a regional currency swap facility to enable the member countries to shield themselves better against any future financial crises. It was initially dismissed for involving only limited amounts of financial resources and requiring most swaps to be congruent with IMF regulations. Its mechanism is also characterized as vague and ambiguous and some critics raise fundamental questions about its relevance for regional monetary affairs because its mere existence does not alter the fact that East Asian states' primary response to the Asian financial crisis was unilateral (Dieter 2009: 129; Webber 2010: 319).

10. Today a total of US$ 120 billion is available, and in May 2009 the CMI was successfully multilateralized, creating a collective centralized reserve fund, with a single contractual agreement, allowing "one-stop shopping" for needed funds. The CMI has also initiated a regional surveillance mechanism called the Economic Review and Policy Dialogue. The Plus Three countries, namely China, Japan, and South Korea, have provided technical assistance and training for the monitoring of capital flows in East Asia's less-developed financial systems. Also, they have begun to develop an enriched Asian Bond Fund through their regional central banks, while the CMI has collectively pushed a separate Asian Bond Market Initiative (ABMI) (Pempel 2010: 217–18).
11. See http://www.aseansec.org/25484.htm.
12. The initial impetus behind the expanded framework was provided by Japan's Prime Minister, Junichiro Koizumi, who advocated during his trip to Singapore in January 2002 the additional inclusion of Australia and New Zealand as core members in the process toward the creation of an East Asian community (Terada 2010: 72).
13. ASEAN was able to take the lead in the APT largely by default, given the continued national rivalries and security competition across Northeast Asia. As David Jones and Michael Smith (2007: 152–3, cited Pempel 2010: 217) point out, "a shared sense of weakness rather than strength facilitated ASEAN's capacity to transform the regional order," leading to a discourse that was "conducted according to the non-legalistic, consensus-oriented ASEAN way that represented a distinctive alternative to European styles of diplomacy."

References

Aggarwal, Vinod K. and Min Gyo Koo, eds. 2008. *Asia's New Institutional Architecture: Evolving Structures for Managing Trade, Financial, and Security Relations*. New York: Springer.

Ball, Desmond. 2000. Multilateral Security Cooperation in the Asia-Pacific Region: Challenges in the Post-Cold War Era. In *The Security Environment in the Asia-Pacific*, Hung-maoTien and Tun-jeCheng, eds. Armonk, NY: M.E. Sharpe.

Bhagwati, Jagdish and Hugh T. Patrick, eds. 1991. *Aggressive Unilateralism: America's 301 Trade Policy and the World Trading System*. Ann Arbor, MI: University of Michigan Press.

Buzan, Barry, Ole Waever and Jaap de Wilde. 1998. *Security: A New Framework for Analysis*. Boulder, CO: Lynn Rienner.

Calder, Kent E. 2004. Securing Security through Prosperity: The San Francisco System in Comparative Perspective. *Pacific Review* 17 (1): 135–57.

Capling, Ann. 2008. Preferential Trade Agreements as Instruments of Foreign Policy: An Australia-Japan Free Trade Agreement and its Implications for the Asia-Pacific Region. *Pacific Review* 21 (1): 27–43.

Chan, Mignonne M.J. 2005. U.S. Trade Strategy of "Competitive Liberalization." *Tamkang Journal of International Affairs* 8 (3), available at: <http://www2.tku.edu.tw/ ti/Journal/8-3/831.pdf>.

Conti, Delia B. 1998. *Reconciling Free Trade, Fair Trade, and Interdependence: The Rhetoric of Presidential Economic Leadership*. Westport, CT: Praeger Publishers.

Cook, Malcolm. 2008. The United States and the East Asia Summit: Finding the Proper Home. *Contemporary Southeast Asia* 30 (2): 293–312.

Cumings, Bruce. 1997. Japan and Northeast Asia into the Twenty First Century. In *Network Power: Japan and Asia*, Peter J. Katzenstein and Takashi Shiraishi, eds. Ithaca, NY: Cornell University Press.

Destler, I.M. 2005. *American Trade Politics*, 4th ed. Washington, DC: Institute for International Economics Press.

Dieter, Heribert. 2009. Changing Patterns of Regional Governance: From Security to Political Economy? *Pacific Review* 22 (1): 73–90.

Goldstein, Avery. 2005. *Rising to the Challenge: China's Grand Strategy and International Security*. Stanford, CA: Stanford University Press.

Goldstein, Judith. 1988. Ideas, Institutions and American Trade Policy. *International Organization* 42 (1): 179–217.

Gowa, Joanne. 1995. *Allies, Adversaries, and International Trade*. Princeton, NJ: Princeton University Press.

Grieco, Joseph M. 1990. *Cooperation among Nations: Europe, America, and Non-tariff Barriers to Trade*. Ithaca, NY: Cornell University Press.

Hatch, Walter and Kozo Yamamura. 1996. *Asia in Japan's Embrace: Building a Regional Production Alliance*. Cambridge: Cambridge University Press.

Higgott, Richard. 2004. U.S. Foreign Policy and the "Securitization" of Economic Globalization. *International Politics* 41: 147–75.

Hund, Markus. 2003. ASEAN Plus Three: Towards a New Age of Pan-East Asian Regionalism? A Skeptic's Appraisal. *Pacific Review* 16 (3): 383–417.

Irwin, Douglas A. 1997. *Managed Trade: The Case against Import Targets*. Washington, DC: American Enterprise Institute Press.

Kim, Keeseok. 2010. How has Korea Imagined its Region? Asia-Pacific, Northeast Asia, and East Asia. *Korean Journal of International Studies* 50 (3): 73–110.

Koo, Min Gyo. 2009a. The Senkaku/Diaoyu Dispute and Sino–Japanese Political Economic Relations: Cold Politics and Hot Economics? *Pacific Review* 22 (2): 205–32.

———. 2009b. *Embracing Asia, South Korean Style: Preferential Trading Arrangements as Instruments of Foreign Policy*. EAI Issue Briefing No. MASI 2009–08, 11 November, available at: <http://www.eai.or.kr/data/bbs/eng_report/2009111215515244.pdf>.

———. 2010. Embracing Free Trade Agreements, Korean Style: From Developmental Mercantilism to Developmental Liberalism. *Korean Journal of Policy Studies* 25 (3): 101–23.

———. 2011. The U.S. Approaches to the Trade–Security Nexus in East Asia: From Securitization to Re-securitization. *Asian Perspective* 35 (1): 37–57.

Kwei, Elaine. 2006. Chinese Bilateralism: Politics Still in Command. In *Bilateral Trade Arrangements in the Asia-Pacific: Origins, Evolution, Implications*, Vinod K. Aggarwal and Shujiro Urata, eds. New York: Routledge.

Mochizuki, Mike M. 2009. Political-security Competition and the FTA Movement: Motivations and Consequences. In *Competitive Regionalism: FTA Diffusion in the Pacific Rim*, Mireya Solís et al. eds. New York: Palgrave Macmillan.

Moon, Chung-in. 2005. Community-building in Northeast Asia: A South Korean Perspective. Paper presented at the conference "Northeast Asia's New Institutional Architecture and Community-Building in a Post-9/11 World," Berkeley APEC Study Center, UC Berkeley, 11 December.

Moon, Chung-in and Sang-young Rhyu. 2010. Rethinking Alliance and the Economy: American Hegemony, Path Dependence, and the South Korean Political Economy. *International Relations of the Asia-Pacific* 10 (3): 441–64.

Moore, Thomas G. 2007. China's Rise in Asia: Regional Cooperation and Grand Strategy. In *The Evolution of Regionalism in Asia: Economic and Security Issues*, HeribertDieter, ed. London and New York: Routledge.

Pempel, T.J. 2008. *Exogenous Shocks and Endogenous Opportunities: The Economics–Security Tradeoff and Regionalism in East Asia. EAI Working Paper Series.* Seoul: East Asia Institute.

———. 2010. Soft Balancing, Hedging, and Institutional Darwinism: The Economic–Security Nexus and East Asian Regionalism. *Journal of East Asian Studies* 10: 209–38.

Presidential Committee on Northeast Asian Cooperation. 2004. *Toward a Peaceful and Prosperous Northeast Asia.* Seoul: Government of Republic of Korea.

Ravenhill, John. 2008. Asia's New Economic Institutions. In *Asia's New Institutional Architecture: Evolving Structures for Managing Trade, Financial, Security Relations,* Vinod K. Aggarwal and MinGyo Koo, eds. Berlin: Springer-Verlag.

Shambaugh, David. 2004. China Engages Asia: Reshaping the Regional Order. *International Security* 29 (3): 64–99.

Sohn, Yul and Min Gyo Koo. 2011. Securitizing Trade: The Case of the Korea–U.S. Free Trade Agreement. *International Relations of the Asia-Pacific* 11 (3): 433–60.

Solís, Mireya and Saori N. Katada. 2007. Understanding East Asian Cross-regionalism: An Analytical Framework. *Pacific Affairs* 80 (2): 229–58.

Stevenson, Richard W. 1997. U.S. Starts Trade Sanction Process against Koreans and 4 Others. *New York Times,* 2 October, available at: <http://www.nytimes.com/1997/10/02/business/us-starts-trade-sanction-process-against-koreans-and-4-others.html>.

Stubbs, Richard. 2002. ASEAN Plus Three: Emerging East Asian Regionalism? *Asian Survey* 42 (3): 440–55.

Terada, Takashi. 2010. The Origins of ASEAN+6 and Japan's Initiatives: China's Rise and the Agent–Structure Analysis. *Pacific Review* 23 (1): 71–92.

Tyson, Laura D'Andrea. 1990. Managed Trade: Making the Best of the Second Best. In *An American Trade Strategy: Options for the 1990s,* Rudiger W. Dornbusch *et al.* eds. Washington, DC: The Brookings Institution Press.

Webber, Douglas. 2001. Two Funerals and a Wedding? The Ups and Downs of Regionalism in East Asia and Asia-Pacific after the Asian Crisis. *Pacific Review* 14 (3): 339–72.

———. 2010. The Regional Integration that Didn't Happen: Cooperation without Integration in Early Twenty-first Century East Asia. *Pacific Review* 23 (3): 313–33.

White House. 2002. *The National Security Strategy of the United States of America.* Washington, DC: The While House, available at: <http://georgewbush-whitehouse.archives.gov/nsc/nss/2002/>.

Yahuda, Michael. 2005. Chinese Dilemmas in Thinking about Regional Security Architecture. *Pacific Review* 16 (2): 189–206.

Zoellick, Robert. 2001. Free Trade and Hemispheric Hope. Remarks before the Council of the Americas, Washington, DC, 7 May.

8 Regional institutions and the economic–security nexus

T.J. Pempel

Introduction

Formal multilateral regional institutions in Northeast Asia are rather recent phenomena. Moreover, until the late 1980s the few embryonic efforts at structured regional cooperation were rarely comprehensive in their memberships while remaining narrowly focused in their action agendas. Since the last years of the twentieth century, a number of bodies have been created that have more comprehensive memberships; however, most remain thinly institutionalized, narrowly specific in their agendas, and limited in their capacity to shape the policy choices of their members. Most importantly for the purposes of this volume, regional multilateral bodies have rarely been empowered to address issues in both the economic and security areas. Only recently have scholars begun to appreciate the potential for such regional institutions to exert much significant influence over the intersecting economic–security relationships in Northeast Asia (see, for example, Ravenhill 2009; Calder and Ye 2010; Pempel 2010).

This chapter examines how and why regional institutions have become more numerous and are playing a larger role in enhancing intra-regional cooperation economically and financially. Further, it examines the fact that while the ability of regional multilateral bodies to shape events on traditional hard security matters has admittedly been less impressive, even in hard security matters regional institutions have gained robustness and are beginning to find non-conflictual solutions to commonly perceived security dilemmas. Furthermore, the chapter argues, in keeping with the findings on the conflict-reducing tendencies and socializing capacity of institutions, the complex of regional bodies, including those with an explicitly economic mandate, is playing an enhanced role in softening many previously brittle state-to-state tensions throughout the region and helping to fuse states' conceptualization of the interactive links between economics and security.

At the same time, the regional institutional matrix in Northeast Asia continues to have what Peter Katzenstein (2005) has labeled "porous borders," that is, most Northeast Asian countries participate in a multitude of institutions whose memberships vary considerably. Some are narrowly inclusive of Northeast Asian states (such as the Trilateral Summit examined by Iida, Chapter 9, this volume, as well as here); others are predominantly Northeast Asian in membership (the Six Party Talks); still others (such as the ASEAN Plus Three) include states from both Northeast and Southeast Asia; while others (such as the Shanghai Cooperation Organization) include Northeast Asian states (such as China and Russia) but also have extra-regional members as core members, in this case four Central Asian republics.

To date, the regional institutions in which Northeast Asian states are engaged typically have agendas concretely devoted to either economics or security. Few bodies are empowered to address issues in both areas or to engage in explicit tradeoffs across these areas. For the most part, this dichotomy is the result of the different types of challenges that led to the creation of these discreet bodies. Virtually all of the new *economic* institutions represent collective regional responses to pressures from the *external* forces of globalized finance. These external forces have spawned a collective regional response. In contrast, security perceptions across Northeast Asia share few common visions concerning hard security threats. Instead, the military and defense views of most Northeast Asian states are shaped by regionally *endogenous* concerns—fears about one another—that have made any collective regional response far more problematic.

East Asian peace and increased economic ties

East Asia's experience over the last fifty or so years reflected a positive and rein-forcing spiral between the easing of security tensions and enhanced economic development, as was argued at length in Chapter 1. Resolution of a number of difficult security tensions created an initial climate that allowed national leaders to shift their focus to economic development and national economic successes. These, in turn, proved conducive to the subsequent rise in regional economic interdependence through cross-border investment, trade, and regional production networks (Ernst and Ravenhill 2000; Katzenstein and Shiraishi 1997, 2006; Pempel 2005, 2008b, 2008c; inter alia). As economic ties across the region flourished, they contributed to the region-wide reduction in security tensions and the growing commitments of most East Asian governments to concentrate policy attention to improving the economic well-being and wealth of their countries rather than biasing policy toward security dilemmas, enhanced military budgets, or the effort to gain contested territory from their neighbors. The collective pursuit of economic development has become an increasingly shared goal among most Northeast Asian governments just as growing cross-border economic ties have enhanced their levels of mutual interdependence (Steinfeld 2008). Security frictions have hardly disappeared, but many prior hot spots have been cooled and the probabilities of overt military conflicts across the region have been consequently reduced.

For the first quarter century following World War II, security tensions were particularly high across all of East Asia, while economic interactions were limited by the overall poverty of much of the region, sharp bipolar ideological divisions, bilateral alliances, and self-referential nationalism that was a logical response to the powerful legacy of colonialism. The region saw few moves toward significant cooperation in either the economic or military spheres. Such "cooperation" as did exist took the form primarily of bilateral alliances between the United States and a number of its allies along with parallel alliances between the Soviet Union and China and theirs. True, five Southeast Asian countries, downplaying their multiple security issues with one another, forged ASEAN as early as 1967 in a united front against the powers whose predacious military and diplomatic muscle they most feared. Such security cooperation and the defense it provided from intervention by larger powers such as the United States, China, or Russia, allowed ASEAN's members to focus increased attention and resources on fostering national economic development (Acharya 2001; Goh 2007–08; Ba 2009).

Counterpart countries in Northeast Asia however were neither invited to join ASEAN nor predisposed to take comparable actions of their own (Hemmer and Katzenstein 2002). There, Cold War divisions cleaved far deeper, excavating more formidable trenches of mutual isolation. These initially separated the pro-Western and pro-Communist regimes; even now they continue to divide the two governments on either side of the Taiwan Straits, they have left an ideological and political chasm that bifurcates the Korean Peninsula, and they contribute to a number of unresolved territorial issues. Nonetheless, as was noted in detail in Chapter 1, military shooting has essentially stopped in Northeast Asia since the time of the Korean Armistice, and Southeast Asia saw its last interstate war end as invading Vietnamese armies pulled out of Cambodia in 1982 (Acharya 2001: chap. 3; Alagappa 2003; Solingen 2007).

Northeast Asia continues to demonstrate a complex relationship between economics and security. Improved relations between the United States, Japan, and South Korea, on the one hand and the People's Republic of China (PRC) on the other gave a great boost to expanding economic links among them all. But equally, these relationships saw the reduction of some of the worst security tensions. The collapse of the Soviet Union further softened many longstanding security dilemmas. Since the early 1980s, Northeast Asian countries (with the conspicuous exception of the Democratic People's Republic of Korea (DPRK)) have generally enjoyed economic growth and expanded regional economic interdependence, in the process of which many of the worst sources of regional security tensions have become less acerbic.

Is this positive spiral irresistible? Has the momentum been such that the chances of its being reversed are low? That is far too teleologically linear and undoubtedly overly optimistic. Economic interdependence has indeed advanced in tandem with a general improvement in the security climate, but the march is pockmarked by periodic outbursts of nationalism, cross-border insults, and bombast, along with the occasional mobilization of military force. Yet economics and security have become increasingly closely linked in Northeast Asia, raising the prospects of some version of Kantian commercial peace. Certainly for the moment, the process of economic interdependence and the expansion of regionalized institutional cooperation appears likely to continue and in the process to contribute to the emerging and positive spiral between economic interdependence and reduced security tensions.

Economic regional institutionalization

Most East Asian governments played catalytic and nurturing roles in the sequence of national economic miracles that cascaded across the region (Johnson 1982; Amsden 1989; Woo 1991; Woo-Cumings 1999; inter alia). But these miracles became regional as well as nation-specific phenomena. The linkages of trade and foreign direct investment that have woven Northeast Asia's increasingly success-ful national economies together and created transnational production networks were fundamentally driven by corporate decisions rather than government dictates. Asian-based multinationals, driven fundamentally by business decisions rather than by politics, integrated themselves more efficiently into the global economy in part by forging closer ties within the East Asian region (Katzenstein and Shiraishi 1997; Pempel 1997; inter alia). In fact as John Ravenhill (2008: 43–4) has argued, the favorable East Asian economic and security climate allowed individual multi-national corporations to operate fluidly across national borders in ways that reduced, rather than accelerated, the temptation for businesses to pressure govern-ments to engage in formal mechanisms of cross-border cooperation. As a result, with the already mentioned exception of sub-regional ASEAN, East Asia, includ-ing Northeast Asia, even up to the end of the Cold War saw far more cross-border linkages through bottom-up and corporate-driven connections than through top-down and government-sponsored institutions (Pempel 2005).

The cumulative effect of such corporate actions was a substantial increase in cross-border production, which in turn has generated the enhanced intra-Asian trade and the deeper regional interdependence as was noted in Chapter 1. By 2011, intra-Asian trade had risen to 56 percent of total Asian trade, a figure close to that of the European Union, while Northeast Asian reliance on the previously dominant U.S. market had been steadily on the decline. Economic interdepend-ence among Japan, China, Taiwan, and the Republic of Korea has grown exponentially. China is now the number one trading partner for all three of the others and burgeoning levels of cross-border investment flow among all of these Northeast Asian economies. Their expanding and interconnected economic link-ages have forged a latticework driven, as noted, less by governments and far more by the commercial activities of transnational firms and investors.

This pattern of mutually-reinforcing market and corporate-driven ties, links to global economic institutions, and minimal governmentally-created regional insti-tutions was challenged by the Asian economic crisis of 1997–98 (Pempel 1999). Prevailing patterns of economic development in many countries of East Asia (most notably South Korea, Indonesia, Thailand, Malaysia, and the Philippines) proved highly vulnerable to extra-regional shocks while internal banking and monetary deficiencies in many East Asian states became nakedly apparent (Hamilton-Hart 2008).

The few rather weak regional bodies in existence at the time of the crisis demonstrated neither the willingness nor the capacity to stem its spread. Both ASEAN and Asia-Pacific Economic Cooperation (APEC) proved feckless as the currencies of several East Asian countries collapsed in the face of concerted speculative attacks. APEC had already begun to lose some of its early luster as U.S. policymakers grappled with the failure of the Early Voluntary Sector Liberalization (EVSL) process they had hoped would open Japanese agricultural markets to American exports (Webber 2001; Krauss 2004). APEC's economic marginalization was furthered by what Richard Higgott (2004) has called the George W. Bush administration's strong-armed efforts to "securitize" economic globalization. At Bush's behest, APEC was pressed to compromise its original economic focus in favor of taking a collective stand in support of the so-called global war on terror.

Japan made an effort to organize collective regional financial assistance to the most deeply troubled countries with its proposal for an Asian Monetary Fund (AMF) (Amyx 2004). Perceived by the United States and the IMF as an action independent of, and challenging to, the IMF and by China as a potential boost to Japan's regional influence, the AMF confronted blistering U.S., Chinese, and IMF opposition and Japan quickly withdrew its proposal. By not engaging in competitive devaluation of its own currency, China emerged from the crisis as something of a backstage regional hero. But the crisis quickly telegraphed to many East Asian elites the collective message that "free markets" could be devastating to their domestic economic agendas, exposing highly vulnerable markets and national currencies to vast quantities of speculative and rapidly moving "hot money" (Winters 1999). Such globalized free markets provided a powerful exogenous shock that stimulated a series of common intra-regional responses.

After Thailand, Indonesia, and South Korea, lacking any viable alternative, were forced to comply with the heavily criticized terms that came with their IMF rescue packages, widespread resentment swept the region against what was seen as the West's and the IMF's doctrinaire adherence to a particular version of capitalism. Regional players saw what they perceived as a short-term currency crisis treated by the United States and the IMF as a series of structural examples of "crony capitalism" that needed correction and that simultaneously provided the West with an opportunity to push their specific interpretations of globalization and thereby to gain easy access to the most economically dynamic region of the world (Higgott 1998; Pempel 1999).

In the aftermath of the crisis, the governments of Asia took a number of steps to forge new institutions that would deepen their regional ties, supplementing, although not bypassing, existing global multilateral fora.

The result was a burst of collective activity across East Asia seeking to develop deeper, more formalized, and more "Asians only" institutional arrangements— well short of the institutionalized levels of bodies found in the European Union, but vastly more comprehensive than what had existed before the crisis. The governments of East Asia initiated an array of new actions designed to take greater control of their (and the region's) foreign economic policies. These represent what I have elsewhere called (2008c) governmental efforts to erect "firewalls" against the forces of unbridled marketization and globalization. Formal institutions were one major response. Regional ties in East Asia ceased to be the exclusive byproducts of bottom-up market connections, nor were they any longer automatically embedded in the pan-Pacific orientation reflected in APEC. Instead, following the crisis, East Asian governments actively embraced an enhanced and integrative regional latticework driven predominantly by Northeast and Southeast Asian governments (MacIntyre *et al.* 2008).

Initially the incentive for creation fell to ASEAN, most notably with the formation of ASEAN Plus Three (APT), a process that began in mid-1995. Starting in 1997, the ASEAN governments pressed to heighten APT's independent role, expanding it from a series of meetings among senior officials to include a meeting of finance and economic ministers and eventually to a more institutionalized set of links with their major northern neighbors that culminated in an annual meeting of heads of state. This thirteen-nation summit has since become a major engine for cooperation on a variety of regional problems, particularly in finance.

As Kim (2004: 35) has argued, APT represents a collective East Asian "search for new and better ways of managing the forces of globalization to the region's advantage by combining the resources of Northeast Asia and Southeast Asia." Since its creation, APT has provided a convenient regional forum within which various combinations of countries could work out particular bilateral problems as well as enter into other cooperative arrangements.

ASEAN was able to take the lead in the APT primarily because of the continued national rivalries and security competition in Northeast Asia. But APT was also an important cog in what Evelyn Goh (2007–08: 121) has labeled "omni enmeshment," namely a Southeast Asian effort to entice its Northeast Asian neighbors into a series of formal institutions and governmental processes. And as Jones and Smith (2007: 152–3) have rightly pointed out in contrast to the predictions of realism, "a shared sense of weakness rather than strength facilitated ASEAN's capacity to transform the regional order," leading to a discourse that was "conducted according to the nonlegalistic, consensus-oriented ASEAN way that represented a distinctive alternative to European styles of diplomacy..."

Of particular note for Northeast Asia, the "plus three" countries, Japan, the Republic of Korea (ROK), and the PRC, have, since first agreeing to do so in October 2003, typically met together for trilateral discussions on the sidelines of the formal meetings. After many such sideline meetings, the "plus three" eventually agreed to hold a leaders' meeting outside the APT framework. The first of these took place in Fukuoka, Japan, in December 2008. Since then the three have met annually, established a secretariat in Seoul, and begun negotiations on a trilateral free trade agreement and a common investment treaty (Pempel 2010; Iida, Chapter 9, this volume). More will be said about this Trilateral Summit below.

APT has moved more concretely to institutionalize and deepen facets of East Asia's interdependence. One of the first new moves was the Chiang Mai Initiative (CMI) of 6 May 2000, begun under the auspices of the APT. CMI expanded existing ASEAN currency swap arrangements and added a network of bilateral swaps among the ASEAN countries, China, Japan, and the ROK. These were to provide emergency liquidity in the event of any future crisis (Pempel 2005; Grimes 2006; Amyx 2008). Though initially criticized as involving only limited amounts of money and requiring that most swaps be congruent with IMF regulations, the original web of bilateral swap agreements has been continually expanded so that as of this writing some $120 billion is committed. In addition, in 2007 an agreement was reached to multilateralize the CMI by creating a collective pool of funds and a single contractual agreement to draw on them. Such an arrangement would transform the series of bilateral swaps into a single reserve fund with a centralized and multilateralized arrangement. China, Japan, and Korea have additionally provided technical assistance and training for the monitoring of capital flows to other Asian countries (Hamilton-Hart 2008: 120), moving East Asia as a region toward a more common technical framework in finance, with the richer Northeast Asian governments becoming collectively the primary lenders of first resort.

An important arrangement was reached among China, Japan, and the ROK concerning the multilateralization of CMI. Both Japan and China sought the prestige of being the largest donor and the country thereby entitled to the largest share of intra-CMIM voting power. The eventual compromise that was struck, driven primarily by South Korea, allowed both to claim a symbolic victory. Japan contributes 32 percent of the funds while China plus Hong Kong contributes an equal 32 percent, allowing Japan and "greater China" to each claim the number one spot. Korea meanwhile gained the right to a 16 percent share (one half of either of the co-number ones). That such a compromise could be brokered to mutual satisfaction unquestionably has a political and symbolic impact well beyond that of the financial arena.

Asian governments have also moved to create bond markets denominated in local currencies. The more advanced economies, largely those in Northeast Asia, have developed an enriched Asian Bond Fund through the regional central banks, while the CMI has also pushed a separate Asian Bond Market Initiative (ABMI). Combined, these two efforts offer another mechanism to enhance regional financial collaboration that is likely to reduce Asian dependence on the U.S. dollar for financial reserves, currency baskets, and international transactions. Important components include a local-currency bond market with a regional clearing and settlement system, a bond-rating agency, a trading system, and other sophisticated features (Grimes 2006; Pempel 2005, 2006a). Asian borrowers will avoid the "double mismatch" problem that arose in 1997–98, that is, borrowing short in foreign currency (mostly dollars) and lending long in domestic currencies. Local currency bond markets would also reduce Asia's vulnerability to U.S. abuse of its position as the issuer of the world's most popular currency.

As Kahler and Lake (2006) point out, regional governmental cooperation continues to lag behind burgeoning corporate linkages. National rivalries, especially in Northeast Asia, continue in economics (not simply in security). Thus most Asian governments, and in particular the four largest economies of Northeast Asia, have aggressively accumulated gargantuan war chests of foreign reserves. By the middle of 2011, their collective reserves had expanded to more than US$ 4 trillion, constituting two-thirds of the world total and more than triple the roughly $1 trillion in 2001. While these accumulations may be viewed as "wasted" capital by neoclassical economists, they have a powerful regional as well as global impact. At the same time, these enhanced foreign reserves have given the Northeast Asian countries a greater collective influence over global credit markets as well as IMF voting power. And the combined buildup enhances the credibility of the Chiang-Mai Initiative and its subsequent multilateralization (CMIM) in the event of future currency crises.

In addition, most of the governments in the region have, since about 2001–02, become active promoters of bilateral and multilateral Free Trade Agreements (FTAs) or Economic Partnership Agreements (EPAs) (Dent 2003; Grimes 2006; Aggarwal and Koo 2008; Amyx 2004, 2008; Pempel 2005, 2008b, 2008c). Virtually non-existent in Asia at the time of the crisis, such trade pacts have quickly become a favored state instrument designed to improve intra-regional trade ties while exerting national influence over trade policies in ways not dependent on the now failed negotiations in the WTO's Doha Round. They provide a regionally anchored counterweight to the global WTO. Not all of these are intra-regional and many form webs of trade arrangements that span the globe.

One of China's most important successes in utilizing its economic power to advance its regional agenda came with its proposal during the 2000 ASEAN Summit for an ASEAN–China FTA. Psychologically, the proposal bolstered the perception that China's rise might generate a win-win economic cooperation with Southeast Asia in what would potentially be a market of some 1.7 billion people. Importantly, Chinese negotiators offered an "early harvest" of lower tariffs for agricultural exports from Southeast Asia to China. With agricultural exports so critical to the growth strategies of most countries in Southeast Asia, particularly ASEAN's newer members, the Chinese move was particularly deft politically. ASEAN trade with China jumped almost 60 percent in 2005 over 2004 due largely to the "early harvest" (Weatherbee 2006: 275). China's moves spurred competitive reactions by Japan and the ROK, though ultimately both were more constrained than China by the extent to which their democratic political systems could constrain the utilization of governmental strategies on trade liberalization as a political tool.

To date, none of these FTAs link the most powerful economies of Northeast Asia to one another, but as noted above the "Plus Three" countries are now exploring a trilateral FTA that, if implemented, could be the largest single agreement in existence and would surely contribute to further institutionalization of the existing trade links being developed in Northeast Asia.

In short, within the economic and financial sphere, post-crisis Asia has moved to expand and deepen both its regional institutions and the actions of its governments in currency and trade protection. None have yet posed any direct challenges either to global institutions such as the World Bank, the IMF, or the WTO (although see Oba, Chapter 6, this volume). Nor have they replaced many of the bilateral security and economic arrangements that continue to keep the United States deeply enmeshed in the region. What they have done is to construct an additional layer of regional fora between national and global institutions that foster primarily greater East Asian interdependence, as well as giving those governments enhanced leverage vis-à-vis the sweeping processes of American-driven financial and trade globalization. And not insignificantly, they demonstrate an expanding network of institutions that bind the Northeast Asian economies more formally to one another, as well as between themselves and Southeast Asia. These pan-Asian moves aimed largely against perceived threats from Western-dominated globalized economic thrusts, however, have not been matched by similar moves in the security arena.

Security: flirting with institutionalized cooperation?

Not surprisingly, the end of the Cold War saw a flurry of predictions that the longstanding tensions in Asia would resurface, making the region a hotbed of rivalries (see Buzan and Segal 1994; Friedberg 1993, 2011). Certain recent events are compatible with these predictions.

Across the region, despite the growth in economic linkages and the formation of economically-focused regional bodies, security tensions in Northeast Asia remain high. No potential hard security challenge poses a more widespread concern than the rise of China and its potential long-term implications. For the first thirty years of its economic modernization, Chinese leaders devoted their principal attention to infrastructure development and exportable, labor-intensive products. This approach was accompanied by a generic "charm offensive" (Kurlantzick 2007), designed to convince its neighbors that China's rise would be peaceful and devoid of any fundamental challenge to the status quo. Yet China has been expanding its military budget at rates faster than its growth in GDP, and it has made significant steps toward a blue-water navy, in space technologies, and in the capacity for cyber-warfare. Such developments, along with an increased assertiveness in Chinese diplomatic and political actions, particularly since early 2010, have exacerbated concerns that military and territorial expansion as well as a challenge to the regional status quo will be forthcoming (Mearsheimer 2001; Shambaugh 2006; Friedberg 2011).

Furthermore, North Korea has been a security thorn in the region's side particularly since it renounced the Nuclear Non-proliferation Treaty, restarted its pluto-nium production, began re-launching long-range missiles, carried out two nuclear tests, and announced that it was developing a highly enriched uranium project that could be used for weapons production over and above its already-demon-strated plutonium capabilities. Even though all parties are nominally committed to the denuclearization of the Korean Peninsula and to encouraging the greater economic integration of the DPRK into the success story of the region as a whole, Japan, China, the United States, Russia, and the ROK all have strongly different priorities regarding the DPRK.

Meanwhile, Japan has tiptoed away from its once "defensive defense" posture, taking on a more active and geographically broader military role, including what Christopher Hughes (2009) has called the "super-sizing" of the DRPK's military threat (see also Soeya 2005; Pempel 2007; Pyle 2007; Samuels 2007; inter alia).

Cross-Straits relations were tense following the election of an independence-minded Democratic Progressive Party (DPP) government in 2000 and China's retaliatory passage of a law threatening military action to prevent Taiwanese separation in March 2005. The combination fueled intense security fears across much of the region. Only with the election of Ma Ying Jeou did bilateral tensions soften and economic and commercial ties grow even deeper, most notably with the 2010 signing of the Economic Cooperation and Free Trade Agreement (ECFA).

Elsewhere, territorial squabbles periodically exacerbate certain already fractious bilateral relationships: Japan and the ROK over Dokdo/Takeshima, Japan and Russia over the Kuriles, China and Japan over the Senkaku/Daioyu islands as well as explorations in what each claims as its "exclusive economic zone," China and Korea over Koguryo, and of course the unresolved cross-Straits problem.

Clearly, a vast number of endogenous security threats exist across Northeast Asia. Not surprisingly, such intra-regional divisiveness has greatly impeded the creation of regional institutional bodies comparable to even the embryonic moves at fostering cross-border cooperation in economics and finance. Instead, Northeast Asian security remains heavily defined by bilateral alliances in place since the early years of the Cold War—America's bilateral ties with Japan, the ROK, and less formally its support for Taiwan on the one hand, and the China–DPRK alliance on the other, along with residual China–Russia and Russia–DPRK cooperative arrangements.

The one formal regional body that has sought to subdue intra-regional conflicts though regularized meetings has been the ASEAN Regional Forum (ARF). Behind ASEAN, Southeast Asia moved substantially closer to becoming a security community than did Northeast Asia (Acharya 2001; Buzan 2003). The ARF was formed in 1994 and today has 27 nations as members. It meets annually but has proven to be of limited security effectiveness, largely because of strong resistance by many of its members against it engaging in either preventive diplomacy or conflict prevention. Instead the bulk of ARF's activities involve merely confidence building measures (CBMs) and little by way of preventive diplomacy or conflict resolution. Yet the ASEAN experience has resonated in Northeast Asia in many ways, including participation in the ARF and the fact that China, Japan, and South Korea (along with Australia, New Zealand, India, Russia, and the United States) have all agreed to the Treaty of Amity and Cooperation, which commits signatories to the peaceful resolution of all interstate conflicts.

One of the more interesting and complicating formal regional bodies with an explicit security focus created since the end of the Cold War is the Shanghai Cooperation Organization (SCO) which brings together China, Russia, and four Central Asian republics (that is, six non-democracies) in a regional body that has occasionally been dubbed an "anti-NATO." The SCO has an economic agenda on compatible developmental cooperation, energy exploration, and intra-national security (mostly aimed at preventing ethnically-driven separatist movements). The SCO remains the only regional institution in East Asia to have conducted collaborative military exercises. The SCO has quite obviously done nothing to reduce any security fears in Japan or South Korea, despite whatever it may do to foster cooperation among its own members. Indeed, while it reduces tensions and fosters cooperation among its six members, it simultaneously exacerbates the longstanding Cold War-based security dilemmas in Northeast Asia.

At the same time, Northeast Asia has seen three additional multilateral bodies that cut across longstanding lines of cleavage in their memberships and that have at least the potential to deal with endogenous security problems: 1) the Six Party Talks; 2) the East Asia Summit; and 3) the Trilateral Summit among Japan, China, and South Korea, mentioned above.

The one endogenous security problem around which a regional institution (or process) has in fact been created is the Six Party Talks (6PT), aimed at dealing with the rising nuclear tensions on the Korean Peninsula. This is not the place to rehash the tensions that led to the creation of the 6PT (see Funabashi 2007; Chinoy 2008; Pempel 2008a; inter alia). After an initial October 2002 U.S.–DPRK confrontation over whether or not the North was adhering to its promises under the 1994 Framework Agreement, the DPRK left the APT, ended the International Atomic Energy Agency (IAEA) inspections, and began a rapid-fire program of both missile and nuclear testing (Pritchard 2007). In combination, these events exacerbated security anxieties across Northeast Asia. Roughly two years of mutual recriminations between the United States and the DPRK eventually led to the process now known as the Six Party Talks. These ushered in a new multilateral process that involved the two Koreas, the United States, Japan, China, and Russia. China has chaired the talks from the start. Addressing the problem through this new mechanism was a signal victory for multilateralism over bilateralism in Northeast Asian security and initially appeared to hold out the prospect of a "concert of regional powers" being formed.

For roughly two years, the talks made little progress, serving instead as a platform for rhetorical mudslinging and temperamental posturing, particularly by the United States and the DPRK. Conditions changed in early July 2006 after the DPRK tested a series of missiles. The result was a strong UN Security Council resolution of condemnation. On 9 October, the DPRK carried out an actual nuclear test followed in less than a week by an even stronger UN Security Council condemnatory resolution (Resolution 1718).

An important breakthrough took place when the United States agreed to meet with DPRK negotiators in bilateral talks *outside* the official Beijing framework, specifically in Berlin in January 2007. The 6PT resumed on 8 February 2007 and a major statement was issued on 13 February, which was largely a reformulation of an earlier September 2005 agreement; both statements had the core elements of any final deal.

The main outlines of the proposed framework involved four central points: 1) the verifiable and peaceful denuclearization of the Korean Peninsula; 2) a return by the DPRK to the Non-proliferation Treaty (NPT) and the IAEA inspection regime; 3) guarantees by the United States not to attack the DPRK, respect for its sovereignty, and the commitment to negotiate a permanent peace regime on the peninsula; and 4) the promotion by all six parties of economic cooperation on a bilateral and multilateral basis.[1]

The agreements managed to fuse several key elements of economics and security. Most importantly, a central objective of any security and peace mechanism for Northeast Asia was to alleviate the DPRK's security fears of "regime change" while making efforts to convince the DPRK regime to integrate itself more fully into the regional economy and to give greater focus to its own economic growth and less to military prowess. As was noted in the section on economics, it is naïve to assume that greater economic interactions alone will eliminate or greatly reduce diplomatic and security differences. But East Asia as a region has demonstrated the ability of its decades-long concentration on rapid economic transformation and improved living standards for its citizens to mitigate some of the region's most extreme security dilemmas. To hold out such a vision of growth and regional economic integration before the DPRK's leaders was presumed to be a powerful motivation—at least for some of the country's leaders—toward changed behavior and closer ties with the immediate neighborhood.

In 2008, however, the 6PT hit a major roadblock, the causes of which are anchored in competing national interests and mutual recriminations about failure to follow through on alleged commitments made in the 2007 agreement. The death of Kim Jong-il further delayed any chance of resuming the talks. As a consequence, the 6PT remain stalled as of mid-2012.

Certainly, the 6PT still hold the prospect of becoming a non-trivial move toward regional security multilateralism. The 6PT was directed less at creating a security community to withstand or offset some external threat, but rather to provide a "community" approach to intra-regional security threats, in this case, the North Korean nuclear buildup and the danger that it might unleash a region-wide arms race, including possibly nuclear proliferation. The Six Party process—and potentially any that might follow in its (if successful) footsteps—promises a protective umbrella under which member states could deal with outstanding issues either on a multilateral or bilateral basis. Also, as students of such organizations have long pointed out, it could provide a potentially powerful mechanism by which to socialize its members into common patterns of conduct and collaborative norms, the end result of which would potentially involve greater understanding of competing national motivations and ideally, reduced security tension and the possibilities of overt conflict (Wendt 1999; Acharya 2001; inter alia).

A second body worth noting is the East Asia Summit (EAS), begun in 2005, originally with the 13 APT members plus Australia, India, and New Zealand. This was one of the first regional bodies involving all of the major Northeast Asian states (Taiwan, not recognized as a state, is not a member) that had a mandate that included both economics and security. Indeed, the EAS is charged with considering economic cooperation and development along with diplomacy and security, as well as issues such as the environment, pandemics, education, and cultural exchange (ASEAN Secretariat 2005; Cody 2005). With the inclusion of the United States and Russia in 2010, the EAS has at least the potential to be another regional institution buffering intra-regional and/or bilateral security divisions.

Finally, the Trilateral Summits should be noted as another potential regional multilateral body with security potential. While not explicitly focused on security, the summits have allowed these three erstwhile security competitors to address, as they have on numerous occasions, their respective security concerns. Starting with the first meeting independent of the APT, the leaders of the three countries have met annually. These meetings led to promises to cooperate on outstanding security issues (Calder and Ye 2010; Iida, Chapter 9, this volume) and following the 2010 meeting the three created a secretariat in Korea and agreed to move toward a common investment treaty as well as a trilateral free trade agreement. As of this writing these moves are being pushed forward.

Of particular interest in these Trilateral Summits is that despite short-term diplomatic and geopolitical tensions among the three, such as the China–Japan confrontation over the Senkaku/Daioyu, the Japan–ROK tensions over Dokdo/Takeshima, or Japanese history texts, the trilateral meetings have typically gone on as scheduled. This suggests that all three countries, rather than using the trilateral meetings as a bargaining chip on such other issues, have a sufficient commitment to their value to ensure that they not be held hostage to, or cancelled because of, other dyadic disputes.

Institutional linkages: hope for reduction of security tensions?

The 6PT, the SCO, the EAS, and the Trilateral Summits all constitute non-trivial moves toward security multilateralism that bring together highly contentious parties, although with very different targets and quite different implications for global security relations. These institutions are not directed specifically at creating an instrumental security community to withstand or offset some external threat, let alone a Grotian community designed to advance a broadly common agenda (see Alagappa 2003). Instead these bodies seek to respond collectively to specific intraregional security challenges—North Korea in the case of the 6PT; separatism and terrorism for the SCO; virtually any security challenge perceived by any one of the Trilateral Summit participants. In all cases the regional bodies cut across prior lines of hard security division and seek to foster at least a mini-concert of powers.

When these security bodies are considered in combination with the bodies taking up region-wide issues of financial integration and regulation, currency protection, and the use of regional capital to support regional development projects, it is clear that a number of relatively new regional bodies are cutting across traditional lines of security division in ways that hold the potential for substantial reductions in tensions and the likelihood of overtly hostile military conflicts.

East Asia's institutional pattern has been a helter-skelter bevy of organizational forms, separate institutional targets, and both overlapping and conflicting membership and institutions that are typically highly constrained in their ability to act. Yet comparative analysis has shown that institutions can evolve over time in both purpose and power (Thelen 2004; Streeck and Thelen 2005) in the process acquiring a prevailing role as the structurer of members' interactions (see North 1990; Steinmos *et al.* 1992). Further, as Yoram Haftel's research (2007) has demonstrated, the combination of economic interdependence and regular meetings among high-level officials has proven to be a powerful combination in mitigating violent conflict among states (see also Pempel 2010).

Despite the limited success of many East Asian multilateral bodies, the very fact of meeting regularly, searching for areas of agreement, and developing patterns of cooperation and trust are all possible outcomes of "institutionalizing cooperation." To the extent that current problems can be resolved, the opportunities and the mutual trust needed to address different and additional problems, whether regional or bilateral, go up. The early ASEAN and the Organization for Security and Cooperation in Europe (OSCE) experiences reinforce this point. Importantly, ASEAN, the ARF, the 6PT, and the SCO also provide powerful mechanisms for the socialization of members into common patterns of conduct and collaborative norms, the end result of which potentially is greater understanding of competing national motivations and, eventually, reduced conflict. Many (Acharya 2001; Buzan 2003; Johnston 2003) have provided compelling evidence that the socialization of originally skeptical members has been a tangible benefit of various multilateral bodies in East Asia.

Furthermore, institutions promise the possibility of spillovers from one functional area to another as it becomes clear to participants that problems in one area cannot be satisfactorily resolved without addressing problems in cognate areas. Certainly East Asia's now-multiple trilateral bodies are being driven by efforts to solve a bevy of functionally different issues and retain the possibility for various fusions and tradeoffs across economic and security issues.

The hope is that East Asia's current state of numerous institutions advancing diverse goals and exercising limited power will evolve over time toward greater institutional consolidation, enhanced member trust, and greater robustness in institutional power. It is apparent that most of these new regional bodies are attempting to tackle shared issues from a regional perspective, even as they contend with nationally-specific and often contradictory agendas by member states. To the extent that such bodies can prove their usefulness, the states of Northeast Asia may well find in them the basis for enhanced mutual trust and increased use of such bodies for further problem-solving, including the possibility that issues normally seen as the responsibility of one institution or another will increasingly spill over to foster solutions involving cooperation in other areas. In such a way, issues of economics and security could well become increasingly interwoven and subject to cross-issue tradeoffs in ways that enhance the currently positive climate in economics and generate a more positive security environment.

Note

1. Full statements and details are on the U.S. State Department's website at <http://www.state.gov/r/pa/prs/ps/2007/february/80479.htm> and <http://www.state.gov/r/pa/prs/ps/2007/february/80479.htm>.

References

Acharya, Amitav. 2001. *Constructing a Security Community in Southeast Asia: ASEAN and the Problem of Regional Order*. London: Routledge.
Aggarwal, Vinod K. and Min Gyo Koo, eds. 2008. *Asia's New Institutional Architecture: Evolving Structures for Managing Trade, Financial, and Security Relations*. Berlin: Springer-Verlag.

Alagappa, Muthiah, ed. 2003. *Asian Security Order: Instrumental and Normative Features*. Stanford, CA: Stanford University Press.

Amsden, Alice M. 1989. *Asia's Next Giant: South Korea and Late Industrialization*. Oxford: Oxford University Press.

Amyx, Jennifer. 2004. Japan and the Evolution of Regional Financial Arrangements in East Asia. In *Beyond Bilateralism: US–Japan Relations in the New Asia-Pacific*, Ellis S. Krauss and T. J. Pempel, eds. Stanford, CA: Stanford University Press.

———. 2008. Stocktaking on Regional Financial Initiatives among the ASEAN+3. In *Crisis as Catalyst: The Dynamics of the East Asian Political Economy*, Andrew MacIntyre, T.J. *et al.* eds. Ithaca, NY: Cornell University Press.

ASEAN Secretariat. 2005. Available at: <http://www.aseansec.org/18098.htm>.

Ba, Alice. 2009. *[Re]Negotiating East and Southeast Asia: Region, Regionalism, and the Association of Southeast Asian Nations*. Stanford, CA: Stanford University Press.

Buzan, Barry. 2003. Security Architecture in Asia: The Interplay of Regional and Global Levels. *Pacific Review* 16 (2): 143–73.

Buzan, Barry and Gerald Segal. 1994. Rethinking East Asian Security. *Survival* 36 (2): 3–21.

Calder, Kent and Min Ye. 2010. *The Making of Northeast Asia*. Stanford, CA: Stanford University Press.

Chinoy, Mike. 2008. *Meltdown: The Inside Story of the North Korean Nuclear Crisis*. New York: St. Martin's Press.

Cody, E. 2005. Asian Leaders Establish New Group. *Washington Post* 15 December, A25, available at: <www.washingtonpost.com/wpdyn/content/article/2005/12/14>.

Dent, C.M. 2003. Networking the Region? The Emergence and Impact of Asia-Pacific Bilateral Trade Agreement Projects. *Pacific Review* 16 (1): 1–28.

Ernst, Dieter and John Ravenhill. 2000. Convergence and Diversity: How Globalization Reshapes Asian Production Networks. In *International Production Networks in Asia: Rivalry or Riches?* M. Borrus *et al.*, eds. London: Routledge.

Friedberg, Aaron. 1993. Ripe for Rivalry: Prospects for Peace in a Multipolar Asia. *International Security* 18 (3): 5–33.

———. 2011. *A Contest for Supremacy: China, America, and the Struggle for Mastery in Asia*. New York: W.W. Norton.

Funabashi, Yoichi. 2007. *The Peninsula Question: A Chronicle of the Second Korean Nuclear Crisis*. Washington, DC: Brookings Institution.

Goh, Evelyn. 2007–08. Great Powers and Hierarchical Order in Southeast Asia. *International Security* 32 (3): 113–57.

Grimes, William W. 2006. East Asian Financial Regionalism in Support of the Global Financial Architecture? The Political Economy of Regional Nesting. *Journal of East Asian Studies* 6: 353–80.

Haftel, Yoram Z. 2007. Designing for Peace: Regional Integration Arrangements, Institutional Variation, and Militarized Interstate Disputes. *International Organization* 61: 217–37.

Hamilton-Hart, Natasha. 2008. Financial Cooperation and Domestic Political Economy in East Asia. In *Advancing East Asia Regionalism*, Melissa G. Curley and Nicholas Thomas, eds. London and New York: Routledge.

Hemmer, Christopher and Peter J. Katzenstein. 2002. Why is there No NATO in Asia? Collective Identity, Regionalism, and the Origins of Multilateralism. *International Organization* 56 (3): 575–608.

Higgott, Richard A. 1998. The Asian Economic Crisis: A Study in the Politics of Resentment. *New Political Economy* 4 (1) 333–56.

———. 2004. U.S. Foreign Policy and the "Securitization" of Economic Globalization. *International Politics* 41: 147–75.

Hughes, Christopher. 2009. "Super-Sizing" the DPRK Threat: Japan's Evolving Military Posture and North Korea. *Asian Survey* 49 (2): 291–311.

Johnson, Chalmers. 1982. *MITI and the Japanese Miracle*. Stanford, CA: Stanford University Press.

Johnston, Ian. 2003. Socialization in International Institutions: The ASEAN Way and International Relations Theory. In *International Relations Theory and the Asia Pacific*, G. John Ikenberry and Michael Mastanduno, eds. New York: Columbia University Press.

Jones, David Martin and Michael L.R. Smith. 2007. Making Process, Not Progress: ASEAN and the Evolving East Asian Regional Order. *International Security* 32 (1): 148–84.

Kahler, Miles and David A. Lake. 2006. Economic Integration and Global Governance: Why So Little Supranationalism? Paper prepared for the Workshop on Explaining Global Regulation. University College, University of Oxford, 20–21 October.

Katzenstein, Peter J. 2005. *A World of Regions: Asia and Europe in the American Imperium*. Ithaca, NY: Cornell University Press.

Katzenstein, Peter J. and Takashi Shiraishi. 1997. *Network Power*. Ithaca, NY: Cornell University Press.

———. 2006. *Beyond Japan: The Dynamics of East Asian Regionalism*. Ithaca, NY: Cornell University Press.

Kim, Samuel S., ed. 2004. *The International Relations of Northeast Asia*. Lanham, MD: Rowman & Littlefield.

Krauss, Ellis S. 2004. The United States and Japan in APEC's EVSL Negotiations: Regional Multilateralism and Trade. In *Beyond Bilateralism: U.S.–Japan Relations in the New Asia-Pacific*, Ellis S. Krauss and T.J. Pempel, eds. Stanford, CA: Stanford University Press.

Kurlantzick, Joshua. 2007. *Charm Offensive: How China's Soft Power is Transforming the World*. New Haven, CT: Yale University Press.

MacIntyre, Andrew, T.J. Pempel, and John Ravenhill. 2008. Conclusion. In *East Asia: Coping with the Crisis*, Andrew MacIntyre *et al.*, eds. Ithaca, NY: Cornell University Press.

Mearsheimer, John J. 2001. *The Tragedy of Great Power Politics*. New York: W.W. Norton.

North, Douglass. 1990. *Institutions, Institutional Change and Economic Performance*, Cambridge: Cambridge University Press.

Pempel, T.J. 1997. Transpacific Torii: Japan and the Emerging Asian Regionalism. In *Network Power*, Peter J. Katzenstein and Shiraishi Takashi, eds. Ithaca, NY: Cornell University Press.

———. 1999. *The Politics of the Asian Economic Crisis*. Ithaca, NY: Cornell University Press.

———. 2005. *Remapping East Asia: The Construction of a Region*. Ithaca, NY: Cornell University Press.

———. 2006a. The Race to Connect East Asia: An Unending Steeplechase. *Asian Economic Policy Review* 2 (autumn): 239–54.

———. 2006b. Japanese Policy under Koizumi. In *Strategic Thinking in Japan*, Gilbert Rozman, ed. London: Routledge.

————. 2007. Japanese Strategy under Koizumi. In *Japanese Strategic Thought toward Asia*, Gilbert Rozman *et al.*, eds. New York: Palgrave.

————. 2008a. Japan: Divided Government; Diminished Resources. In *Strategic Asia 2007–2008: What the Next President Should Know about Asia*, Ashley Tellis and Mercy Kuo, eds. Washington, DC: National Bureau of Asian Research.

————. 2008b. Restructuring Regional Ties. In *Crisis as Catalyst: The Dynamics of the East Asian Political Economy*, Andrew MacIntyre *et al.*, eds. Ithaca, NY: Cornell University Press.

————. 2008c. Firebreak: East Asia Institutionalizes its Finances. In *Institutionalizing Northeast Asia: Making the Impossible Possible?* Martina Timmermann and Jitsuo Tsuchiuyama, eds. Tokyo: United Nations University Press.

————. 2010. Soft Balancing, Hedging, and Institutional Darwinism: The Economic–Security Nexus and East Asian Regionalism. *Journal of East Asian Studies* 10: 209–38.

Pierson, Paul. 2000. The Limits of Design: Explaining Institutional Origins and Design. *Governance* 13 (4): 475–99.

————. 2004. *Politics in Time*. Princeton, NJ: Princeton University Press.

Pritchard, Charles L. 2007. *Failed Diplomacy: The Tragic Story of How North Korea Got the Bomb*. Washington, DC: Brookings Institution.

Pyle, Kenneth B. 2007. *Japan Rising: The Resurgence of Japanese Power and Purpose*. New York: Century Foundation.

Ravenhill, John. 2008. Asia's New Economic Institutions. In *Asia's New Institutional Architecture: Evolving Structures for Managing Trade, Financial, Security Relations*, Vinod K. Aggarwal and MinGyo Koo, eds. Berlin: Springer-Verlag.

————. 2009. The Economic–Security Nexus in the Asia-Pacific Region. In *Security Politics in the Asia-Pacific: A Regional–Global Nexus*, William T. Tow, ed. Cambridge: Cambridge University Press.

Samuels, Richard J. 2007. *Securing Japan: Tokyo's Grand Strategy and the Future of East Asia*. Ithaca, NY: Cornell University Press.

Shambaugh, David, ed. 2006. *Power Shift: China and Asia's New Dynamics*. Berkeley, CA: University of California Press.

Soeya, Yoshihide. 2005. Japanese Security Policy in Transition: The Rise of International and Human Security. *Asia-Pacific Review* 12 (1): 103–16.

Solingen, Etel. 2007. Pax Asiatica versus Bella Levantina: The Foundations of War and Peace in East Asia and the Middle East. *American Political Science Review* 101 (4): 757–80.

Steinfeld, Edward. 2008. The Capitalist Embrace: China Ten Years after the Asian Financial Crisis. In *East Asia: Coping with the Crisis*, Andrew MacIntyre *et al.*, eds. Ithaca, NY: Cornell University Press.

Steinmo, Sven, Kathleen Thelen and Frank Longstreth, eds. 1992. *Structuring Politics: Historical Institutionalism in Comparative Analysis*. Cambridge: Cambridge University Press.

Streeck, Wolfgang and Kathleen Thelen, eds. 2005. *Beyond Continuity: Institutional Change in Advanced Political Economies*. Oxford: Oxford University Press.

Thelen, Kathleen. 2004. *How Institutions Evolve: The Political Economy of Skills in Germany, Britain, the United States and Japan*. Cambridge: Cambridge University Press.

Weatherbee, Donald E. 2006. Strategic Dimensions of Economic Interdependence in Southeast Asia. In *Strategic Asia 2006–2007: Trade Interdependence, and Security*,

Ashley J. Tellis and Michael Wills, eds. Seattle, WA and Washington, DC: National Bureau of Asian Research.

Webber, Douglas. 2001. Two Funerals and a Wedding? The Ups and Downs of Regionalism in East Asia and Asia-Pacific after the Asian Crisis. *Pacific Review* 14 (3): 339–72.

Wendt, Alex. 1999. *Social Theory of International Politics*. Cambridge: Cambridge University Press.

Winters, Jeffrey A. 1999. The Determinants of Financial Crisis in Asia. In *The Politics of the Asian Economic Crisis*, T.J. Pempel, ed. Ithaca, NY: Cornell University Press.

Woo, Jung-en [Meredith Woo-Cumings]. 1991. *Race to the Swift: State and Finance in Korean Industrialization*. New York: Columbia University Press.

Woo-Cumings, Meredith, ed. 1999. *The Developmental State*. Ithaca, NY: Cornell University Press.

9 Trilateral dialogue in Northeast Asia

A case of spillover from economic to security cooperation?

Keisuke Iida

Introduction

This chapter focuses on community-building efforts though trilateral dialogue in Northeast Asia. I find intriguing patterns of reciprocal effects between economics and security. Regionalism in East Asia is a popular topic these days and the literature is rapidly expanding,[1] but few have so far focused on regionalism in the sub-region of Northeast Asia.[2] In particular, to the best of my knowledge, trilateral dialogue among China, Japan, and Korea has not been analyzed extensively elsewhere. Therefore, this will be the first attempt to describe and analyze the political economy of trilateral summits/dialogue in Northeast Asia.

The short history of trilateral dialogue among the People's Republic of China (PRC), Japan, and the Republic of Korea (ROK) shows that the causation between economic and security cooperation is not unidirectional. Consistent with liberal hypotheses, economic cooperation seems to encourage security cooperation, but states also require security cooperation as a precursor to economic cooperation, a relationship more consistent with realism. Therefore, a more comprehensive theory of the linkages between economic and security cooperation is needed to explain the pattern of cooperation in Northeast Asia.

Also, the history of these trilateral dialogues goes against some of the clichéd notions about regional cooperation in East Asia in general and Northeast Asia in particular. First, the contrast between Southeast Asia and Northeast Asia in terms of institutionalization, the former having the Association of Southeast Asian Nations (ASEAN) and its related institutions while the latter having none at all, is rapidly becoming obsolete. By now, the three countries under discussion have built a vast number of ministerial, agency-chief, and subcabinet-level channels of regular dialogue and cooperation. Second, the idea that cooperation in East Asia is non-legal or very informal is also becoming obsolete, now that the three countries are about to conclude a trilateral investment treaty while actively considering a trilateral free trade agreement (FTA). Third, the idea that Northeast Asian cooperation is doomed to remain informal because it lacks bureaucratization has become obsolete now that the three countries have agreed to establish a secretariat for trilateral cooperation.

Theory

Various theories and hypotheses on the economic–security nexus already exist. How does economic interdependence affect security and how do security concerns and considerations affect patterns of economic cooperation and conflict?

The hypotheses can be divided into two classes: the first takes economic inter-dependence as an independent variable and treats security as a dependent varia-ble; the second starts with economic interdependence as a dependent variable and treats security as an independent variable. Of course, many would readily admit that these causes and effects are reciprocal and hence do not allow such facile distinctions.

The most well-known hypothesis or conjecture on the economic–security nexus in international relations theory is the Kantian hypothesis: economic inter-dependence leads to the reduction of war. Kant argued that the development of a "spirit of commerce" among nations would contribute to "perpetual peace." Montesquieu also held that "Peace is the natural effect of trade" (cited in Doyle 1983: 225). Norman Angell stated, in a well-known—but often misunderstood—prediction that failed, that in an interdependent world as in pre-World War I Europe, war had become a useless instrument of policy to further economic welfare (Angell 1913). Russet and Oneal (2001) have done extensive analyses of this hypothesis and conclude that it is valid (Russett and Oneal).

A similar hypothesis emerges with the notion of a "security community" in the literature on regional integration (Deutsch *et al.* 1957; Adler and Barnett 1998). If sufficient economic interdependence proceeds, it will lead to the formation of a security community—a community of nations among which war is no longer conceivable.[3]

The process through which this happens is based heavily on purported spillo-vers, a phenomenon first explored by Ernst Haas, who argued that regional integration starts from relatively technical and politically innocuous issue-areas, but if there are tight functional connections between one issue and another, greater integration becomes necessary and spills over from the former to the latter (Haas 1958). He also entertained the possibility of tactical linkage, in which functionally independent issues are linked deliberately as a quid pro quo—cooperation in one issue area is used as the price for cooperation in another. Later he elaborated on the process more minutely (Haas and Schmitter 1964). If such spillovers proceed to a sufficient degree, they will lead to security cooperation.

As statistics show, economic interdependence in Northeast Asia, especially among China, Japan, and South Korea, has increased by leaps and bounds in recent years. However, this economic interdependence has not led to the emer-gence of a security community in this sub-region. Distrust toward the Japanese is still very strong in China and South Korea, not to mention North Korea. Longstanding territorial disputes, historical memories, Sino–Japanese rivalry, and other negative factors account for the overall lack of trust, but these do not explain why the liberal hypothesis does not apply to this region. On the other hand, there has been a modicum of effort in the direction of community building in Northeast Asia in recent years; hence, process tracing may help us to identify some of the effects of economic interdependence on security.

In contrast to these "liberal" theories, realists tend to take security concerns as primary and to interpret international economic interdependence as a dependent variable, something that is a consequence of security enhancement. For instance, mercantilists take economic interdependence as an instrument for the pursuit of national power or a means to national security.[4] Thus, European monarchs, before the rise of the free trade ideology, engaged extensively in restrictions on international trade flows because they believed that trade surpluses would help them hoard gold bullion, which in turn increased their national power.

Today no serious theorists believe that gold or trade surpluses will contribute to national power, but a modern reincarnation of mercantilism is, for lack of a better word, the theory of economic statecraft—how to use economic means to attain security goals.[5] For instance, the ideas of containment and engagement both involve economic statecraft (Mastanduno 1992). Various ideas about economic sanctions, including ideas about whether or not economic sanctions are useful, can be also considered to belong to this class of theories.[6]

Finally, a more positive or empirical theory, which is an intellectual cousin of economic statecraft, is the idea that trade follows the flag (Pollins 1989). In this theory, trade thrives only when international security is attained. Thus, trade flourishes among allies but not among adversaries (Gowa 1994).

All in all, these realist theories hypothesize that security leads to high economic interdependence or increased economic cooperation while insecurity has the opposite effects. The former is evidenced by the emergence of high economic interdependence in East Asia and in Northeast Asia in the post-Cold War period. Mutual recognition between South Korea and China has led to a tremendous increase in interdependence between the two countries. Sino–Japanese economic interdependence preceded China–Korea interdependence. Alternatively, the remaining hostility between Japan, South Korea, and the United States on the one hand and North Korea on the other hand impedes the development of economic relations between North Korea and the United States and its Northeast Asia allies.

However, our concern in this chapter is not security or insecurity per se, but the effects of security cooperation on economic cooperation and vice versa. Extrapolating from the realist position that states may use economics as an instrument to attain security and power goals, it is natural to hypothesize that realism also predicts that security cooperation can lead to economic cooperation. Once states decide to cooperate on security matters, they will try to "lock in" that cooperative relationship by using other means such as economic interdependence. If that is true, security cooperation is an independent variable designed to induce economic cooperation.

In the rest of the chapter, I trace the evolution of top-level dialogue and community-building efforts among the three major powers of Northeast Asia— China, Japan, and South Korea. To foreshadow the conclusions, I find the following patterns.

One of the prominent motives behind the Japanese initiative to start the trilateral dialogue was to participate in the evolving multilateral talks on North Korea. In this case, Japanese motivations confirm the realist hypothesis: economics is subordinated to security concerns. But in this case, the independent variable was not security concerns per se, which were low key in the late 1990s when the nations believed that the Democratic People's Republic of Korea (DPRK) was still in compliance with the Agreed Framework, but lack of political influence on the part of Japan due to exclusion from the talks with North Korea; and the dependent variable was less economic interdependence and more official dialogue or cooperation aimed at promoting economic interdependence.

The liberal theory of "spillover"—expansion of a policy agenda from economic affairs to other, more politically sensitive issues—has proven to be true in Northeast Asia. The trilateral summit was initially confined to purely economic and technical issues, but soon security issues were included in the agenda. However, the logic did not follow the exact theory of spillover. There was no impediment to promoting economic cooperation per se in the early 2000s. The eruption of two security crises—9/11 in 2001 and the second Korean Peninsula nuclear crisis in 2002—fostered common interest among the trilateral countries, and it was very natural to include these topics in the trilateral setting subsequently without their having been driven by efforts at furthering economic cooperation.

However, the start of the regular foreign ministers' meeting in 2007 and the regularization of meetings among different layers of high-ranking officials of foreign ministries added more layers of dialogue where the trilateral summit and security intersect: these meetings were used both to prepare for trilateral summit talks (including a mechanism to monitor the progress of trilateral cooperation) and a forum to discuss each other's strategies toward the North Korean nuclear problem. The 2003 Joint Declaration institutionalized the foreign ministers' meetings among the trilateral countries by creating the Three-Party Committee, and the first Three-Party Committee meeting took place in Qingdao, China, in 2004. However, even before then, there had been informal trilateral foreign ministers' meetings on the sidelines of the ASEAN Plus Three (APT) foreign ministers' meeting. Therefore, the trilateral foreign ministers' meeting really emerges as a spillover or spin-off from both trilateral dialogue and APT cooperation.

History of the trilateral summit

Genesis

The trilateral summit meetings began as a Japanese idea. Prime Minister Keizo Obuchi first floated the idea of holding such a trilateral summit in a meeting with Kim Dae-jung following a 1998summit in Hanoi of leaders of ASEAN and the leaders of the three Northeast Asian countries. Obuchi told Kim that trilateral summit talks on issues surrounding the DPRK could be held when the three nations—China, Japan, and Korea—participated in gatherings such as the Hanoi meeting. Kim responded by saying that the North should be urged to cooperate in four-way talks involving the North, South Korea, the United States, and China (Obuchi Presses for Trilateral Talks, *Asahi Evening News*, 17 December 1998). It is clear from this brief conversation between Obuchi and Kim that security cooperation was high on the agenda of these leaders when they conceived of trilateral talks.

China seemed wary of such talks at the outset. After proposing the idea of a trilateral summit in Hanoi, Obuchi asked President Clinton and President Kim for cooperation, and in July 1999, when Obuchi visited China, he suggested the idea to the Chinese government, which did not agree. At the Asia-Pacific Economic Cooperation (APEC) meeting in September 1999, Japanese foreign ministry officials suggested the idea to Chinese Foreign Minister Tang Jiaxuan, but he did not accept the idea either. According to the Japanese Ministry of Foreign Affairs, it was apparently Prime Minister Zhu Rongji's own decision that spurred China to participate in the trilateral meeting. Zhu, however, gave three preconditions—no host, no agenda, free discussion only (*Mainichi Shimbun* [*Mainichi* hereafter], 29 November 1999). China agreed to the summit because the relations between North Korea and its neighbors, as well as the United States, had been improving and because the summit could help China strengthen its economic ties with Japan and South Korea (Japan, China, ROK Leaders to Meet for 1st Summit, *Daily Yomiuri*, 20 November 1999: 1). It was only a few days before the actual meeting that the Chinese acceptance arrived (*Asahi*, 29 November 1999; *Nihon Keizai Shimbun* [*Nikkei* hereafter], 29 November 1999).

In contrast to China's tepid attitude, South Korea was very enthusiastic about promoting trilateral economic cooperation, and at the first meeting in Manila, President Kim Dae-Jung suggested joint research on trilateral economic cooperation among the research institutes of the three countries. However, political questions were another matter. At an interview the night before, Prime Minister Obuchi said that the trilateral meeting would be a forum to discuss political questions (*Nikkei*, 29 November 1999). In particular, Tokyo was interested in discussing how to maintain security in Northeast Asia, specifically with reference to North Korea (*Daily Yomiuri*, 20 November 1999). At that time, Japan had been excluded from the four-party talks over the North Korean nuclear issue among the DPRK, China, the ROK, and the United States, and Japan was interested in participating in the dialogue. China, and to some extent, the ROK were very cautious about broadening the agenda to include political matters (*Mainichi*, 29 November 1999).

Another sensitive matter at the beginning was how to deal with possible U.S. objections. The United States had a history of disagreeing with the creation of Asia-only forums, and there was concern that the United States might be alarmed if the leaders of the three major countries in Asia assembled together without U.S. participation. Therefore, the Japanese government carefully selected the APT as an opportunity for the trilateral summit. According to the Japanese foreign ministry officials, the three leaders could meet "in a non-contrived manner (*shizen na katachi*)." Of course, out of courtesy, they did not forget to inform the United States of the meeting in advance (*Asahi*, 29 November 1999).

As this section has shown, the origin of the trilateral summit or dialogue can be traced to the Japanese preference to be included in security talks in Northeast Asia, but nonetheless, the dialogue centered on economic and functional issues, at least initially. This can be either interpreted as a confirmation of the liberal hypothesis of spillover: economic cooperation is antecedent to security cooperation. Or alternatively, it can be interpreted as evidence in favor of the realist hypothesis about the instrumentality of economic cooperation: economic cooperation is used as a carrot to induce security cooperation. Either way, it confirms the tight linkage between economics and security in Northeast Asia.

The first three breakfast meetings

The three leaders met in the Philippine capital of Manila on the morning of 28 November 1999. Given the Chinese wariness about discussing security issues at the summit, it was natural for the three leaders to focus on economic issues. In particular, Kim, Zhu, and Obuchi agreed to conduct joint research to seek ways of institutionalizing economic cooperation among their three countries (*Korea Times*, 26 November 1999). The discussion yielded an agreement on commissioning the three nations' top economic think tanks to study ways of promoting collaboration in ten sectors, including trade, fisheries, maritime affairs, and the environment (Editorial, *Korea Herald*, 30 November 1999). According to a post-summit briefing, heads of the think tanks of the three countries would meet to explore ways to work out concrete steps to boost trilateral economic cooperation (*Korea Times*, 26 November 1999). Also, the three leaders took up the issue of China's membership of the World Trade Organization (WTO) during the hour-long meeting, with Obuchi and Kim expressing support for Beijing's early entry into the world-trade governing body (Japan Economic Newswire, 27 November 1999).

Obuchi proposed holding the three-way summit regularly. This was supported by Kim, but Zhu was noncommittal (Jiji Press Ticker Service, 29 November 1999). At the end of the first meeting, the three leaders managed to agree to meet once again. Per this agreement, it was decided that they would meet in Singapore, again on the sidelines of APT meetings in November 2000.

Although the first-ever trilateral summit had skirted security issues, the political motive behind it was criticized by North Korea. A report by the state-run Korea Central News Agency stated: "The Japanese and South Korean authorities attempted to turn the three-nation summit held in Manila... into a forum to discuss the Korean issue," calling their act a "sinister attempt." The report continued to warn against further politicizing the forum: "If the Korean issue is discussed at that summit in the future, it will not be of any help to solving it but will make it complicated and put a brake on its solution" (Japan Economic Newswire, 10 December 1999).

Meanwhile, Japan was busy trying to make the forum more political. According to Japan's Foreign Ministry, Japan made informal proposals in the spring of 2000 to China and Korea about the trilateral foreign ministerial meeting, and both countries responded positively. The talks were planned to coincide with the meeting in Bangkok of the APT and would allow Japan to brief Beijing and Seoul on the proceedings of the Group of Eight summit to be held in July in Okinawa, Japan. But Japan was careful not to include sensitive regional issues such as the situation on the Korean Peninsula (Japan Economic Newswire, 5 March 2000).

Prime Minister Obuchi suddenly died of a stroke in May, and Yoshiro Mori, his successor, attended the second trilateral summit meeting in Singapore. The PRC had become more forthcoming about holding a trilateral summit, and in particular, more willing to discuss politically sensitive questions (*Yomiuri*, 22 November 2000). In the end, however, no political items were discussed at the second trilateral summit. However, the Chinese government had notified the other governments in advance that "if the North Korean problem or Northeast Asian affairs are to be put on the agenda, our leader will be ready to discuss them" (*Yomiuri*, 25 November 2000).

The Chinese government was much more aggressive in enhancing trilateral cooperation this time. Zhu Rongji told Kim and Mori that the conditions for enhancing trilateral cooperation among Japan, South Korea, and China were gradually maturing, and in particular, he proposed that they give more support to encourage Chinese, Japanese, and South Korean enterprises to establish links. Mori and Kim agreed. Zhu also proposed to set 2002 as the personnel exchange year of China, Japan, and South Korea and also to increase environmental coop-eration among the three countries (Xinhua General News Service, 24 November 2000). Thus, 2002 was designated the "Year of Contacts of the Personnel of China, Japan, and Korea" because it coincided with the Soccer World Cup co-hosted by Japan and Korea, as well as being the 30th anniversary of the normalization of diplomatic relations between China and Japan.[7] The leaders also agreed that the trilateral meetings would be held regularly on the sidelines of APT meetings from then on (*Asahi*, 24 November 2000). They also agreed that the think tanks of the three countries—Japan's National Institute for Research Advancement (NIRA), the Development Research Center of the PRC State Council, and the Korean Institute for International Economic Policy (KIEP)—would start a joint research project on trilateral economic cooperation in the wake of China's accession to the WTO (*Asahi*, 24 November 2000).

Kim Dae-jung hosted the breakfast talks at a Singapore hotel, and the three leaders decided that Japan would host the next year's summit. Note that in Manila the Chinese had objected to any country "hosting" the summit, and their guard was already down on this issue.

The third trilateral summit meeting took place in Brunei. Prime Minister Junichiro Koizumi, who succeeded Mori in April, was very upbeat about the trilateral summit. He proposed that the trilateral summit be more formal than a breakfast meeting and that the foreign ministers of the three countries also meet at the time of the APT Foreign Ministers' Meeting (*Yomiuri*, 4 November 2001). Koizumi called for cooperation in antiterrorism efforts following the September 11 attacks on the United States. The leaders agreed to enhance surveillance of the transnational movements and funding of terrorists (Matsunaga 2001). This was clearly the first step in broadening the trilateral agenda to include more politically sensitive questions.

On economics, the joint report drawn up by the economic think tanks of the three countries, which was endorsed by Koizumi, Zhu, and Kim, proposed four short-term measures to boost trade—mutual notification about changes in trade laws or regulations; creating a training program for customs, inspection, and quarantine institutions; establishing an early warning system for trade disputes; and improving the mobility of business people (Aoki 2001). The report also called for regular meetings of the economic ministers from Japan, China, and South Korea, and the three leaders agreed that they would hold trilateral Economic Ministers' meetings regularly and would increase mutual notifications of changes in trade-related laws (*Yomiuri*, 5 November 2001). Thus, there were two instances of spillover or spin-offs at this time—from the summit to the economic ministers' and foreign ministers' meetings.

The first three breakfast meetings had provided an inkling of what was to come. Despite initial Chinese reluctance to discuss anything remotely politically sensitive in this forum, security was put on the agenda in 2001 by accident. The 9/11 terrorist attacks had galvanized this meeting into a forum to discuss security cooperation in the field of counterterrorism. Needless to say, China was much more forthcoming, even aggressive, in promoting economic cooperation. Therefore, by the end of this period, China had become a true believer in trilateral cooperation.

Koizumi and the cancellation of the trilateral summit

There were two developments during the Koizumi years that had opposite effects for trilateral cooperation: the second Korean Peninsula crisis and the deterioration in Sino–Japanese relations. In October 2002, North Korea allegedly admitted to the existence of a nuclear program, triggering the second Korean nuclear crisis. Given the leadership of China in shepherding the Six-Party Talks, trilateral security and foreign policy cooperation became all the more important. On the other hand, Sino–Japanese and Korean–Japanese relations steadily deteriorated during the Koizumi years because of his repeated visits to the Yasukuni Shrine, a shrine which memorializes the Japanese war dead, including convicted war criminals. Mutual visits between Chinese and Japanese state leaders stopped, but Koizumi managed to hold three more trilateral summit meetings on the sidelines of the APT.

Koizumi's second trilateral summit was held in Phnom Penh, the capital of Cambodia on 4 November 2002, only a few weeks after the outbreak of the second Korean Peninsula nuclear crisis. China was very eager to use the trilateral summit to open channels of discussion on the North Korean problem. It was Beijing, not Tokyo, which suggested switching the style from an informal breakfast meeting to a formal, business-like meeting (*Asahi*, 5 November 2002). Sensing Chinese enthusiasm, Koizumi told reporters that:

> China does not want to see a nuclear-armed North Korea. It is hopeful that we could share the same view at the trilateral meeting, namely that it would

be a plus for the DPRK if the DPRK became a responsible world citizen (*Yomiuri*, 4 November 2002).

Prime Minister Zhu Rongji admitted that the PRC had not been informed of North Korea's nuclear program, adding that China supported the denuclearization of the Korean Peninsula (*Yomiuri*, 5 November 2002).

However, more surprising was Zhu's suggestion that the three countries start research on the establishment of a trilateral FTA (*Yomiuri*, 5 November 2002). Japan and Korea were extremely cautious, however. Referring to the fact that China had just joined the WTO, Koizumi said that "we should look into it from a medium- to long-term perspective." ROK Foreign Minister Kim expressed a similar view, adding that research on the subject at the semi-official think-tank level should be continued (*Asahi*, 5 November 2002; *Yomiuri*, 5 November 2002).

This Phnom Penh meeting is noteworthy in three respects. First, this was the first time that security issues were discussed extensively in the trilateral context. Second, the three countries were united regarding the need for working to make the DPRK abandon its nuclear ambition. Third, there was more cooperation on this security issue than on economics.

In the spring of 2003, China made forays into arranging multilateral talks to deal with the DPRK's nuclear program, and initially set the stage for trilateral talks among North Korea, the United States, and China in April. China and the United States were interested in expanding the talks to four parties to include South Korea or to six-party talks to include Japan and Russia. However, North Korea, which considered the nuclear issue to be a bilateral problem between itself and the United States, opposed any such expansion. The United States considered the April three-way talks to have been ineffective, and by June, the United States, Japan, and Korea were in agreement that the new round of nuclear talks must be enlarged to include Seoul and Tokyo. Finally, after much cajoling, China agreed to expand the three-party talks to six-party talks, which started in August. It is not clear whether the existing trilateral dialogue through the summit talks and foreign ministers' meetings helped Japan participate in the Six-Party Talks, but at the least it did not hurt. All we can say is that the second Korean Peninsula nuclear crisis and the start of the Six-Party Talks set the stage for regular security dialogue on this question at the trilateral summit and foreign ministers' meetings.

The next trilateral summit in Bali in October 2003 was noteworthy because of its greater institutionalization. It was decided early in that year that the three leaders would issue a Joint Declaration for the first time.[8] This indicates that advance preparation became more elaborate than before. Reportedly, it was a Chinese initiative to issue a Joint Declaration, and its motive was to co-opt Japan and Korea into the project to stabilize Northeast Asian security (*Mainichi*, 8 October 2003).

As in the previous year, security was high on the agenda of the trilateral summit. Koizumi said in advance of the summit that he would seek to "closely coordinate and share the view on how to deal with North Korea's nuclear standoff" (Japan Economic Newswire, 6 October 2003). The more explicitly political nature of the Bali summit is also demonstrated by the fact that the Joint Declaration referred to the promotion of exchanges among the militaries of the three countries.[9] The Joint Declaration reconfirmed that the trilateral countries would seek to cooperate for the peaceful solution of the North Korean nuclear crisis (*Mainichi*, 7 October 2003). Korean President Roh Moo-hyun, Chinese premier Wen Jiabao, and Koizumi, mindful of the North's nuclear weapons program, also agreed on the need to boost cooperation to promote disarmament and prevent the spread of weapons of mass destruction (*Korea Times*, 8 October 2003). They also agreed to enhance their cooperation in such transnational crimes as terrorism, maritime piracy, human trafficking, and drug smuggling.

Taking advantage of the growing consensus on North Korea, Koizumi also tried to use this summit to gain understanding from China and Korea on the abduction issue. From the very beginning of the meeting, he tabled the nuclear and abduction issues simultaneously (*Yomiuri*, 8 October 2003). However, reflecting Chinese and Korean cautiousness on the abduction issue, the Joint Declaration only obliquely referred to it in the broader context of as "each country's concerns" (ibid.). The leaders also decided to institutionalize the trilateral foreign ministers' meeting by establishing a Three-Party Committee during the Bali meeting.[10] The Three-Party Committee would be headed by foreign ministers and would meet once or twice a year to monitor their cooperation projects and fine-tune an annual report that would be presented henceforth at trilateral summit talks (*Korea Herald*, 29 December 2003).

On economics, the three leaders launched a joint study with the aim of concluding an investment treaty among themselves (*Asahi*, 7 October 2003). Because the WTO's ministerial meeting in Mexico in September had failed to reach an accord over investment, it was feared that the new round of WTO talks would remain deadlocked for a while. As a result, the Japanese government was trying to gain benefits in the field of cross-border investment (Fukazawa 2003). Also, the think tanks of China (DRC), Japan (NIRA), and Korea (KIEP) submitted their joint report on the trilateral FTA (*Nikkei*, 7 October 2003). The questionnaire they administered among the major firms in the three countries showed high support for the FTA (85.3 percent of Chinese firms, 78.7 percent of Japanese firms, and 70.9 percent of Korean firms) (ibid.). However, Japanese and Korean commitment to the realization of the FTA remained tepid, in contrast to Prime Minister Wen Jiabao's enthusiasm (*Yomiuri*, 8 October 2003). Japan was not only worried about the economic effects of the trilateral FTA on vulnerable sectors in Japan, but also about the political motive behind the Chinese initiative. As one high-ranking Japanese official said: "China aims to grab the initiative of economic integration in the entire Asian region, including ASEAN" (Fukazawa 2003). The Joint Declaration also referred to strengthening of cooperation in environment and many other sub-regional issues. All in all, the Bali summit was the first summit in which China was in the driver's seat.

Between the Bali meeting and the next summit in Vientiane, the second and third rounds of the Six-Party Talks were held (February and June 2004), but progress was elusive and extremely slow. When Japanese Foreign Minister Yoriko Kawaguchi and Chinese Foreign Minister Li Zhaoxing met in Beijing in

April, they agreed to have regular trilateral dialogues involving China, Japan, and South Korea to strengthen cooperation on North Korea's nuclear ambitions. Kawaguchi also met with Premier Wen, but Wen slammed Koizumi's repeated visits to the Yasukuni Shrine (Japan Economic Newswire, 4 April 2004). Kawaguchi, Li, and South Korean Foreign Affairs and Trade Minister Ban Ki Moon inaugurated the Three-Party Committee by meeting in Qingdao on 21 June.[11] They agreed to create a trilateral cooperation strategy to be presented to their top leaders during their summit talks in November. They also agreed to encourage the joint study being conducted on a possible investment pact (Japan Economic Newswire, 21 June 2004). The foreign ministers of the three countries (Japan was represented by the new foreign minister Nobutaka Machimura) met in Vientiane two days before the summit on the sidelines of the ASEAN meetings (Japan Economic Newswire, 27 November 2004). Aside from putting the finishing touches on the Action Strategy to be adopted by the top leaders two days later, they reaffirmed their vow to call North Korea back to the stalled Six-Party Talks at an early date (ibid.).

The trilateral summit in Vientiane on 29 November 2004 was the last one for Koizumi. Koizumi, Wen, and Roh agreed on the early resumption of the Six-Party Talks and cooperation in the reconstruction of Iraq. They also agreed to promote reform of the United Nations (*Yomiuri*, 29 November 2004). They adopted an "Action Strategy" on trilateral cooperation, covering fourteen different areas of cooperation (Three-Party Committee 2004). In security, they agreed to further encourage exchanges among military officials (*Asahi*, 29 November 2004).

On economic issues, Japan was most interested in a trilateral investment treaty, and an unofficial group of experts from Japan, China, and South Korea met in Tokyo, Seoul, and Beijing during 2004 to report to the summit. Japan had just concluded a bilateral investment treaty with the ROK, and Tokyo was interested in seeing the same rights extended to investors doing business in China. The study panel set up by the Bali summit met for the fourth time in Tokyo for a two-day meeting, and it was agreed that the three countries should work together to conclude a trilateral agreement on promoting investment (Japan Economic Newswire, 17 September 2004). [12]

At the Vientiane summit meeting, President Roh made a proposal to hold the trilateral summit independently from the APT meetings. Koizumi and Wen agreed to take his proposal under advisement, although the idea did not materialize until 2008 (*Nikkei*, 29 November 2004).

The trilateral summit was suspended for more than a year after Vientiane. The breakdown was foreshadowed by events at the disastrous trilateral foreign ministers' meeting in Kyoto, which was held on the sidelines of the Asia-Europe Meeting (ASEM) in May 2005. China and Korea put the history issues on the table without prior warning to Japan. Foreign Minister Machimura wanted to confine all history issues to strictly bilateral forums (Editorial, *Nikkei*, 8 May 2005). Furthermore, Machimura asked his Chinese and Korean counterparts for their support for Japan's bid to gain a permanent seat at the UN Security Council, but both countries remained noncommittal. The only modest accomplishment of this meeting was an agreement to start government-level discussions on the trilateral investment treaty (*Nikkei*, 8 May 2005).

Koizumi visited the Yasukuni Shrine on 17 October 2005, an event that became a direct trigger for the cancellation of the 2005 trilateral summit, which had been scheduled for Kuala Lumpur in December on the sidelines of the APT. Cui Tiankai, head of the Chinese Foreign Ministry's Asian Affairs Department, declared that "China–Japan relations are currently facing difficulties, the reason for it being the Japanese leader's repeated visits to the Yasukuni Shrine" (Japan Economic Newswire, 30 November 2005). China denied Koizumi a bilateral meeting with Chinese President Hu Jintao during the summit of the Asia-Pacific Economic Cooperation in South Korea in October, although Koizumi did hold a bilateral meeting with South Korean President Roh Moo-hyun. Yet Roh told him that he found the shrine visits unacceptable (ibid.). On 4 December, the Chinese foreign ministry announced that the summit among Japan, South Korea, and China planned for December would be postponed (Japan Economic Newswire, 3 December 2005). China and Korea took a united stand in refusing to meet with Koizumi (*Yomiuri*, 5 December 2005). Roh and Wen met in Kuala Lumpur on 12 December (the day when the trilateral summit was scheduled), and they agreed that Koizumi was to blame for the cancellation of the summit (Japan Economic Newswire, 11 December 2005; *Nikkei*, 12 December 2005). For his part, Koizumi rejected any attempt by China and South Korea to pressure him into not visiting Yasukuni.[13] The trilateral foreign ministers' meeting to be held on the sidelines of Asian meetings in Kuala Lumpur was also postponed (Japan Economic Newswire, 8 December 2005). The main casualty from this breakdown in cooperation was the delay in starting negotiations for a trilateral investment treaty (*Asahi*, 7 December 2005; *Mainichi*, 9 December 2006). This is a typical case of security (or political) issues putting the brakes on economic cooperation.

This second period in the story of trilateral dialogue contains simultaneous evidence for both the liberal hypothesis about spillovers from economics to security and the realist view that economic cooperation can only proceed as far as security conditions will foster. Evidence in favor of the liberal hypothesis is provided by the fact that security became an increasingly important agenda item in this forum after the outbreak of the second Korean Peninsula crisis. This was natural after security had already become a familiar topic in 2001 in the aftermath of the 9/11 terrorist attacks. A spin-off (the creation of an institution as a byproduct of another institution) is also suggestive of a spillover effect: the Joint Declaration of 2003 formally established a Three-Party Committee, which took the form of a regularized meeting of foreign ministers of the trilateral powers. Foreign ministers from the three countries had met informally before, but this firmly institutionalized the forum in which security issues would be discussed on a regular basis. At the same time, realism gets some vindication in the sense that economic cooperation was hampered by negative political cooperation. The breakdown in political cooperation or political trust among the three countries, triggered by Koizumi's Yasukuni visits, led to a temporary demise of cooperation over economic matters.

Rejuvenation

Koizumi retired as prime minister in September 2006, and his successor Shinzo Abe was eager to repair the damaged relations with China and Korea. In October, immediately after taking office, he made visits to Seoul and Beijing. In Seoul, Abe and Roh agreed to hold a trilateral summit in the Philippines on the sidelines of APT scheduled later that year. The economic ministers of the three governments met in Cebu in the Philippines on 9 December 2006, and agreed to start formal negotiations for a trilateral investment treaty early in 2007 (*Nikkei*, 7 December 2006). The science ministers met in Seoul for their first trilateral ministerial meeting on 12 January 2007 and promised to strengthen ties in various technological fields including atomic energy and disaster prevention (Japan Economic Newswire, 13 January 2007).

The trilateral summit was rescheduled to January 2007 because of a typhoon. The second East Asia Summit was also delayed. After meeting Japanese Deputy Foreign Minister Katsuhiko Asano and South Korean Foreign Minister Song in-soon on 12 January, Chinese Foreign Minister Li Zhaoxing declared that "Relations between the three countries are showing fresh impetus for development" (Torode 2007). Abe met with Roh and Wen on 14 January 2007. They issued a Joint Press Statement in which they agreed to start negotiations on the trilateral investment treaty in 2007 (TCCS 2007). On the other hand, the leaders merely "took note" of their progress toward the trilateral FTA (Japan Economic Newswire, 14 January 2007). The Joint Press Statement also included the establishment of a high-level forum for officials of foreign affairs, increased cooperation over environmental problems, and support for UN Security Council reform.

Security was again an important agenda at the reopened trilateral summit. The three leaders expressed their concern over the DPRK, which had launched Taepodong missiles in July and conducted a nuclear test in October of 2006. Abe, Wen, and Roh called on North Korea to take concrete and effective steps toward the denuclearization of the Korean Peninsula and toward implementation of a Six-Party Joint Statement (Japan Economic Newswire, 14 January 2007). In addition, Japan won the inclusion of the abduction issue in the Joint Statement.[14] In an oblique way, the leaders stressed the importance of addressing the international community's "humanitarian concerns"—a phrase that can be taken to mean North Korea's abductions of Japanese nationals (Japan Economic Newswire, 14 January 2007). China offered to provide help for the resolution of the abduction issue. This was the first time that the Chinese government officially made a cooperative gesture on the abduction issue (*Asahi*, 15 January 2007).[15]

Reflecting the upbeat mood among the three countries, the Northeast Asia Trilateral Forum—an eminent persons' group—issued a number of recommendations to the three governments in the spring of 2007. Former Japanese Prime Minister Yasuhiro Nakasone called for regular summits involving Japan, China, and South Korea (*Nikkei Weekly*, 23 April 2007). Former Korean Prime Minister Lee Hong-Koo went so far as to propose creating a Northeast Asian Community, with the possible participation of the DPRK and Mongolia in the future (*Nikkei*, 16 April 2007).

As we have seen, there had been calls for institutionalizing the trilateral summit, making it independent from the APT meetings. It was Yasuo Fukuda, Abe's successor, who took the initiative to make this happen. Fukuda met with Prime Minister Wen Jiabao of the PRC and President Roh Moo-hyun of the ROK in Singapore on 20 November 2007, and at this trilateral meeting, he proposed to host the foreign ministers' meeting in Japan in 2008 (*Mainichi*, 20 November 2007). The three leaders also agreed that the trilateral summit would henceforth be independent from the APT framework (*Nikkei*, 20 November 2007).

On North Korea, which had the second inter-Korean summit in Pyongyang on 2–4 October, the leaders agreed on the need to ensure that North Korea would fulfill its denuclearization promises, and Wen and Roh expressed again their support for Japan in resolving the abductions and other issues with Pyongyang (Japan Economic Newswire, 20 November 2007). They did not issue a Joint Statement at this meeting, but nevertheless announced cooperative programs in thirteen different issue areas. They also discussed the possible establishment of a new forum for security dialogue in Northeast Asia (*Nikkei*, 20 November 2007).

By the spring of 2008, it was decided that the first standalone trilateral summit would be held in Japan (*Yomiuri*, 19 April 2008). Fukuda decided to confirm this decision with Lee Myun-bak and Hu Jintao at top-level bilateral meetings in the spring. First, Fukuda met with Lee Myun-bak in Tokyo on 21 April 2008, and suggested the hosting of the first Trilateral Summit in Japan (*Yomiuri*, 21 April 2008).[16] They agreed to hold the summit in the three countries in rotation from then on (*Yomiuri*, 21 April 2008). In May President Hu Jintao visited Japan, the first time in ten years that the head of the Chinese government had visited Japan. On this occasion, Fukuda garnered Chinese approval for the first standalone Trilateral Summit in Japan. The final step was Lee's visit to China, where the two governments agreed on holding the summit, and they also agreed that the foreign ministers' meeting would be held in rotation in the three countries (*Asahi*, 29 May 2008).

In June 2008, foreign ministers Masahiko Komura, Yang Jiechi, and Yu Myung-Hwan met in Tokyo. They agreed to intensify their cooperation in the progress of the second phase of the nuclear dismantlement in North Korea (*Mainichi*, 15 June 2008). They also agreed to hold the meeting in rotation, with China as a host in 2009.

Another big issue at the foreign ministers' meeting was climate change, which was due to be discussed at the G8 Hokkaido Toyako summit. The three ministers formed a consensus that an effective framework for greenhouse gas reductions in the post-Kyoto era was necessary. They also called for acceleration in the negotiations over the trilateral investment treaty (ibid.).

However, between this foreign ministers' meeting and the summit, an unfortunate turn of events intervened. The Japanese Ministry of Education prepared teaching guidelines for the new middle-school curriculum, in which teachers were obligated to discuss the Takeshima/Dokdo problem in social-studies classes. At the last minute, ministers decided to delete the most controversial phrase to assuage Korean fears, but that was not enough. The ROK Ambassador to Japan went back to Seoul in protest, and the Korean–Japanese relations were strained once again.

The summit was scheduled for September, but it became politically difficult for Lee Myun-bak to visit Tokyo (*Mainichi*, 18 July 2008; *Nikkei*, 16 July 2008, 6 August 2008). Also, on 1 September, Prime Minister Fukuda abruptly announced that he would resign, creating an inevitable delay in the scheduling of the summit. As a result, Chief Cabinet Secretary Nobutaka Machimura formally announced the postponement of the summit. Foreign Minister Hirofumi Nakasone met with his Chinese counterpart Yang Jiechi in New York, and they agreed that the Trilateral Summit should be held by the end of the year (*Nikkei*, 27 September 2008).

At the same time, Korea's resistance softened due to the financial crisis. In October, the Korean won hit an all-time low against the dollar since the Asian financial crisis of 1997, and Korea desperately needed financial help from its economic partners. Thus, Lee Myun-bak proposed that an emergency Trilateral Summit be held in Beijing on the sidelines of ASEM in October (*Mainichi*, 7 October 2008).

However, Prime Minister Taro Aso, who had just succeeded Fukuda, had another idea. He sounded out China and South Korea about hosting a Trilateral Summit in Fukuoka in December (Japan Economic Newswire, 21 October 2008; *Mainichi*, 21 October 2008). This was in part in response to Chinese and Korean entreaties that the summit be held before the end of the year (*Mainichi*, 22 October 2008). Aso met with Lee Myun-bak in Beijing on the sidelines of the ASEM meetings and proposed that a Trilateral Summit be held in December, to which Lee readily agreed (*Asahi*, 24 October 2008). PRC Prime Minister Wen also agreed (*Mainichi*, 25 October 2008). Aso also met with President Hu Jintao in Beijing, and they reconfirmed their recognition of the need for Sino–Japanese cooperation to cope with the financial crisis (*Asahi*, 25 October 2008).

Aso sent his special emissaries to the ROK in November, and the two governments agreed on the need to expand the bilateral swap agreements, which were part of the Chiang Mai Initiative established through the APT process in 2000. The ROK had already concluded a swap agreement to the tune of US$ 30 billion with the United States.[17] By November, the trilateral governments also came to an agreement that the trilateral ministerial-level meeting of disaster management ministers should be established. In the wake of the earthquake in Sichuan in May 2008, the Japanese government had suggested such an idea (*Asahi*, 27 November 2008).

The first standalone Trilateral Summit in Dazaifu, Fukuoka, on 13 December 2009 naturally revolved around financial cooperation, but there were some other breakthroughs. Meeting ahead of the summit, Aso and Lee welcomed a deal reached the night before to increase a bilateral currency swap arrangement to the equivalent of US$ 20 billion. The Bank of Korea also announced a deal with the PRC worth about US$ 26 billion (Talmadge 2008). The leaders promised new stimulus spending to increase domestic demand and pick up the slack in global growth left by the slowdown in the United States (Fackler 2008).

Another breakthrough occurred on the abduction issue. The Roh administration, given its sunshine policy toward the DPRK, had been reluctant to endorse Japanese demands to include the abduction issue on the agenda of the

Trilateral Summit. However, the Lee administration was much more forth-coming. Therefore, China and Korea pledged they would support the Japanese efforts to resolve the abduction issue (*Yomiuri*, 14 December 2008).

However, on the North Korean nuclear issue, there was a slight strain. Japan and Korea were on the same page in terms of "regretting the lack of progress in the verification of denuclearization in the Six-Party Talks," but Prime Minister Wen did not express "regret," provoking a concern that China was turning pro-DPRK once again (*Yomiuri*, 14 December 2008). Also, two Chinese survey ships had entered into Japanese territorial waters in the East China Sea on 8 December, reigniting tensions between Beijing and Tokyo over disputed islands (Japan Economic Newswire, 12 December 2008). In a bilateral meeting with Wen, Aso expressed concern over the incident (Talmadge 2008).

The summit talks ended by issuing three statements: one on trilateral partnership, one on international finance and the economy, and the third on disaster manage-ment cooperation.[18] The crown jewel of the achievements at the summit was clearly the doubling of the swap line between Japan and the ROK and the seven-fold increase of the swap line between the PRC and the ROK. Compared to this, other agreements were minor (*Nikkei*, 14 December 2008). The three countries agreed to hold the second (standalone) Trilateral Summit in China in 2009 and the third one in South Korea in 2010 (Japan Economic Newswire, 13 December 2008). Aso stated that the three-way summit was a "revolutionary" event that would greatly contribute to global stability and prosperity (*Yonhap*, 14 December 2008).

Emergency Trilateral Summit talks, outside the three-year rotation cycle that had been agreed to at the Fukuoka Summit, took place in April 2009, immedi-ately after the flight test of a Taepodong 2 missile by the DPRK on 5 April. The three leaders happened to be in Pattaya, Thailand, to attend the fourth East Asia Summit. On 11 April they agreed that the UN Security Council should issue the strongest message (against North Korea) in a timely manner. At the time, the UN Security Council was putting together a united stance against North Korea. Japan and Korea had called for a Security Council resolution while China had wanted to limit it to a nonbinding presidential statement. Aso suggested shortly before leaving Tokyo on 10 April that his government might make concessions and settle for a nonbinding presidential statement at the Council (Japan Economic Newswire, 10 April 2009). Indeed, at the Pattaya meeting, Aso agreed that Japan would be content with such a presidential statement (*Yomiuri*, 12 April 2009).

The third period, which saw finally the weaning of the trilateral dialogue from the APT process, again confirms the liberal hypothesis. First, the political damage caused by the cancellation of the 2005 summit was easily repaired by Koizumi's successors, who tried to depoliticize the Yasukuni issue. The imperative of economic cooperation does not allow for a lapse in political dialogue at the top level among the highly interdependent Northeast Asian economies. For a short while, security concerns, this time over the Takeshima/Dokdo issue, almost derailed the first standalone Trilateral Summit, but the financial crisis triggered by the failure of Lehman Brothers in September 2008 had a strong effect on the Korean economy in the fall of 2008, and that led to enhanced trilateral economic cooperation at the 2008 summit in the form of expansion of bilateral swap agreements between Japan and China on the one hand and Korea on the other.

Change in Japan

The Trilateral Summit meeting had to be rescheduled again due to changes in the Japanese government. The Aso government called general elections for the lower house of the Diet to be held on 30 August 2009, and at the elections, the Democratic Party of Japan (DPJ) won 308 seats, an overwhelming majority, in the 480-member chamber. However, since the DPJ lacked a majority in the upper house, it had to form a coalition government with the People's New Party and the Social Democratic Party. Yukio Hatoyama, the DPJ party leader, was named prime minister by the Diet on 16 September. The original Chinese plan had been to hold a Trilateral Summit in Tianjin, Prime Minister Wen's hometown, on 30 August, but this had to be postponed because of its conflict with the Japanese elections. After the Japanese elections, the Chinese called for a summit in October and sent Wu Dawei, Deputy Foreign Minister, to Japan to invite Prime Minister Hatoyama to the summit talks.[19]

The summit was finally held in Beijing on 10 October 2009. In preparation for the summit, Chinese Foreign Minister Yang Jiechi, South Korean Foreign Minister Yu Myung-hwan, and Japanese Foreign Minister Katsuya Okadamet in Shanghai on 28 September agreed to hold the summit meeting in Beijing. There were three major issues at this time: Hatoyama's proposal for an "East Asian Community," the DPRK problem, and climate change. Already at this foreign ministers' meeting, a modicum of consensus on the East Asian Community and the DPRK problem was reached while differences remained on climate change. The foreign ministers agreed on the need for cooperation for the formation of the East Asian Community and the recognition that the nuclear program of North Korea is a threat to the peace and stability of the Northeast Asian region (*Nikkei*, 29 September 2009).

In the monthly magazine *Voice*, Yukio Hatoyama had envisioned the formation of an East Asian Community, and it was placed in the pre-election party manifesto of the DPJ (Hatoyama 2009). Hatoyama floated the idea at a meeting with Hu Jintao in New York on 21 September, when they visited the United Nations to address the General Assembly. Hu was elated when Hatoyama expressed deep regret for the history of colonial rule and invasion of China, referring specifically to the Murayama commentary of 1995. Hatoyama also asked for Chinese cooperation in creating an East Asian Community (*Yomiuri*, 23 September 2009). In his address to the UN General Assembly, Hatoyama further elaborated on the East Asian Community idea.[20] His idea included not only the FTA in East Asia, but also cooperation in finance, currency, energy, environment, and disaster relief.

At the beginning of the summit in Beijing, Hatoyama said that China, Japan, and Korea would form the core of his East Asian Community (*Yomiuri*, 10 October 2009). It seems that this was a faux pas on the part of Hatoyama, for the Japanese government had gone to great lengths at the time of the previous

Trilateral Summit to make sure that the standalone Trilateral Summit would not make ASEAN countries nervous. ASEAN countries, while welcoming the East Asian Community idea, were concerned by Hatoyama's remarks. This challenged ASEAN's long perception of itself as the core of Asian regionalism. Therefore, the chairman's statement at the ASEAN leaders' meeting referred to a regional structure with ASEAN at its core (*Yomiuri*, 25 October 2009).

Meanwhile, the business communities of the three countries were pushing for the creation of a trilateral FTA, and they had decided to hold the first-ever trilateral business summit simultaneously in Beijing while the leaders met. The Business Summit adopted a joint declaration calling for greater efforts toward the trilateral FTA (Jiji Press Ticker Service, 11 October 2009; *Yomiuri*, 11 October 2009). At the summit, China and Japan were very enthusiastic about the formation of the trilateral FTA, while Lee said that they should continue their joint academic research. Nevertheless, the leaders agreed on the start of research on the FTA at the governmental level and agreed to aim for the conclusion of the Trilateral Investment Agreement early in 2010, prior to any FTA (*Nikkei*, 11 October 2009; *Yomiuri*, 10 October 2009). The economic ministers' meeting in Hua Hin, Thailand, on 25 October, agreed on the start of the tripartite joint research involving industrialists, academics, and government officials (*Nikkei*, 25 October 2009).

Another hot issue at this summit was the DPRK, which had been upsetting the security climate since the beginning of 2009. On 5 April, it had test-fired a Taepodong 2 missile in the direction of Japan. In retaliation for the UN sanctions, North Korea vowed not to return to the Six-Party Talks, and on 13 June, it admitted to having a highly enriched uranium program (in addition to its better known plutonium program), which it had been denying until that time.

In the lead-up to the first successful Trilateral Summit hosted in China, the Chinese government made efforts to bring the DPRK back to the Six-Party Talks. First, China sent State Councilor Dai Bingguo to Pyongyang in September as a special emissary for Hu Jintao to meet with First Vice-Minister of Foreign Affairs Kang Sok-ju. At that time, Pyongyang expressed the intention to engage in "bilateral" and "multilateral" talks, but was not explicit about the Six-Party Talks. However, when Prime Minister Wen met with Kim Jong-il in Pyongyang on 5 October, Chairman Kim reportedly expressed his readiness to return to the Six-Party Talks if the North's relations with the United States improved (Japan Economic Newswire, 7 October 2009). The Chinese media reported that Kim pledged to participate in multilateral talks including the Six-Party Talks after assessing the nature of bilateral talks with the United States (*Mainichi*, 7 October 2009).[21] This was considered a gift from Kim to Wen (*Mainichi*, 6 October 2009). However, the DPRK's commitment to the Six-Party Talks was conditioned on the success of bilateral talks between North Korea and the United States (ibid.). At the Trilateral Summit, Wen explained his meeting with Kim Jong-il in Pyongyang in detail, saying that the DPRK was interested in improving its relations with Japan and the ROK (*Nikkei*, 11 October 2009).

South Korea had its own initiative, proposing a "grand bargain" with North Korea. The idea was to settle the North Korean nuclear issue in one single step

instead of in phases, that is, ending the cycle in which the DPRK agreed to denuclearization steps only to return to provocations (Kim 2009). At the Trilateral
Summit, Lee Myun-bak explained his "grand bargain" with respect to the DPRK's
nuclear program. His idea consisted of granting a great deal of economic assistance to the DPRK if North Korea agreed to dismantle the central part of its
nuclear program. He also said that North Korea was interested in this idea
(*Yomiuri*, 11 October 2009). However, Wen was noncommittal about such a grand
bargain (*Mainichi*, 11 October 2009). Indeed, North Korea was highly critical of
the grand bargain idea, saying that the intent was to interfere with the resolution
of the nuclear issue between the DPRK and the United States (Korea Central News
Agency, cited in *Mainichi*, 11 October 2009). Hatoyama agreed with Lee's view
on withholding aid to Pyongyang. "Unless there is a precise change in North
Korea's actions, we should not provide economic cooperation. North Korea's will
to change must be seen," he said at the joint news conference. On the other hand,
he declared that Lee's proposal to offer a one-time "grand bargain" of aid and
concessions in exchange for denuclearization was "completely correct" (Global
News Wire (Chinadaily.com.cn), 10 October 2009).

The United Nations was scheduled to convene the 15th Conference of the
Parties (COP15) to the UN Framework Convention on Climate Change and the
5th Meeting of the Parties (MOP5) to the Kyoto Protocol in Copenhagen in
December of 2009, and it was expected that the parties would sign a document to
create a post-Kyoto framework for climate change with mid-term emission reduction goals. However, the negotiations had been in a stalemate largely due to
disagreement between developed and developing countries. Prime Minister
Hatoyama pledged that Japan would aim at an ambitious mid-term reduction
goal—that of reducing greenhouse gas emissions by 25 percent by 2020 relative
to the 1990 level.

After the summit, Hatoyama held a bilateral meeting with Premier Wen and
asked the latter for cooperation for the success of COP15, and Wen promised that
he would do his utmost for a successful meeting (*Sankei*, 11 October 2009). This
led to the joint statement on sustainable development issued after the summit
committing the three countries to "work closely together… to contribute to the
successful achievement of the Copenhagen Conference" (Ministry of Foreign
Affairs 2009). Finally on 26 November in a lead-up to the COP15 meeting in
Copenhagen, Beijing announced that it would cut carbon intensity—carbon emissions per unit of GDP—by 40 to 45 percent by 2020 relative to the 2005 level.
The change in China's attitudes can be attributed to many factors, but one of them
seems to have been pressure from Japan.[22]

The three leaders met again on Jeju Island 29–30 May for the third Trilateral
Summit. Since only half a year had elapsed since the previous meeting, one could
not hope to see much progress, and on both economic and security issues, results
were meager, but there was one notable achievement: agreement on the establishment of a trilateral secretariat.

In the security arena, the *Cheonan* incident dominated the discussion at the
summit and all the other bilateral talks on the sidelines. The South Korean patrol

ship, carrying 104 personnel, sank in the Yellow Sea on 26 March 2010, and 46 people died. Having already concluded that the evidence of the North Korean involvement in the sinking of the ship was conclusive, the Lee Myun-bak government sought to consolidate international support for its position denouncing North Korea in the UN Security Council. However, the Chinese government refused to admit that North Korea was to blame for the incident and resisted the call for fresh sanctions on the DPRK. Finally, at the summit, the three governments pledged to "cooperate" on the matter, but China would concede nothing further.

On economic issues, the trilateral investment treaty under negotiation and the trilateral free trade agreement, which is under study, were the most important items on the agenda. On the investment treaty, the three leaders pledged to make efforts to conclude the negotiations, while on the trilateral FTA, they merely promised to conclude the joint study by 2012 (TCCS 2010a).

In contrast to these paltry results on security and economic cooperation, one of the major achievements made in this summit meeting was an agreement on the establishment of the Secretariat for Trilateral Cooperation (TCCS 2010b). Celebrating the fact that "there are 17 Ministerial Meetings as well as over 50 exchange and dialogue mechanisms among the three countries," the governments decided it was "necessary to plan and coordinate the trilateral cooperation in various fields..." Korea, which has always been the most enthusiastic of the three nations concerning the formalization of trilateral dialogue, will provide the premises for the secretariat. There is no doubt that this secretariat will assume an increasingly important role in further fostering trilateral cooperation.

Conclusions

The history of the trilateral summit shows that although no security community exists in Northeast Asia as of yet, there have been various spillovers from economic cooperation to security cooperation. The evidence is as follows.

The trilateral summit started out by discussing economic issues only in a very informal manner, but soon security issues began to be discussed. In 2001, the nations discussed and promised cooperation in counterterrorism. From 2002 on, the nuclear program of North Korea was put on the agenda of the summit, and especially from 2003 onwards, after the Six-Party Talks processes started, it became standard fare for the trilateral summit to promise enhanced cooperation on this matter.

This is reconfirmed by one of the regular participants in the trilateral summit: Chinese Premier Wen. He reportedly talked about a "proper sequence" in 2004. Stressing that the three countries should make greater efforts to expand the scope of trilateral cooperation, he said at the 2004 meeting that the three sides should agree on "[a] proper sequence based on respective advantage: Priorities for cooperation should be given to the important sectors in sequence, first to the convenient ones and gradually expand to other fields" (Xinhua General News Service, 29 September 2004). The "convenient ones" presumably refer to various economic and other technical issues while "other fields" refer to more politically sensitive issues such as security cooperation. Indeed, this is in perfect harmony with Obuchi's original objective of starting the trilateral summit to help Japan participate in the security dialogue on North Korea.

In terms of spillovers and spin-offs, the summit created additional forums for foreign ministry officials to interact with one another on many issues, including security. This happened almost by accident in the early years. For example, when the Six-Party Talks started in 2003, Asian affairs officials of the trilateral countries got together to prepare for the trilateral summit; at the same time, they discussed the North Korean problem (Jiji Press Ticker Service, 4 October 2003).

The summit, with an eye toward making sure that progress is made toward the fulfillment of their 2003 Joint Declaration, created a Three-Party Committee, headed by foreign ministers of the three countries. Each year, the Committee met once in the intercessional period and immediately before the summit to prepare their report.

The 2003 Joint Declaration also institutionalized the foreign ministers' meetings among the trilateral countries, and the first trilateral foreign ministers' meeting took place in Jintao in 2004. However, informal trilateral foreign ministers' meetings had previously been held on the sidelines of APT foreign ministers' meeting. Therefore, the trilateral foreign ministers' meeting was clearly a spillover or spin-off from the trilateral summit as well as from the APT.

High-ranking officials of the three countries met very frequently, partly for preparation for the Six-Party Talks, but also for the preparation of the summit talks. The summit in 2008 further institutionalized this process by calling for an annual Trilateral Senior Foreign Officials' Meeting, which "aims to facilitate the strategic exchange of opinions on regional trends and global issues" (Ministry of Foreign Affairs 2008). The 2008 Action Plan also stated that "other working level consultations including Director-Generals and lower-level officials should continue" (ibid.). Similarly, the trilateral summit has repeatedly called for the increase in interactions among defense personnel of the three countries (TCCS 2003; Three-Party Committee 2004; Ministry of Foreign Affairs 2009; TCCS 2010a).

The summit itself experienced a spillover from a regular summit to an emergency summit. In the spring of 2008, in response to the escalation of the North Korean crisis, the top leaders of the three countries held an emergency meeting in Pattaya, Thailand, because they happened to be there to attend the East Asia Summit. How frequently these emergency meetings will be held remains to be seen.

On the other hand, the realist notion that economic cooperation remains dependent or subordinated to security concerns is also validated to some extent. For example, Koizumi's experience of the cancelled trilateral meeting in 2005 is congruent with realist expectations. Koizumi's repeated visits to the Yasukuni Shrine had damaged the Sino–Japanese and Korea–Japan relations, and his visit on October 2005 became a trigger for the cancellation of the trilateral summit two months later. One can dispute whether the distrust toward Japan created by Koizumi's behavior is a security concern or a more fundamental political concern, but the fact remains that the main casualty of this disaster was a delay in the start of negotiations over the trilateral investment accord, which was supposed to be approved at the December 2005 summit.[23] Thus, economic cooperation in this clear instance was at the mercy of security considerations or the lack of political trust. This episode suggests that the lack of security cooperation could derail economic cooperation easily, thereby turning the clock backwards.

The political economy of Northeast Asian cooperation is complex and defies simple explanations based on deductive principles drawn from either liberalism or realism, standard tools to analyze international relations in the West. On the whole, the liberal spillover hypothesis is supported by considerable evidence, but there is certainly an important component of realist instrumentality in the use of economics for political advantages as well. Therefore, a more comprehensive theory to include all these considerations is needed to understand the dynamics of Northeast Asian cooperation in economic and security affairs.

Notes

1. The literature on East Asian regionalism and multilateralism is too numerous to mention, but some of the most prominent recent examples include: Katzenstein (2005), Pempel (2005), Katzenstein and Shiraishi (2006), Calder and Fukuyama (2008), Acharya (2009), and Green and Gates (2009).
2. The few exceptions include Timmermann and Tsuchiyama (2007), Aggarwal and Koo (2008), and Aggarwal *et al.* (2008).
3. Originally, the security community was defined as "a group of people that had become integrated to the point that there is a real assurance that the members of the community will not fight each other physically, but will settle their disputes some other way" (Adler and Barnett 1998: 6).
4. This is a conventional understanding of mercantilism. However, Viner argues that the relationship between power and wealth in the minds of mercantilists was in fact more reciprocal. See Viner (1948).
5. Drawing on Lasswell, Baldwin defines economic statecraft as "influence attempts relying on primarily on resources which have a reasonable semblance of a market price in terms of money" (1985: 13–14). The goals of influence attempts in economic statecraft do not have security. Any goals, economic and non-economic, of the state are included.
6. As examples of (negative) economic sanctions, Baldwin lists the following: embargoes, boycotts, tariff increases, tariff discrimination, withdrawal of most-favored-nation treatment, blacklist, quotas, license denial, dumping, preclusive buying, freezing of assets, controls on import/export, aid suspension, expropriation, taxation, withholding dues to international organization, and the threats of all the above (Baldwin 1985: 41).
7. *Yomiuri* (24 November 2000). For an overview of this series of events, see Ministry of Foreign Affairs (2002).
8. *Yomiuri* (31 July 2003). For the text of the Declaration, see TCCS (2003).
9. *Yomiuri* (4 October 2003). Paragraph V.13 of the Joint Declaration reads, "The three countries will strengthen security dialogue and facilitate exchange and cooperation among the defense or military personnel of the three countries."
10. In accordance with this agreement, the foreign ministers of the trilateral countries met in Qingdao, China, in June 2004 (*Asahi*, 2 June 2004). The foreign ministers prepared an "Action Strategy" with the pillar of economic cooperation (*Nikkei*, 13 June 2004). The three foreign ministers also met at the time of the trilateral summit meeting in Vientiane in November.
11. According to the joint statement after this meeting, the foreign ministers confirmed that the meeting of the Three-Party Committee would be held at least once a year and

that the meeting should be held in the three countries in rotation. They also confirmed that in addition to diplomatic officials, officials from other departments of the three countries should participate in the meeting of the Trilateral Committee at an appropriate time in accordance with the need of the agenda (full text of the joint statement issued by South Korea, Japan, China, *BBC Monitoring Asia Pacific*, 22 June 2004).

12. For the text of the report, see Ministry of Economy, Trade, and Industry (2004).

13. "Yasukuni can't be made into a diplomatic card" Koizumi told reporters at his office. "Even if China and South Korea try to make it a diplomatic card, there is no way" (Japan Economic Newswire, 4 December 2005).

14. Japanese Ministry of Foreign Affairs officials said that this was the first time that the trilateral summit referred to the abduction issue (*Mainichi*, 15 January 2007).

15. Chinese officials had thus far expressed "understanding" but had never offered to "help."

16. To distinguish it from its earlier meetings held on the sidelines of APT, the "Trilateral Summit" will be capitalized from here on.

17. Before the summit was held, it was agreed that Japan would expand its bilateral swap line with the ROK from US$ 13 to 30 billion (*Asahi*, 12 December 2008).

18. See Trilateral Summit (2008a, 2008b, 2008c) for the text of the statements.

19. In a bilateral summit meeting with Lee Myun-bak in New York, Hu Jintao announced that the leaders from China, Japan, and Korea would hold their second summit meeting in Beijing on October 10 (Xinhua General News Service, 23 September 2009).

20. For the text of his UN speech, see <http://www.kantei.go.jp/foreign/hatoyama/statement/200909/ehat_0924c_e.html>.

21. Wen explained that North was not opposed to the Six-Party Talks at the post-summit press conference (*Nikkei*, 11 October 2009).

22. After the Chinese announcement, Prime Minister Hatoyama told reporters that in creating the mood to have a successful COP15, Japan took a substantive leading role (*Asahi*, 27 November 2009).

23. When the Chairman of the Keidanren Hiroshi Okuda visited Beijing in September 2005, Prime Minister Wen Jiabao sent a clear signal that China was willing to enter into negotiations (*Nikkei*, 8 October 2005).

References

Acharya, Amitav. 2009. *Whose Ideas Matter? Agency and Power in Asian Regionalism.* Ithaca, NY: Cornell University Press.

Adler, Emanuel and Michael Barnett, eds. 1998. *Security Communities.* Cambridge: Cambridge University Press.

Aggarwal, Vinod K. and Min Gyo Koo. 2008. An Institutional Path: Community Building in Northeast Asia. In *The United States and Northeast Asia: Debate, Issues, and New Order*, G. John Ikenberry and Chung-In Moon, eds. Lanham, MD: Rowman & Littlefield.

Aggarwal, Vinod K., Min Gyo Koo, Seungjoo Lee, and Chung-in Moon, eds. 2008. *Northeast Asia: Ripe for Integration?* Berlin and Heidelberg: Springer.

Angell, Norman. 1913. *The Great Illusion: A Study of the Relation of Military Power to National Advantage*, 4th ed. New York: Putnam's.

Aoki, Naoko. 2001. Report Calls for Meeting of Economic Ministers. *Japan Economic Newswire*, 4 November.

Baldwin, David A. 1985. *Economic Statecraft.* Princeton, NJ: Princeton University Press.

Calder, Kent F. and Francis Fukuyama. 2008. *East Asian Multilateralism: Prospects for Regional Stability.* Baltimore, MD: Johns Hopkins University Press.

Deutsch, Karl W., *et al.* 1957. *Political Community and the North Atlantic Area: International Organization in the Light of Historical Experience.* New York: Greenwood.

Doyle, Michael W. 1983. Kant, Liberal Legacies, and Foreign Affairs. *Philosophy and Public Affairs* 12 (3): 205–35.

Fackler, Martin. 2008. Asian Leaders Focus on Growth at a 3-Nation Summit-Meeting. *New York Times*, 14 December.

Fukazawa, Junichi. 2003. Japan, ROK Wary of China-led FTA. *Daily Yomiuri*, 9 October.

Gowa, Joanne. 1994. *Allies, Adversaries, and International Trade*. Princeton, NJ: Princeton University Press.

Green, Michael J. and Jill Gates, eds. 2009. *Asia's New Multilateralism: Cooperation, Competition and the Search for Community*. New York: Columbia University Press.

Haas, Ernst B. 1958. *The Uniting of Europe: Political, Social and Economic Forces, 1950–1957*. Stanford, CA: Stanford University Press.

Haas, Ernst B. and Philippe C. Schmitter. 1964. Economics and Differential Patterns of Political Integration: Projections about Unity in Latin America. *International Organization* 18: 705–37.

Hatoyama, Yukio. 2009. Watashi no Seiji Tetsugaku [My Political Philosophy]. *Voice* September: 132–41.

Katzenstein, Peter J. 2005. *A World of Regions: Asia and Europe in the American Imperium*. Ithaca, NY: Cornell University Press.

Katzenstein, Peter J. and Takashi Shiraishi, eds. 2006. *Beyond Japan: The Dynamics of East Asian Regionalism*. Ithaca, NY: Cornell University Press.

Kim, So-hyun. 2009. Lee-Hatoyama Summit Today. *Korea Herald* 9 October.

Mastanduno, Michael. 1992. *Economic Containment: CoCom and the Politics of East–West Trade*. Ithaca, NY: Cornell University Press.

Matsunaga, Hiroaki. 2001. Japan, China, S. Korea Discuss Fighting Terror. *Daily Yomiuri* 6 November: 1.

Ministry of Economy, Trade, and Industry. 2004. Nichichukan Toshi Torikime no Ariubeki Keitai ni Kansuru Kyodo Kenkyu Hokokusho [Joint Study Report on the Desirable Form of CJK Investment Agreement]. Available at: <http://www.meti.go.jp/policy/trade_policy/asia/jck/data/041129ifdi-j.pdf>.

Ministry of Foreign Affairs. 2000. 2002-nen nicchukan kokumin koryu nen toha [What is the Year of Contacts of Personnel among the People's Republic of China, Japan, and the Republic of Korea?] Available at: <http://www.mofa.go.jp/mofaj/area/2002jck/gaiyo.html>.

———. 2008. Action Plan for Promoting Trilateral Cooperation among the People's Republic of China, Japan and the Republic of Korea, 13 December, available at: <http://www.mofa.go.jp/region/asia-paci/jck/summit0812/action.html>.

———. 2009. Joint Statement on Sustainable Development among the People's Republic of China, Japan, and the Republic of Korea, 10 October, available at: <http://www.mofa.go.jp/region/asia-paci/jck/meet0910/joint-2.pdf>.

Pempel, T.J. 2005. *Remapping East Asia: The Construction of a Region*. Ithaca, NY: Cornell University Press.

Pollins, Brian M. 1989. Does Trade Still Follow the Flag? *American Political Science Review* 83 (2): 465–80.

Russett, Bruce and John R. Oneal. 2001. *Triangulating Peace: Democracy, Interdependence and International Organizations*. New York: W.W. Norton.

Talmadge, Eric. 2008. S Korea, China, Japan Show Unity at First Summit. Associated Press, 13 December.

Three-Party Committee. 2004. The Action Strategy on Trilateral Cooperation among the People's Republic of China, Japan, and the Republic of Korea. Adopted 27 November

by the Three-Party Committee, available at: <http://www.mofa.go.jp/region/asia-paci/
asean/conference/asean3/action0411.html>.

Timmermann, Martina and Jitsuo Tsuchiyama. 2007. *Institutionalizing Northeast Asia: Regional Steps towards Global Governance.* Tokyo: UNU Press.

Torode, Greg. 2007. China Welcomes Closer Trilateral Ties; Links with Tokyo and Seoul Improving, Says Foreign Minister. *South China Morning Post* 13 January: 13, 10.

Trilateral Cooperation Cyber Secretariat (TCCS). 2003. Joint Declaration on the Promotion of Tripartite Cooperation among the People's Republic of China, Japan, and the Republic of Korea. Bali, 7 October 2003, available at: <http://www.tccs.asia/documents/documents_view.php?&start=5&seq=553&mode=view&s_gubun=&s_text=&s_section=>.

———. 2007. Joint Press Statement of the Seventh Summit Meeting among the People's Republic of China, Japan, and the Republic of Korea. Cebu, 14 January, available at: <http://www.tccs.asia/documents/documents_view.php?&start=0&seq=554&mode=view&s_gubun=&s_text=&s_section=>.

———. 2010a. Trilateral Cooperation VISION 2020, available at: <http://www.tccs.asia/documents/documents_view.php?&start=0&seq=604&mode=view&s_gubun=&s_text=&s_section=>.

———. 2010b. Memorandum on the Establishment of the Trilateral Cooperation Secretariat among the Governments of the People's Republic of China, Japan and the Republic of Korea (2010), available at: <http://www.tccs.asia/documents/documents_view.php?&start=0&seq=603&mode=view&s_gubun=&s_text=&s_section=>.

Trilateral Summit. 2008a. Japan–China–ROK Trilateral Summit: Joint Announcement on Disaster Management Cooperation. Fukuoka, 13 December, available at: <http://www.mofa.go.jp/region/asia-paci/jck/summit0812/disaster.html>.

———. 2008b. Japan–China–ROK Trilateral Summit: Joint Statement for Trilateral Partnership. Fukuoka, 13 December, available at: <http://www.mofa.go.jp/region/asia-paci/jck/summit0812/partner.html>.

———. 2008c. Japan–China–ROK Trilateral Summit: Joint Statement on the International Finance and Economy. Fukuoka, 13 December, available at: <http://www.mofa.go.jp/region/asia-paci/jck/summit0812/economy.html>.

Viner, Jacob. 1948. Power versus Plenty as Objectives of Foreign Policy in the Seventeenth and Eighteenth Centuries. *World Politics* 1: 1–29.

10 Conclusion

The uneasy dance of economics and security

T.J. Pempel

Introduction

The preceding chapters have analyzed some of the myriad ways in which economics and security have interacted within Northeast Asia since the end of the Cold War. They demonstrate how intimately the two spheres are linked and how their intersecting roles have shaped regional events. This chapter does not attempt to summarize their collective findings. Rather it underscores several key implications derived from the preceding research material. My aim is to capture several key trends surrounding the economic–security nexus within the region, both for insights into the region itself and also to suggest their implications for ongoing discussions about the interplay of economics and security in international relations more generally. Five broad conclusions are given particular attention.

First, the chapters suggest the benefits of stepping down a rung from the clouds of macro-theoretical analyses that focus on global power balances and system-wide relationships, valuable as these can be for certain purposes, and instead to examine *Northeast Asia as a regional security complex*. It is clear from the findings in the chapters that the primary interactions in Northeast Asia center on relations among geographical neighbors more than on global power relationships. At the same time, a Northeast Asian regional security complex makes sense if, and only if, one treats the United States as a key component of that complex. The United States, as a global power with ongoing involvement in the region, plays a huge role in its affairs. For that reason the United States constitutes an essential actor in the Northeast Asian regional security complex. And while global forces periodically shape regional events, it is the mutual interactions among this core regional group—the United States, China, Japan, the two Koreas, Taiwan, and periodically Russia—that are most central to the dynamics of the economic–security nexus within Northeast Asia.

Second, although economics and security are clearly interrelated in Northeast Asia, *neither sphere consistently drives the other*. Instead, the relationship between the two emerges as highly variegated, issue specific, and subject to the shifting preferences of different governmental leaders.

Third, economic relationships in Northeast Asia have become far *deeper and more intimate than simple trade ties*; they include cross-border investment, global production networks (GPNs), and global intellectual networks (GINs), as well as complex financial webs. Consequently, economic interdependence across the region is far deeper and more economically complex than anything captured in the typically analyzed relationships between "trade" and "war."

Fourth, and related, the leadership in most Northeast Asian countries has increasingly engaged in *multilateral regional approaches* to problems that encourage cross-border cooperation rather than conflict. In East Asia as a whole, it has been ASEAN and Southeast Asia that have driven broader efforts at regional multilateralism. Northeast Asia has been far slower to multilateralize. At the same time, Northeast Asian governments have joined with their Southeast Asian counterparts in a rising number of multilateral bodies that span the broader East Asian region (e.g. Lincoln 2004; Beeson 2007; Pempel 2005, 2006, 2008; Calder and Ye 2010, inter alia). Within East Asia, multilateralism has been far more prevalent in economics, finance, and trade than it has been in defense and foreign policy. And when it comes to formal institution making, Northeast Asian approaches to multilateral institutions have kept the two spheres rather insulated from one another, except in a limited number of cases such as the new Trilateral Dialogue examined in detail by Iida in Chapter 9.

Fifth, and finally, despite rising levels of both economic interdependence and regional multilateralism, *Northeast Asia remains pockmarked by security tensions and the continuation of coercive diplomacy*. Though Northeast Asia has seen no state-to-state wars since the end of the Korean Conflict in 1953, any current peace remains tenuous. War has by no means become "unimaginable" within the region, as would be the case within a deeply entrenched security community. Repeating what was noted in Chapter 1, and as Alagappa (2003) has underscored, the security order in Northeast Asia remains "instrumental" and is far from "normative" or "solidarist." It is, as Kahler (2011: 19) put it, the "peace of the prudent." Meanwhile, U.S.–China relations bristle with mutual suspicions (e.g. Jacques 2009; Friedberg 2011) and the region as a whole struggles with security uncertainties focused on a rising China, a nuclear North Korea, an introspective Japan, and a distracted America. Thus while state-to-state warfare remains improbable in Northeast Asia, coercive diplomacy resulting from traditional clashes of national interest and the mustering of military force continues to be extensive across the region (on coercive diplomacy, see Christensen 2011).

The following sections explore each of these points in greater detail. Collectively they should shed Northeast Asian light on broad issues of debate in international relations, including the value of the regional level of analysis; the complex causal relationships among economics, security, and regional multilateralism; and the ways in which all of these forces are intersecting with changing regional power relations. Collectively, they highlight the competing forces shaping future prospects for conflict escalation or conflict reduction.

Northeast Asia as a security complex

A first point to emerge from the chapters above is the value of conceptualizing *Northeast Asia as a regional security complex*. The benefits of thinking about regional security complexes was most powerfully raised by the Copenhagen School of international relations, most notably in the work of Barry Buzan and Ole Waever (2003, especially chaps 3, 5, 6; see also Buzan 2003). Seeking to forge a middle-level theoretic understanding of contemporary international security, they make a compelling case that security problems are most frequently geographically constricted. As they put it, security problems do not travel well, and as they note for Northeast Asia, "Once the struggle for decolonization was over, the European powers ceased to matter much as players" (ibid.: 138).

For most of the Cold War, events in the Northeast were overwhelmingly shaped by two major "outside" powers, the United States and the Soviet Union. The collapse of the USSR and the end of the Cold War left the United States as the major outside influence on the region. And especially since the end of the Cold War, as Lake and Morgan (1997: 7) detail in depth, regions, including Northeast Asia, have become "substantially more important" sites of conflicts and cooperation than was true under the pervasive bipolarity of U.S.–Soviet global competition. As Michael Yahuda (2004: 229) points out, "the defenses of most East Asian countries are directed against one another." In a similar vein, Peter Katzenstein (2005) unravels the primacy of regional orders under what he calls the American Imperium.

For some, East Asia is composed of two discrete security complexes— Northeast and Southeast Asia—but others stress the ways in which these previously rather discrete security complexes are becoming increasingly fused into a single regional complex. Without much question, on the most important hard security tensions and foreign policy issues affecting Northeast Asia, Southeast Asia remains peripheral. These tensions and policies have been driven by, and remain largely under the influence of, the states within the region.

Yet as one speaks of a regional security complex it is difficult to do so without underscoring the continued influence of the most prominent extra-regional actor, the United States, which remains an unmistakable shaper of events in both the security and economic realms across the Asia-Pacific and throughout Northeast Asia. That America's capacity to shape financial and economic activities unilaterally has dwindled from its preeminence during the period from World War II until at least the Plaza Accord of 1985 is undeniable. And Asia's collective weight in global GDP has risen substantially since then, even as the U.S. share of global GDP has remained relatively constant at around 25 percent. Yet the rapid rise of the developing economies, and particularly the economic successes of China and the rest of Asia, have meant *relative* declines in America's economic influence (Luce 2012). Nonetheless, American influences, both unilaterally and through American-dominated institutions such as the IMF, the World Bank, and the WTO, are undeniable.

American economic muscle, while still impressive, is but a shadow of the U.S. preeminence in areas of hard security. There, its unsurpassed military budget and its military sophistication, its bilateral alliances with both Japan and South Korea, its basing architecture, and its capacity for forward deployment all dwarf the competitive capabilities of any other country or combination of countries in the region. When combined with the military strengths of countries with which the United States shares its hub-and-spoke security alliances, notably Japan and

Korea, the combined force vis-à-vis potential challengers is multiplied even further. The United States is a de facto, if not a de locus, member of any Northeast Asian security complex.

That said, virtually all of the empirical problems that were examined in this volume's research underscore the centrality of interactions among Northeast Asian countries themselves along with their links to the United States. Geography and regional historical legacies have been the preeminent shapers of the most pressing economic and security problems these countries confront. Clear examples would include the economic and political relations between the People's Republic of China (PRC) and Taiwan; the ongoing jockeying over historical memories driven largely by interactions among China, the two Koreas, and Japan; techno-nationalist competitions across the region; the growing preponderance of free trade agreements; and the bulk of the new regional multilateral bodies that have been forged. In addition, complex economic linkages within Northeast Asia have also been exploding in the form of foreign direct investment, trade, and regional production networks, and these regional ties have come to take on an ever greater share of the total economic activity of most states in the region.

As but one indicator of this growing economic interdependence, China has become the main export market for Taiwan, South Korea, and Japan, replacing the United States in all three instances. Equally, cross-border investment among these countries reflects similar trends. These market-driven interactions are supplemented by the dozens of more formally structured interactions among the states of Northeast Asia identified by Calder and Ye (2010: 19–22). In short, intra-regional interactions have become increasingly dense for all of the major nation-states in the region, reflecting their geographical proximity and interdependence.

Perhaps most symbolically significant, as Iida demonstrates in Chapter 9, the top leaders from Japan, Korea, and China have been holding annual summits since 2008 and more recently institutionalized these ties by creating and staffing a trilateral secretariat to serve the three in their collective interactions. Both economic and security concerns are regularly on the agenda and the three have come increasingly to concentrate on their mutual interactions.

The region is by no means sealed off from the broader globe and other regions. Without question, as Oba's analysis (Chapter 6) shows, global forces periodically impinge on the region, a message that was delivered with a bludgeon by the global financial crises of 1997–98 and of 2007–10. Problems of global warming, terrorism, pandemics, and nuclear proliferation present additional examples of global problems that the region must deal with. ASEAN and the individual countries of Southeast Asia are often regular partners with their neighbors to the North in the larger regional dynamics of East Asia, playing a particularly critical linkage in economic and production networks as well as in the supply chains that span the entire Western Pacific. ASEAN has also been an important catalyst behind the burgeoning number of regional institutions and arrangements that are increasingly engulfing most of the states of Northeast Asia. Similarly, Central Asian republics periodically gain Northeast Asian salience through issues such as energy, Muslim fundamentalism, and their economic and security ties to Russia and China through the Shanghai Cooperation Organization (SCO). And Northeast Asian states, in their investment policies and free trade agreements, frequently engage with extra-regional partners.

Such qualifications demonstrate the porous nature of the region's borders, both geographically and functionally. Still, the governing elites in Northeast Asia's core states are most typically preoccupied with their mutual interactions. For students of international relations anxious to move beyond the narrow confines of European experiences, examining the activities of Northeast Asia through such a regional security lens suggests a set of experiences over the last 30–40 years that do not match up neatly with general conclusions drawn from the far more frequently studied experiences of Western Europe (e.g. Alagappa 2003; Ikenberry and Mastanduno 2003; Kang 2003; Katzenstein 2005).

The salience of treating Northeast Asia as a security complex is also clear in the increasing efforts of the region to project itself collectively outward to the globe at large (Tow 2009). Notably, the countries of Northeast Asia have moved to enhance their collective influence in certain global multilateral bodies, most particularly the IMF. Cognizant of how negatively the IMF's actions were viewed by most Asian countries in the wake of the 1997–98 financial crisis, and how these actions threatened the developmental strategies of the IMF bailout countries, Japan, China, and Korea in particular have pressed for a greater collective voice in decision-making within that global body.

Thus, despite many possible qualifications, the intensity and specificity of the interactions among the states of the region highlight the value of treating Northeast Asia as a regional security complex and using that notion as the logical starting point for examining the dynamics of relations among the states of that region. In turn, this also allows one to consider how these regional experiences may offer fresh lessons for international relations theory (see Buzan and Waever 2003; Kang 2003; Acharya and Buzan 2007, inter alia).

The economic–security nexus: dancing together but with neither partner leading

The international relations literature bristles with debates over the links between economics and security. A primary emphasis is on which drives the other. A longstanding debate in international relations has ensued over the extent to which trade relations between nation-states mitigate any incentives they may have to engage in military conflicts with one another. The usual arguments center on whether "trade follows the flag" or whether "commercial ties prohibitively raise the costs of war." This debate traces back at least to the "commercial peace theory" advanced by Immanuel Kant. Varying boundary conditions and sub-debates have qualified the central argument over time and this is by no means the place to reopen that debate (see Layne 1994; Mansfield and Pollins 1999; Anderton and Carter 2001; Gartzke *et al.* 2001; Barbieri 2002; Oneal *et al.* 2003; Souva and Prins 2006; Barbieri *et al.* 2008; Arena and Palmer 2009; Böhmelt 2010, inter alia).

At the same time, the chapters in this book support the notion that "economics" and "security" interact quite symbiotically in Northeast Asia, but in ways that defy any credible claim that one consistently drives the other or that one or the other is the prime shaper of events. Rather, economics and security resemble closely entwined dancers dipping, spinning, and rotating in close synchronicity across the Northeast Asian dance floor, with neither one consistently leading or alternatively moving backwards passively following the other's lead. Who leads and who follows in any particular sequence is a function of the music being played and at least as importantly, on the preferences of the dancers themselves. As Moravcsik (1997) has reminded us, while structural forces—whether economic or military—set broad parameters for any nation's grand strategy, the preferences of state actors are critical in the directions a state eventually pursues. Domestic political factors and leadership preferences remain central molders of any country's foreign policy choices both strategically and operationally. The relationship between structure and agency is clearly symbiotic but rarely hierarchical.

As but one example, Cheung (Chapter 4) shows the pervasive commitments by all governments across the region to techno-nationalism, perhaps the most obvious manifestation of how closely the two realms are fused in the minds and policies of national leaders. But as he also shows, leaders in different countries pursue quite distinct versions of techno-nationalism. To cite only two of the more extreme patterns, some, for example, privilege military industries and heightened nationalism while others center their efforts on civilian industries and globalization. Such differences shape the pressures for regional cooperation or conflict.

A different facet of the economic–security nexus emerges from Oba's treatment (Chapter 6) of Northeast Asian responses to the two financial crises that engulfed the region in 1997–98 and 2008–10. Both shocks saw regimes in Northeast Asia responding with a vigor and concentration of policy resources that raised national economic protection to an existentially critical level akin to military security. Such attention to finance and economic security was congruent with the pervasive commitment made by most Northeast Asian leaders to treat economic development as a core component of regime legitimacy that was examined in Chapter 1. Yet if economics drives most leaders, the regime in North Korea with its unparalleled devotion of state resources to the military has been a conspicuous exception; there, as Imamura (Chapter 3) shows, economic policies, including basic agricultural reforms and minimal marketization, have been subordinated to the overweening demands of the military.

Taking still another example, economic and security relations are intimately connected in the cross-Strait strategies of leaders in both the PRC and Taiwan, as Kastner (Chapter 2) demonstrates, but the specific interactions in that bilateral relationship have in recent years reflected cordiality or confrontation largely as a function of whether an independence-minded or integration-minded government is in power in Taipei. Taiwanese governments anxious to reach accommodation with Beijing have found a welcoming partner, and trade, tourism, and other economic linkages have blossomed. In contrast, when Taipei has been under more independence-minded leadership, security tensions have expanded and economic interactions have slowed. And throughout the process, governments in both Taiwan and the PRC have continually wrestled with their own assessments of which side would, in the long run, most benefit from closer economic and cultural ties.

Shifting one's focus slightly, the number of free trade agreements across the region has soared since 2000 but in most instances, political and security calculations have trumped economic incentives in the choice of trade partners. Once it became clear that the WTO's Doha round was unlikely to reach any comprehensive global agreement, most East Asian governments became active promoters of bilateral and multilateral free trade agreements (FTAs) or Economic Partnership Agreements (EPAs) (Dent 2003; Amyx 2004; Aggarwal and Koo 2008; Pempel 2008; Grimes 2009; Suominen 2009). Certainly, as Koo makes clear in Chapter 7, this has been true for South Korea as that country has sought recently to offset its previously U.S.-dominated foreign policy by expanding its ties to neighbors in both Northeast and Southeast Asia through bilateral FTAs and thus to enhance its influence as a regional "middle power." Yet as East Asia generally rushes forward with FTAs, no such agreement yet exists among the big three in Northeast Asia, and security competition, domestic politics, and techno-nationalist impulses impede trilateral trade cooperation.

While the two spheres intersect constantly, neither consistently drives the decisions of state leaders across the region. If there is one trend that emerges region-wide it is that economic issues have been given greater priority in the policy calculations of such political elites than have security concerns. Northeast Asian elites, particularly since the Deng reforms in China and the democratization of both Taiwan and South Korea in the late 1980s, self-consciously devote far more effort and resources to sustaining national development, economic enhancements, and the delivery of tangible job and welfare benefits to their citizens than they do to projecting national military preeminence (Overholt 2008). Hard security problems remain of considerable concern across the region, particularly for military planners, and mutual trust among the key states of the region is fragile at best. And as will be discussed below, coercion remains an ongoing option for most states in Northeast Asia. At the same time, security worries and military threats have tipped down in the centrality of the foreign policy orientations of most states from the preeminence they held two or three decades ago.

Clearly this has been true in South Korea. As Koo notes, for most of the Cold War period, the economic–security nexus of South Korea was concentrated on military and security concerns and the recurrent threat of attack or infiltration by the North. Yet following democratization and the end of the Cold War, South Korea began to give greater emphasis to enhancing its national economic prowess and fusing its traditional security concerns with an emphasis on trade and economics. Relations with China were normalized and China became the Republic of Korea's (ROK) main trading partner and investment destination by 2006. The administrations of Kim Dae-jung and Roh Moo-hyun both pursued policies of economic engagement with the North—critics would say with limited change in North Korean behavior. But in fact, hard security confrontations between North and South declined substantially during the ten years of their combined presidencies, only to rise again during the tenure of the more security-oriented governance of Lee Myung-bak. Equally, Korean elites pressed hard for the Korea–U.S. FTA (KORUS) as an agreement that would serve both economic and security purposes. The South Korean shift toward more emphasis on economics and finance has been reflected in the country's drop in military spending as a percent of GDP from 4.5 percent in 1989 to 2.7 percent in 2010.

Similarly, Taiwan has reduced the primacy of its hard security focus as reflected in a drop in the percentage of its GDP devoted to military and defense expenditures. These fell from a level of 4.9 percent in 1990 to 2.1 percent in 2010. Just as with South Korea, enhanced economic links to China have resulted in making China the main export destination for goods from both Taiwan as well as Japan.

Somewhat surprisingly given the systematic attention given to an alleged Chinese military expansion and the undeniable efforts by China to expand its air and naval capabilities substantially, the Chinese expansion merely parallels the country's overall growth and, as a percentage of GDP China's military spending has actually dropped. The most typically reliable estimate suggests that the figure is 2.1 percent today compared to 2.5 percent in 1990 (all figures from SIPRI 2012).

Rather ironically, if there is one power—in addition to the United States—that is expanding its focus on hard security over economic diplomacy, it is Japan. For most of the postwar period Japan has been more oriented toward economics as a tool of international influence than its Chinese, South Korean, and Taiwanese neighbors. Relying heavily on its alliance with the United States for traditional security assurances, Japan pursued a systematic "dollar diplomacy" through, among other things, investment, overseas development assistance, and technology sharing. As Cheung notes in Chapter 4, Japan's approach to techno-nationalism has been predominantly civilian and globalized. Yet, as Samuels (2007) has noted, rising worries about North Korean and Chinese military threats, combined with ongoing U.S. pressures for Japan to engage in greater burden sharing have resulted in a revisionist group of policymakers consolidating power in Japan (Pempel 2007; Hughes 2009). As a consequence, particularly since 2002, Japan has made a number of moves away from its long-dominant pacifism, among other things by upgrading the status of the Defense Agency to that of a ministry, expanding the missions of its military, engaging in closer military coordination with the United States, and developing enhanced cyber-warfare and satellite surveillance capabilities. Yet despite such moves, Japan continues to maintain virtually the same spending levels for military and defense in both yen and U.S. dollars as well as in percent of GDP that it has appropriated since 1990. In this regard, Japan's military enhancements, like those of China, do not signal a sharp reprioritization of security over economics. Instead they are aimed at recalibrating strategy and upgrading capabilities without signaling a major refocus of the national grand strategy. Moreover, as the militaries of both China and Japan enhance their capabilities they risk triggering the classical security dilemmas, despite what both might claim are purely defensive endeavors.

The most obvious exception to the regional predisposition to favor economic prioritization over hard security remains the Democratic People's Republic of Korea (DPRK). Imamura (Chapter 3) shows that the "military first" policy has enjoyed unchallenged primacy among the ruling elites and that even efforts at improving agricultural production have failed due to a reluctance to break with the Stalinist model of a command economy allegedly prioritizing industrialization. Military prioritization continues despite the deprived and depressed living standards of most of the country's citizens, and despite the continued imprecations of China to shift away from aspects of the longstanding command economy and to inject greater market forces (Haggard and Noland 2007; Lankov 2008). Nor has the North been particularly responsive to either the experiences or blandishments of its more prosperous neighbors, including the "sunshine policy" of economic engagement attempted by two successive South Korean regimes between 1998 and 2008. Instead periodic bursts of brinksmanship and military provocation provide unwelcome challenges to the otherwise economically-focused predisposition of the region as a whole (Michishita 2009).

Nevertheless, as noted in Chapter 1, despite tensions on the Korean Peninsula as well as others throughout the region, the Asia-Pacific continues to enjoy the most broadly peaceful era in its history (Wainwright 2010). Economics has by no means displaced security worries across Northeast Asia, but classical security dilemmas and a hard security focus have surrendered some of their sharpness in the face of an enhanced economic focus and greater cross-border economic and financial connections.

Economic interdependence in Northeast Asia: deeper than trade

Northeast Asia's economic interactions far transcend country-to-country trade in goods, as is the case for East Asia as a whole. Chapter 1 underscored many of the ways in which the region's economic interdependence extends deeper than simple exchanges through trade. Historical investment ties from Japan to the rest of the region that began in the 1970s and accelerated during the 1980s have further deepened and have subsequently been mirrored by similarly complex linkages by Korean, Taiwanese, and Chinese firms. As well, much of the region is knitted together by the economic–cultural networks that constitute the various "China circles" that connect ethnic Chinese businesspeople and financiers in different parts of the region to one another through a variety of investment and joint production facilities.

Today the most important economic linchpins across Northeast Asia are those that transcend individual national borders. Global production networks involve multinational corporations connected to localized networks of producers that span multiple country borders (Ernst and Kim 2002). Such global production networks involve substantial capital investments by the parent multinational corporation that go far deeper into a nation's economy than single standalone plants; rather the investments are in partnership (albeit hierarchically favorable to the multinational corporation in most cases) with various locally-situated subcontractors and they transfer knowledge and technology, along with goods and components. Their overall result is to forge far tighter economic bonds than those developed by simple market-priced exchanges of goods through trade.

Similarly, as Tai Ming Cheung underscores in Chapter 4, East Asia has witnessed the rise of GINs that "integrate dispersed engineering, product development, and research activities across geographic borders." As Ernst and Kim (2002: 1418) argue, such networks have "changed dramatically the international geography of production and innovation." Both GPNs and GINs weave elaborate webs of extensive cross-border linkages among providers of goods or services in Northeast Asia, and East Asia more generally, that are far more valuable to state actors and far more difficult to replace or dislodge than the traded goods reflected in bilateral trade statistics. The result is that the complex economic ties across Northeast Asia, rooted as they in these new GPNs and GINs, may well exert a more profound constraining influence over governments tempted to escalate conflicts with their neighbors through military actions. Yet too often it is these bilateral trade statistics that drive debates in the international relations analysis about the economic–security nexus.

These deeper economic interdependencies by no means completely deter governments from opting for military confrontations with those to whom they are linked. As noted in the previous section, the economic–security nexus in Northeast Asia often finds security considerations trumping economic ties. It is difficult to envision, for example, any degree of economic interdependence between Taiwan and China that would lead either to surrender their concerns over, respectively, political autonomy or residual sovereignty. Yet, the deeper and more complex the networks of economic dependence become, the more difficult and costly it is to gamble on their loss. Trade, investment, and other financial ties across Northeast Asia—and throughout East Asia more broadly—forge highly complex interdependencies that are not easy to disentangle for short-term political purposes, such as Choi (Chapter 5) makes clear, demonstrating national unhappiness over issues that trigger negative historical memories or unresolved territorial disputes.

Regional institution building

The collective successes of so many countries across East Asia, and the worldwide embrace of the story line of an "East Asian miracle" along with the growing importance of deepening intra-regional economic ties, made it easy to minimize the potential impact of extra-regional financial influences. Yet, as Oba's analysis in Chapter 6 of the Asian financial crisis and the Lehman crisis and their impact on Northeast Asia demonstrates, and as Pempel (2012) argues independently and in his treatment of regional institutions in Chapter 8, the collective vulnerability of the region's nation-states to the sloshing of global capital was unmistakable. As a result, in the wake of the 1997–98 crisis those governments took numerous individual and collective steps to buffer themselves against future capital threats with the result that Northeast Asia emerged far less devastated by the Lehman crisis than it did in 1997–98.

Prior to the 1997–98 financial crisis East Asian and Northeast Asian moves toward collective action and regional multilateralism were minimal. The few that existed were largely pan-Pacific (Pempel 2005). The devastating economic and social effects of the crisis, however, stimulated greater collective efforts at creating buffers against the most potentially devastating consequences of the forces of global capitalism, particularly those unleashed by the most sophisticated products of global finance: rapid-fire currency transfers, derivatives, sweeping trade liberalization, securitization, and, even in some cases, short-term stock market speculation. If there has been a common "enemy" against which East Asian governments have moved to enhance their regional cooperation, deeper networks, and collective institutions, it is this exogenous force of global capitalism. States throughout the region have enhanced the mechanisms and venues for intra-regional cooperation among "Asians only" while simultaneously erecting borders against "outsiders." These moves broke with the earlier institutional pattern of creating bodies made up of members from both sides of the Pacific. As treated in detail in Chapter 8, the new moves include the ASEAN Plus Three, the Asian Bond Market Initiative, common enhancement of foreign reserve holdings, and the explosion of intra-Asian FTAs, to mention only the most noteworthy. In all of these, the countries of Northeast Asia (with the noteworthy exception of the DPRK) have been central players.

Regional multilateral bodies have been far more pervasive and successful in the economic and financial spheres than in hard security, however. In the latter sphere, bilateral relationships continue to be the primary instruments of military and defense cooperation, although as noted some build-out from bilateralism to trilateralism can be seen in U.S.–Japan–Australia and U.S.–Japan–Korea ties, and in the more complex China–Russian links through the SCO and by both to the DPRK. In some respects these ties sharpen, rather than reduce, the residual cleavages of the Cold War.

Furthermore, as is often noted by students of Asian regionalism (Beeson 2007; Grimes 2009), the institutional developments that have occurred so far remain administratively thin and have limited abilities to ensure compliance. At the same time, they have fostered an enhanced sense of intra-Asian cooperation and as institutions they have the potential to enhance mutual trust and socialize members into increasingly common perspectives on specific problems and their possible solutions. Ernst Haas (1964) long ago suggested that multilateralism and cooperation in one functional area such as economics might "spill over" to spawn positive cooperation and trust in another area, such as security. Whether or not that will happen in the relationship between economics and security in Northeast Asia through enhanced communication and institutional socialization remains of course an open question but early indications are that such spillover has begun (see Deutsch *et al.* 1957 on the general issue; Acharya and Johnston 2007 on how this has played out in East Asia).

Another promising sign for cooperation among the three leading countries in Northeast Asia may be found in the Trilateral Dialogue which has continued to advance despite the systematic dust-ups around Japanese textbooks or Yasukuni visits, or periodic xenophobic outbursts in China, Korea, or Japan. This Trilateral Dialogue has not been the political football that military-to-military arrangements have been, suspended at the slightest hint of national insult. Furthermore, the Trilateral Dialogue now has a secretariat in Seoul and an explicit agenda to pursue—both a common investment treaty and a joint trade pact among Japan, China, and South Korea. Moreover, a heads-of-state meeting has a catalyzing impact on the government agencies beneath them: summits demand "deliverables," however symbolic, and that usually lubricates previously slow-moving decision-making processes. To the extent that the top leaders of all three countries continue to build on these summits and as other government agencies are woven into the cooperative process, as appears to be taking place, the three countries may be able to begin negotiating settlements to complex and longstanding disputes by engaging in tradeoffs that erode the traditional boundaries between economics and security. Similarly, with the United States now making stronger efforts to reengage with the multilateral processes in East Asia, particularly through membership in the East Asia Summit, regional multilateralism may be layered on top of, and serve as a complement to, traditional bilateral alliances. If so, the result is likely to be less conflict and enhanced cooperation.

Continued security tensions and coercive diplomacy

Important as enriched economic interdependence and regional institutions have become, the nation-state continues to be the preeminent actor in the dynamics of both economic and security interactions across Northeast Asia (Katzenstein 2005). China is at the center of both the new economic links and most regional institutions, but its official policies adhere adamantly to the importance of sovereignty in virtually all aspects of the country's foreign affairs, from resolutions in the United Nations to territorial questions in its surrounding maritime areas. Japan and South Korea, though highly globalized in many aspects, retain strong streaks of protectionism and nationalism. North Korea's economy is disengaged from those of most others in the region with the notable exception of China—though as Imamura (Chapter 3) notes, it is increasingly tied to the economies of a number of Middle Eastern countries such as Iran, Syria, and Egypt. The DPRK also holds membership in very few of the emerging regional bodies beyond the security-focused ASEAN Regional Forum. Taiwan is essentially banned from all regional institutions except for Asia-Pacific Economic Cooperation (APEC), where it holds membership as an "economy" rather than as a state, and most of Taiwan's neighbors remain reluctant to engage with it too closely for fear of alienating China. Russia's traditional European concentration has been complemented in the post-Cold War period by enhanced engagement in both Central Asia and Northeast Asia but its regional multilateral and economic interdependence linkages are thin.

Techno-nationalism, as Tai Ming Cheung demonstrates in Chapter 4, remains a tantalizing goal for the major states of the region. And issues linked to historical memories rankle on a regular basis, even if they do not actually shatter existing ties. Even in areas such as trade relations, as Min Gyo Koo (Chapter 7) shows, states remain the key drivers of any bargains eventually struck in FTAs and their priorities continue to take precedence over multilateral or region-wide arrangements. Moreover, political and security relations between signatories to FTAs are typically more compelling drivers than economic considerations per se.

As was noted in the section on the relationship between economics and security, the states of Northeast Asia are generally reducing their military budgets as a percentage of GDP. At the same time, most are endeavoring to upgrade the forces they have. Furthermore, the region remains vexed by transnational security problems from piracy and drug trafficking to global warming and disease pandemics. Northeast Asia's regional linkages and capacity for security cooperation are not remotely close to the levels reached in the European Union where regional wars have now become implausible despite the region's history as a tinderbox of clashing militaries.

Governments in Northeast Asia also remain relatively untrusting of one another, particularly as regards long-term intentions. The current elite focus on economics could change quickly given the appropriate provocations, and governments continue to be sensitive to the prospects for individual or coercive diplomatic maneuverings by their neighbors.

As noted throughout, despite moves to enhance cooperation particularly across a range of economic sub-fields, Northeast Asia has by no means been transformed into a genuine security community. Competing national interests, rather than any collective vision of cooperation, remain key shapers of the economic–security nexus throughout Northeast Asia and are likely to continue to hold that power in the short to medium term.

As a result, even if its probability is low, state-to-state conflict has by no means become unimaginable in the region and various examples of coercive diplomacy remain a disruptive staple of the region (Yahuda 2004; Christensen 2011, inter alia). Security threats percolate throughout the region and the level of trust across national borders remains low (see the surveys at Asian Barometer). Thus, a number of military or Coast Guard skirmishes or standoffs have regularly broken out within the region, the most recent and deadly of which include the sinking of the ROK's corvette, the *Cheonan*, in March 2010 and the DPRK shelling of Yeonpyeong Island in December of that same year. A major dust-up followed the ramming of a Japanese Coast Guard cutter by a Chinese fishing vessel in disputed waters near the Senkaku/Diaoyu Islands in the East China Sea in September 2010. Equally, Japanese fishing boats have been fired at by Russian ships as they trolled in waters around the disputed Northern Territories. And U.S. and Chinese ships confronted one another in waters just off China's coast in March 2009 as the USNS *Impeccable*, an unarmed American research vessel was harassed by Chinese vessels for violating China's EEZ as well as what the Chinese government claimed was international and Chinese law (Pedroza 2009).

Without question, despite the high levels of economic interaction among the jostling states, security challenges have frequently interrupted, such as when tensions have boiled up in the East China Sea, when North Korea has engaged in missile or nuclear tests, or when the American emphasis on "freedom of the seas" clashes with contradictory Chinese demands for acknowledgment of their sovereignty over coastal waters and restrictions on U.S. vessels trolling for military data in close proximity to China's coast. But equally, it is clear that other tensions, such as those surrounding historical memory issues as demonstrated by Choi, or between Taiwan and China, as shown by Kastner, while marked by sometimes blistering and shrill rhetorical exchanges, typically unfold with few if any disruptions in the decades-long trajectory of expanding trade and investment linkages.

Northeast Asia must also deal continually with the regionally idiosyncratic and provocative actions of the DPRK: its military first policy; the challenges to regional security posed by its nuclear and missile programs; its rejection of domestic economic transformation; the corrosively venal and self-serving character of the ruling elite; and the apparent disdain of the regime for the economic well-being of its citizens.

All of these pose systemic and ongoing challenges to comprehensive regional cooperation in economics or security. There also continue to be security tensions concerning sovereignty over contested islands in the East China and South China Seas. On opposing sides of the Taiwan Strait, a democratically-elected government overseeing an economy with a per capita GDP of $21,600 and an authoritarian political elite steering the region's fastest-growing economy with a per capital GDP one-quarter that of Taiwan, offer competing visions of the "one China" they both notionally embrace. Contested historical memories spawn regularized disputes and nationalist outbursts in Japan, Korea, and China. Security dilemmas continue to haunt security planners throughout the region. For the most part, however, hard security problems may generate manifestations of coercive diplomacy but only infrequently have they led to sustained exchanges of deadly force.

Swords have by no means replaced regional plowshares in Northeast Asia, as any survey of military boundary testing in any single year will show. Yet it is vital to remind ourselves that state-to-state military confrontations have largely been avoided and military budgets have been on a slow decline as a proportion of GDP in almost all countries. The reduction in hard security conflicts across Northeast Asia has been paralleled by the increased attention that political elites have been devoting to domestic economic development, as shown by their conspicuous, if often slightly different attention to techno-nationalism, as well as by their collective, if often tentative efforts at regional economic and financial cooperation. And as Northeast Asia's collective efforts to enhance domestic development have become more effective, the collective global influence of the region has risen commensurately. As the 2009 US National Intelligence Community Estimate phrased it, the region is "poised to become the long-term power center of the world" (Blair 2009: 21).

While China has its share of saber rattlers and an eighteen-month period in 2010–11 saw the country taking a number of steps seen as militarily aggressive, the broad direction of that country's policy has been domestic economic development; foreign policy decisions have been orchestrated to convince neighbors of China's peaceful rise for the preceding decade. Seemingly in rejection of the interlude of pushiness, subsequent policies have centered far more on economic and security cooperation with the United States and across the region, suggesting perhaps a political elite cognizant of having overplayed its coercive diplomatic hand.

Looking ahead

In thinking about the future of the economic–security nexus in Northeast Asia, optimists and pessimists have in front of them myriad shards of potential evidence from which to build their cases. In a stimulating essay on the future of U.S.–China relations, Aaron Friedberg (2005) notes how even self-described realists can find reasons to be optimistic or pessimistic as is true of institutionalists and constructivists as well. In all cases prediction is a function of how one selects the evidence and the particular trends one chooses to emphasize.

Similarly, William Overholt (2008) lays out several alternative scenarios of how economics and security might evolve in Northeast Asia. As he indicates, the scenarios are not attempts to predict the future so much as they are designed to provide policymakers with competing visions of alternative end points that they could try to reach or to avoid.

What is critical to take from both perspectives is the importance of the lenses through which we examine developments and trends in Northeast Asia as well as the continued opportunity for human choice. Certainly, the analyses in the chapters above demonstrate the extent to which past interactions between security and economics in Northeast Asia have been powerfully shaped by the agency of domestic political forces and national governments. In the case of Taiwan, Kastner shows the myriad ways in which bilateral Taiwanese–Chinese economic and security relations twisted and turned during different presidencies and the relative strength or weakness of pan-Green or pan-Blue legislatures. Similarly volatile swings in relations between the two Koreas, as well as between South Korea and the United States, were directly attributable to changes in government within the ROK as well as within the United States. How historical issues have been framed by governments and how they have anchored their collective actions in the soil of nationalistic publics have been critical in raising or lowering tensions across the region, although as Jong Kun Choi shows, these ebbs and flows have rarely been sufficiently powerful to upend ongoing economic relations, often as the consequence of top-level political interventions to stem public protests. Moves toward multilateral cooperation may have had their structural drivers but ultimately whether to join or not, and more importantly how to advance one's position within such bodies, are clearly matters involving political choice.

My own views, and probably those of most of the authors, on the economic United States security nexus in Northeast Asia would incline toward "optimistic institutionalism." We have stressed the rising importance and deepening of economic interdependence as well as the expansion and enrichment of multilateral institutions. Clearly, these now afford the region's leaders greater opportunities and incentives to search for peaceful and cooperative ways with which to interact and to resolve their differences. At the same time, there is little that is teleological, or even easy, in the choice of such a path. Multiple fears and opportunities will surely surface that could result in confrontation and military conflicts. The role of political choice will remain paramount and one can only hope that those making the choices will be mindful of their longer-term implications.

References

Acharya, Amitav and Barry Buzan. 2007. Why is there no Non-Western International Relations Theory? *International Relations of the Asia-Pacific* 7 (3): 287–312.

Acharya Amitav and Alastair Iain Johnston. 2007. *Crafting Cooperation: Regional International Institutions in Comparative Perspective*. Cambridge: Cambridge University Press.

Aggarwal, VinodK. and MinGyo Koo, eds. 2008. *Asia's New Institutional Architecture: Evolving Structures for Managing Trade, Financial, and Security Relations*. Berlin: Springer-Verlag.

Alagappa, Muthiah, ed. 2003. *Asian Security Order: Instrumental and Normative Features*. Stanford, CA: Stanford University Press.

Amyx, Jennifer. 2004. Japan and the Evolution of Regional Financial Arrangements in East Asia. In *Beyond Bilateralism: U.S.–Japan Relations in the New Asia-Pacific*, EllisS.Krauss and T. J.Pempel, eds. Stanford, CA: Stanford University Press.

Anderton, Charles H. and John R. Carter. 2001. The Impact of War on Trade: An Interrupted Times-Series Study. *Journal of Peace Research* 38 (5): 625–8.

Arena, P. and G. Palmer. 2009. Politics or the Economy? Domestic Correlates of Dispute Involvement in Developed Democracies. *International Studies Quarterly* 53 (4): 955–75.

Asian Barometer. n.d. Available at<http://www.asianbarometer.org/newenglish/surveys/>.

Barbieri, Katherine. 2002. *The Liberal Illusion: Does Trade Promote Peace?* Ann Arbor, MI: University of Michigan Press.

Barbieri, Katherine, Omar Keshk, and Brian Pollins. 2008. Correlates of War Project Trade Data Set Codebook, Version 2.0, available at: <http://correlatesofwar.org>.

Beeson, Mark. 2007. *Regionalism and Globalization in East Asia: Politics, Economics, Security, and Economic Development*. New York: Palgrave Macmillan.

Blair, Dennis C. 2009. *Annual Threat Assessment of the Intelligence Community for the Senate Select Committee on Intelligence. 12 February*. Washington, DC: Director of the Office of National Intelligence.

Böhmelt, T. 2010. The Impact of Trade on International Mediation. *Journal of Conflict Resolution* 54 (4): 566–92.

Buzan, Barry. 2003. Security Architecture in Asia: The Interplay of Regional and Global Levels. *Pacific Review* 16 (2): 143–73.

Buzan, Barry and Ole Waever. 2003. *Regions and Power: The Structure of International Security*. Cambridge: Cambridge University Press.

Calder, Kent and Min Ye. 2010. *The Making of Northeast Asia.* Stanford, CA: Stanford University Press.

Christensen, Thomas J. 2011. *Worse than a Monolith: Alliance Politics and Problems of Coercive Diplomacy in Asia.* Princeton, NJ: Princeton University Press.

Dent, C.M. 2003. Networking the Region? The Emergence and Impact of Asia-Pacific Bilateral Trade Agreement Projects. *Pacific Review* 16 (1): 1–28.

Deutsch, Karl, *et al.* 1957. *Political Community in the North Atlantic Area.* Princeton, NJ: Princeton University Press.

Ernst, Dieter and Linsu Kim. 2002. Global Production Networks, Knowledge Diffusion, and Local Capability Formation. *Research Policy* 31: 1417–29.

Friedberg, Aaron. 2005. The Future of U.S.–China Relations: Is Conflict Inevitable? *International Security* 30 (2): 7–45.

———. 2011. *A Contest for Supremacy: China, America, and the Struggle for Mastery in Asia.* New York: W.W. Norton.

Gartzke, Erik, Quan Li, and Charles Boehmer. 2001. Investing in the Peace: Economic Interdependence and International Conflict. *International Organization* 55 (2): 391–438.

Grimes, William W. 2009. *Currency and Contest in East Asia: The Great Power Politics of Financial Regionalism.* Ithaca, NY: Cornell University Press.

Haas, E.B. 1964. *The Uniting of Europe: Political, Economic and Social Forces, 1950– 1957.* Stanford, CA: Stanford University Press.

Haggard, Stephan and Marcus Noland. 2007. *Famine in North Korea: Markets, Aid, and Reform.* New York: Columbia University Press.

Hughes, Christopher. 2009. *Japan's Remilitarization.* London: Routledge.

Ikenberry, G.John and Michael Mastanduno, eds. 2003. *International Relations Theory and the Asia Pacific.* New York: Columbia University Press.

Jacques, Martin. 2009. *When China Rules the World: The End of the Western World and the Birth of a New Global Order.* New York: Penguin Books.

Kahler, Miles. 2011. Weak Ties Don't Bind: Asia Needs Stronger Structures to Build Lasting Peace. *Global Asia* 6 (2): 14–23.

Kang, David. 2003. Hierarchy and Stability in Asian International Relations. In *International Relations Theory and the Asia Pacific*, G.John Ikenberry and Michael Mastanduno, eds. New York: Columbia University Press.

Katzenstein, Peter J. 2005. A World of Regions. Ithaca, NY: Cornell University Press.

Lake, David A. and Patrick M. Morgan. 1997. The New Regionalism in Security Affairs. In *Regional Orders: Building Security in a New World*, David A. Lake and Patrick M. Morgan, eds. University Park, PA: Pennsylvania State University Press.

Lankov, Andrei. 2008. Pyongyang Puts Politics Above Dollars. *Asia Times*, 26 November, available at: <http://www.atimes.com/atimes/Korea/JK26Dg01.html>.

Layne, Christopher. 1994. Kant or Cant: The Myth of the Democratic Peace. *International Security* 19 (2): 5–49.

Lincoln, Edward J. 2004. *East Asian Economic Regionalism.* Washington, DC: Brookings Institution.

Luce, Edward. 2012. *The Big Bang: Time to Start Thinking.* New York: Atlantic Monthly Press.

Mansfield, Edward D. and Brian M. Pollins. 1999. *Economic Interdependence and International Conflict: New Perspectives on an Enduring Debate.* Ann Arbor, MI: University of Michigan Press.

Michishita, Narushige. 2009. Playing the Same Game: North Korea's Coercive Attempt at U.S. Reconciliation. *Washington Quarterly* 32 (4): 139–52, available at: <http://www.twq.com/09october/docs/09oct_Michishita.pdf>.

Moravcsik, Andrew. 1997. Taking Preferences Seriously: A Liberal Theory of International Politics. *International Organization* 51 (4): 513–53.

Oneal, John R., Bruce Russett, and Michael L. Berbaum. 2003. Causes of Peace: Democracy, Interdependence, and International Organizations, 1885–1992. *International Studies Quarterly* 47 (3): 301–481.

Overholt, William H. 2008. *Asia, America, and the Transformation of Geopolitics.* Cambridge: Cambridge University Press.

Pedroza, Raul. 2009. Close Encounters at Sea: The USNS *Impeccable* Incident. *Naval War College Review* 62 (3): 101–11.

Pempel, T.J. 2005. *Remapping East Asia: The Construction of a Region.* Ithaca, NY: Cornell University Press.

———. 2006. The Race to Connect East Asia: An Unending Steeplechase. *Asian Economic Policy Review* 2 (autumn): 239–54.

———. 2007. Japanese Strategy under Koizumi. In *Japanese Strategic Thought toward Asia*, GilbertRozman *et al.*, eds. New York: Palgrave.

———. 2008. Firebreak: East Asia Institutionalizes its Finances. In *Institutionalizing Northeast Asia: Regional Steps toward Global Governance*, Martina Timmermann and Jitsuya Tsuchiyama, eds. Tokyo: United Nations University.

———. 2012. Global Finance and Two Asian Crises. Paper prepared for the JICA-RI Conference on The Second Asia Miracle, Tokyo, 27 February.

Samuels, Richard J. 2007. *Securing Japan: Tokyo's Grand Strategy and the Future of East Asia.* Ithaca, NY: Cornell University Press.

SIPRI (Stockholm Peace Research Institute). 2012. SIPRI Military Expenditure Database, available at: <http://milexdata.sipri.org/result.php4>.

Souva, M. and B. Prins. 2006. The Liberal Peace Revisited: The Role of Democracy, Dependence, and Development in Militarized Interstate Dispute Initiation, 1950–1999. *International Interactions* 32 (2): 183–200.

Suominen, Kati. 2009. The Changing Anatomy of Regional Trade Agreements in East Asia. *Journal of East Asian Studies* 9: 29–56.

Tow, William, ed. 2009. *Security Politics in the Asia-Pacific: A Regional–Global Nexus.* Cambridge: Cambridge University Press.

Wainwright, Elsina. 2010. Conflict Prevention in Southeast Asia and the Asia-Pacific. Center on International Cooperation, New York University, available at: <http://www.cic.nyu.edu/peacekeeping/conflict/docs/wainwright_conflict_asia.pdf>.

Yahuda, Michael B. 2004. *The International Politics of the Asia-Pacific, 1945–1995.* 2nd ed. London and New York: Routledge Curzon.

Index

Added to a page number 'n' denotes notes.